Praise for *A Vindication of Love*

"An ambitious polemic. . . . In a fresh reading of literary and historical figures from the Wife of Bath to Emily Dickinson, Nehring sets out to show us the many benefits of throwing ourselves headlong into love—not least, she reveals, deeper powers of insight. . . . Her view . . . restores a vision of love as itself the quest that rewards brave vulnerability."

—Meghan O'Rourke, *Slate*

"After reading Nehring's rousing defense of imprudent ardor and romantic excess . . . it's difficult to deny that she's on to something. . . . Ms. Nehring reveals (and revels in) the rich inner agonies of the love-tossed."   —Meghan Cox, *Wall Street Journal*

"This book will have you rethinking the meaning of true love and how to find it."   —*More* magazine

"*A Vindication of Love* makes an ardent and engaging case for attraction in its rawest form—where lust, emotion, and the intellect converge. Feminism, Nehring acknowledges, has given us innumerable opportunities. Now how about the right to be romantic? . . . A sharp new polemic."   —Maud Newton, NPR

A Vindication of Love

Reclaiming Romance for the Twenty-first Century

Cristina Nehring

HARPER ● PERENNIAL

NEW YORK ● LONDON ● TORONTO ● SYDNEY ● NEW DELHI ● AUCKLAND

HARPER ⬤ PERENNIAL

A hardcover edition of this book was published in 2009 by HarperCollins Publishers.

P.S.™ is a registered trademark of HarperCollins Publishers.

HarperCollins books may be purchased for educational, business, or sales promotional use. For information please write: Special Markets Department, Harper-Collins Publishers, 10 East 53rd Street, New York, NY 10022.

The Library of Congress has catalogued the hardcover edition as follows:
Nehring, Cristina.
  A vindication of love: reclaiming romance for the 21st century/Cristina Nehring.—1st ed.
     p. cm.
  Includes bibliographical references and index.
  ISBN 978-0-06-076503-3
1. Love. I. Title.
  BD436.N445 2009
  128'.46—dc22   2008035012

ISBN 978-0-06-076504-0 (pbk.)

10 11 12 13 14   OV/RRD   10 9 8 7 6 5 4 3 2 1

Passerby, lover, warrior, idealist:
This book is for you.

It is also for Eurydice Rafaella Tess,
my newborn beauty.

Contents

INTRODUCTION

Women in Love

NO SOONER HAD HER CORPSE cooled than the stoning began. The thirty-eight-year-old author had been a "whore," a "hyena in petticoats." Venerable poets suggested she had wished to mate with an elephant. Women's rights advocates damned her "imprudence and impolicy." Nineteenth-century suffragettes dismissed her as a "silly victim of passion" and strained to sever their cause from hers. Twenty-first-century feminists still frequently assail her "misogyny"—or simply pass her over in embarrassed silence.[1]

Yet, Mary Wollstonecraft is the mother of modern feminism. Her *A Vindication of the Rights of Woman* (1792) was the first tract of its kind in English; it provoked more admiration than opposition even in the benighted eighteenth century. This admiration only grew as the Western world came to accept—even to assume—

Wollstonecraft's argument. The problem with Wollstonecraft for many modern feminists is not what she wrote; it is how she lived—or rather, how she loved.[2] At once passionate and profoundly loyal, Wollstonecraft loved without stint, prudence, or reserve—and often without luck.

"There are few crimes which exact a worse punishment than this generous fault: to put oneself entirely in another's hands and thus be at his mercy."[3] So wrote Simone de Beauvoir in *The Second Sex* (1949)—and so it has been for Wollstonecraft. If her life was nearly ended by the dashing American businessman who broke her heart, her reputation was nearly buried by a censorious international readership. And not only—or mainly—by defenders of patriarchy, but by defenders of female emancipation: "Her own sex, her own sisters" exclaims one critic, "condemned her pitilessly."[4] To some degree, one can understand this: They did not want to make a model of a woman who—while writing of female independence—twice attempted suicide for a man. The problem is more vexed than this, though; for feminists, over the decades, have damned not only those of their colleagues and foremothers who were unlucky in love, but those who were lucky.

Take Edna St. Vincent Millay. Ostensibly a poster girl for gender equality, Millay smoked a cigar, won a Pulitzer in poetry (the first ever accorded a woman), supported herself and several family members with her writing, entertained the occasional lesbian lover, consigned housework to her husband, and kept any number of important men permanently at her command. The problem is: She liked them—the men, that is. She liked them a lot, so much that she wrote many poems about them and expended not a little effort at cultivating an alluring sexual persona. She was a success at both: The premier literary critic of the day called her one of the most important American poets of all time.[5] Men adored, obeyed, and afforded her much enjoyment. Hers may be as happy a love life as literary history allows us to glimpse. But after her death, she was punished for it.[6]

The onslaught started more subtly than with Wollstonecraft. A critic would remark upon her sexy demeanor, her sultry voice, and suggest that without it her poetry was rather bare. Another would wonder whether if all those men had not been so besotted with her she'd have made it into the literary canon—conveniently disregarding that her judges and admirers overwhelmingly had never laid eyes on her. Before long, Millay's love life had eclipsed her literary achievement as effectively—and disastrously—as Wollstonecraft's *amours* had eclipsed *A Vindication of the Rights of Woman* 150 years earlier. Millay's poetry—so recently regarded as masterful and wry—was dismissed as lightweight and frivolous—as inconsequential as its pretty, primping, sexually overactive author.[7]

An insidious dynamic seems to be at work here. For women authors in general, love—whether it be reciprocal or spurned, happy or sad, chaste or promiscuous—seems to be a public relations gaffe, a death blow to one's credibility as a thinker. It does not matter whether the woman in question made a mess or a model of her love life, the fact that she *had one*—and assigned it obvious importance in her emotional household—suffices to explode her intellectual credibility. If she felt deeply, she cannot, we seem to assume, have *thought* deeply.

To be respected as a thinker in our world, a woman must cease to be a lover. To pass for an intellectual of any distinction, she must either renounce romantic love altogether or box it into a space so small in her life that it attracts no attention. If a man, as William Butler Yeats once claimed, "is forced to choose / Perfection of the life or of the work," a woman is too often forced to choose perfection of the *heart* or of the *head*.[8] Should she choose to follow her heart, she needn't bother her head about philosophy or feminism because the world will mock her efforts. A strong mind, we've come to believe, precludes a strong heart. This, at least, is the mantra under which female artists have labored for centuries, and continue, to some extent, to labor still.

It has never been the mantra of male artists. Over the centuries, we find, in fact, almost the opposite assumptions shaping the valuation of male writers. From Ovid, Petrarch, and Dante, to Hemingway, Henry Miller, Norman Mailer, and Michel Houellebecq, literary men have been admired rather than punished for their active amorous lives—whether or not their overtures were crowned with success. It does not diminish our respect for Petrarch that he spent his life in hopeless despondence over a married girl who would not give him the time of day. We do not see him as humiliated for this reason, as we see Wollstonecraft. His artistic and philosophical credentials are untainted by the turmoil of his erotic biography; indeed, they are strengthened. Generations of sonneteers and statesmen rushed to imitate his eloquent heartache during the English Renaissance—often inventing a cruel mistress when they could not find one in real life, the better to prostrate themselves before her. It was part of one's *manliness* to surrender to love in the Renaissance, part of one's wealth as a human being. How lucky for us: The literature of amorous surrender has inspired many of the most resplendent poems of the English language. And it is rare indeed for its authors—from Shakespeare (who pined in vain for "Dark Ladies" and bright boys alike) to John Donne (who plunged into decades of poverty after eloping with his boss's niece)—to be belittled by posterity as "silly victims of passion."[9]

Nor are men penalized for promiscuity. Who has ever heard of a Boswell, Byron, or Shelley, a Jean-Paul Sartre or a Philip Roth being demoted as writers because of the number of their erotic adventures? Once in a while a moral reservation may be implied: it is unfortunate that Shelley's teenage bride committed suicide after he abandoned her, or that Byron placed his illegitimate daughter in a nunnery where she starved. But the moral admonition—if even ventured—never touches the work. It occurs to no one to think less of "Mont Blanc" because of Shelley's emotional fiascos, or to discount the poetry of Byron as frivolous fluff because its author numbered his one-night stands in multiples of a hundred (as did Millay). Sartre's temperament has provoked increasing criticism in recent years, but nobody dismisses his *philosophy* because he bedded dozens of groupies while paired with Simone de Beauvoir. No, it is *her* work whose seriousness is questioned for this reason. Why did *she* put up with it, we want to know—and how does it compromise *her* theories?[10]

The reputation of a male thinker is either untouched or improved by an erotically charged biography. The reputation of a female thinker is either subtly undermined or squarely destroyed. Is this the legacy of patriarchy? In part, but it is also the legacy of feminism, which since the eighteenth century has sported an antiromantic bias. In the twentieth century, however, the critique was stepped up. As early as the 1910s and 1920s, women's rights activists summoned their sex to abandon heterosexual love since "there could be no mating between the spiritually developed women of this day and men who . . . are their inferiors."[11] It was in the 1970s that the antiromantic chorus really swelled: from Germaine Greer and Kate Millett to Shulamith Firestone and Andrea Dworkin, articulate, energetic, and often bestselling feminist writers declared sex a glorified form of rape and romance a patriarchal ploy to enslave women.[12] Such voices created a climate in which intellectual women who also loved were regarded as dupes.

"Love," proclaims Shulamith Firestone in a book whose 1970 cover announces it "might change your life," ". . . is the pivot of women's oppression today."[13] Love is "a frenzied passion which compels women to submit to a diminishing life in chains," adds Andrea Dworkin in 1976.[14] It's a "pathological condition," according to a group called simply "The Feminists." After all, "the basic elements of rape are involved in all heterosexual relationships," avers Susan Griffin.[15] Griffin's is a thesis that got a lot of mileage for decades; anticipated in Kate Millett's 1969 literary study, *Sexual Politics*, it was developed at greatest length in Andrea Dworkin's 1987 book *Intercourse*. "Rape," Dworkin concludes, "is becoming a central paradigm for intercourse in our time."[16]

With rhetoric like this, it is no wonder that card-carrying women's advocates were apologetic, at best, about practicing heterosexual love. Lesbianism in the 1970s was "almost a categorical imperative for all women truly interested in the welfare and progress of other women," claims Lillian Faderman.[17]

We have come a long way since—and we haven't. On one hand, it is no longer acceptable to stigmatize women across the board for having male partners. On the other, books continue to appear that, like Mary Evans's 2003 *Love: An Unromantic Discussion*, count love "a four-letter word" or, like Laura Kipnis's 2003 *Against Love: A Polemic*, an oath of "chronic dissatisfaction."[18] These books suggest something.

Love at the beginning of the twenty-first century has been defused and discredited. Feminism is partly to blame, but only partly. We inhabit a world in which every aspect of romance from meeting to mating has been streamlined, safety-checked, and emptied of spiritual consequence. The result is that we imagine we live in an erotic culture of unprecedented opportunity when, in fact, we live in an erotic culture that is almost unendurably bland.

Romance in our day is a poor and shrunken thing. To some, it remains an explicit embarrassment, a discredited myth, the deceptive sugar that once coated the pill of women's servility. To others, romance has become a recreational sport. Stripped of big meanings, it has become simply another innocuous pastime. It has become "safe sex," harmless fun, a good-natured grasping for physical pleasure with a convenient companion—or, indeed, with an object. The sex toy market has gone mainstream. Every emancipated young woman is assumed to own a vibrator—or two. Magazines are full of advice on which one will accessorize most pleasantly with your handbag, fit most snugly into your jeans pocket, or lend itself most easily to a quick fling with a second party. (See the remote-controlled vibrator that can be operated from another room by your cat.) Among older American housewives, the Tupperware party has—we are told in bestsellers like

Gail Sheehy's *Sex and the Seasoned Woman*—been replaced by the sex toy party.[19] Overstated or not, such reports suggest a commodification of eroticism such as the world has not seen before.

To still others, love has become a simple strategy for garnering public attention—a media tool. Teenage girls strip off their shirts and make out for the film crews of *Girls Gone Wild*, as Ariel Levy laments in *Female Chauvinist Pigs: Women and the Rise of Raunch Culture*.[20] On weekends they provide Lewinsky-like favors to Casanova-like numbers of mates. "Love" at this level is no longer *even* about sexual gratification anymore—at least not for the girls. It is about boasting, about stealing a little limelight. It is also about rejecting the fuddy-duddy feminisms of one's elders and showing that one is happy to be a sex object.

The problem is not that it's undignified to be a sex object. We are all sex objects, men as well as women—which in no way precludes our simultaneously being intellectual agents. The issue lies elsewhere. It is the trivialization of love that is the tragedy of our time. It is the methodical demystification, recreationalization, automization, commercialization, medicalization, and domestication of Eros that is making today's world a so much flatter place. For however much is won by making sex (in its widest sense) "safe," however much is gained by making orgasms available on tap and bed partners accessible by the click of a mouse, more—far more—is lost.

We have submitted Eros so relentlessly to our enlightened agendas of self-protection and indulgence today that it has grown anemic. We have restricted and tweaked, humbled and caged it so consistently that the poor beast has become as impotent as it is domestic. No longer able to bite, it has also lost the power to sweep us up, to take us for a flight in the heavens, a twirl into the unknown.

To salvage romantic relations we have had, paradoxically, to bleed the romance out of them. We have had (1) to ironize them, (2) to egotize them, and (3) to circumscribe them. We have had to ironize them because we could no longer be gulls of male "mystification." To look at love as a sublime union of souls, as Wollstonecraft did (as well as Shakespeare and Donne and D.H. Lawrence, but that is another matter) was to succumb to the fictions of the oppressor. According to author Barbara Ehrenreich, physical love is at its best these days when it "provides an ironic commentary on what has traditionally been understood as normal heterosexuality"—that is, when it mocks the old domination-and-submission dynamics dramatized in classic love-making by replacing it with a smorgasbord of new and presumably value-neutral activities like masturbation and sex-toy employment. And should this sap some of sexuality's visceral power, its almost mystical resonance? So much the better, says Ehrenreich: "We [as women] had come to understand that the 'mystery' was simply a form of obfuscation. The grand and magical meanings—eternal love, romance, and, always, 'surrender'—were there in part to distract us from the paucity of pleasure."[21]

Fair enough. Pleasure is a desirable commodity, and we've gotten better at its procurement—but at what price? If indeed the ideas of eternal romance and surrender were able to "distract" us for so long from our important bedroom business, then perhaps it is because they are inherently more exciting than even the most successful sleight of the sexual hand. And perhaps this can be men's experience as readily as women's—especially now that female emancipation has made it so much easier for lovers to be confidants as well as collaborators in erotic ecstasy. In a century—like the fifteenth—when a philosopher like Montaigne still believed women "incapable of friendship," a man might be forgiven for thinking he must segregate his mental from his physical pleasures.[22] But today that man has every invitation to unite them, making heterosexual intimacy, for both sexes, that much more potent and encompassing.

To knock the stigma off romance, one need not roll back pleasure, power, economic self-sufficiency, philosophical enfranchisement, or any of the other successes of the women's movement. We need not trash feminism's flowers to dispose of the rotting fruit in its cellar. Romantic love is better between partners with equal rights; sex is superior after some of the new anatomy lessons. We can *have* both knowledge and mystery, equality and abandon. To succeed in this, we must, however, stop reading erotic relationships as elaborate allegories of one-upmanship.

But what happens when love *is* glaringly unequal? What happens when it is altogether unreciprocated? They sometimes failed: the lovers profiled in the examination of love that ensues in these pages did not always "succeed." The object of their affections was not always their equal. And when he was, he still could not always respond at the level they desired. Sometimes the force of their emotions simply left him reeling, flustered. Sometimes he was otherwise committed. But it is not for this reason that their passion was unproductive or ignoble. To the contrary: It endowed them not merely with an emotional wisdom inaccessible to their more prudent colleagues, but also with richly variegated and dramatic lives. Where many a writer is the sum of his texts, the writers whose loves will come under scrutiny in the chapters that follow were more. Their books are writ in blood as well as ink; their biographies rival their bibliographies.

"It never troubles the sun," wrote Ralph Waldo Emerson in one of his later essays, "that some of his rays fall wide and vain into ungrateful space, and only a small part on the reflecting planet. Let your greatness educate the cold and crude companion. If he is unequal, he will presently pass away; but thou, *thou art enlarged by thy own shining.*"[23] Shakespeare's Dark Lady is forgotten today, but Shakespeare lives. Wollstonecraft's lover, Gilbert Imlay, is full of dust today, but the lines he provoked her to write—and the philosophies he caused her to formulate and reformulate—*live.* Such relationships show that love can be a form of strength, of emotional entrepreneurship, of creative enlargement. In fact, *love can be a form of feminism.*

* * *

THE MOST ardent agents of women's advancement have often been the most ardent entrepreneurs of love. They knew that, far from representing an act of weakness or docility, women's love— like men's—is struggle. It is conquest and self-conquest. Far from proving incompatible with a muscular intellectual life, it is its natural counterpart. Strong thoughts engender strong emotions. A woman accustomed to reasoning for herself is unlikely to leave courting, desiring, sacrificing, swaggering, or indeed self-drama-tizing to the opposite sex. She is unlikely to shrink from a fight.

In her bestselling book, *Writing a Woman's Life*, the late Carolyn Heilbrun laments the fact that the biographies of women—even creatively prolific and professionally successful women—are typically written to revolve around a "romance plot," while the biographies of men are organized as "quest narratives." Men, in other words, are defined by the missions they have accomplished, the dragons they have slain, the prizes they have won, while women are defined by the men they have loved. This is indeed unforgivably reductive; it is an error that Heilbrun exposes with force, but where she herself falls into error is in the antagonism she posits between "quest" and "romance."[24]

There are hundreds of quests, of course, and women ought to pursue as broad a spectrum as men. But is not the highest and hardest quest of all, in fact, that of love? It is in the service of love, of "romance," that knights have slain the fiercest monsters, heroes have won the hardest contests, poets have penned the greatest verses. Far from being the opposite of a quest, is not romantic love the mother of all quests?

"Marriage," Phyllis Rose stated memorably in *Parallel Lives*, is the "primary political experience in which most of us engage as adults. . . ."[25] Why, then, do we flinch to call it quest, end, intrepid undertaking? Equality is not about making women equal to men in foot-soldierdom, but equal in access to the grail. It is in the name of love that both sexes have shown their greatest mettle. The methods they embrace have changed; there is no reason to cling to the old choreography of resistance and pursuit, coyness and command assigned, at one time, to women and men respectively. But there is every reason to retain the hunt for the holy chalice itself, for whether lost or found, embraced or only brushed, it invokes the fiercest courage, the finest expression, the highest achievement.

"The tragedy of the self-supporting . . . woman does not lie in too many, but in too few experiences,"[26] wrote the prescient Emma Goldman in the first half of the twentieth century. The problem is not that today's woman does too many things once reserved for men—that she runs for public office, lifts weights, and has one-night stands. The problem is that she does too few *important* things. And high among the important things she doesn't do—or seek—is love that transcends surgical sex; that transcends frivolous exhibitionism; that transcends pragmatic marriage for the purpose of social stability or family planning.

At its strongest and wildest and most authentic, love is a demon. It is a religion, a high-risk adventure, an act of heroism. Love is ecstasy and injury, transcendence and danger, altruism and excess. In many ways, it is a divine madness—and was recognized exactly as that as early as the time of Plato. To enclose it with AA batteries and sell it over the counter is a terrific loss. To flag it as a form of weakness, as a blotch on the résumé of an otherwise strong woman, an otherwise formidable thinker is an egregious mistake. To turn it into a form of political correctness —or, perhaps worse, into a jokey rebellion *against* political correctness—is a crime.

What sustained Dante when he serenaded the long-dead Beatrice or Marc Antony when he sacrificed his career for Cleopatra, what fueled the lifelong hunger of Emily Dickinson and Elizabeth Barrett Browning, what made Frida Kahlo and Diego Rivera remarry each other even after decades of turmoil is nearly defunct.[27] That combination of a sense of destiny and a willingness to sacrifice, of spirituality and adventure—is dead as a doornail. It is an antiquarian artifact. A historical curiosity.

Romantic love was always a *faith*. It was never a reasoned response to *fact*, never a carefully constructed "lifestyle choice." Petrarch did not love Laura because he had taken her measurements and found her appropriate; Heloise did not love Abelard because she had passed a compatibility quiz. In all likelihood she was *not* compatible with Abelard.[28] And yet the sparks flew. The commitment was real. The magic was beyond dispute. The dignity and meaning it conferred upon both lives were immeasurable.

The problem with faith is that when it disappears it is not always (as we like to imagine) replaced with something higher and more reasonable, but often with something lower and more vapid. "When a man ceases to believe in God, he doesn't believe in nothing. He believes in anything," said G. K. Chesterton in the early 1900s. Umberto Eco has expanded on this point: "We are," he wrote in the British *Telegraph*, "supposed to live in a skeptical age. In fact, we live in an age of outrageous credulity. The 'death of God' . . . has been accompanied by the birth of a plethora of new idols. They have multiplied like bacteria on the corpse of the . . . church—from strange pagan cults and sects to the silly, sub-Christian superstitions of *The Da Vinci Code*."[29] Whether or not this is accurate of religious faith, it may well be true of romantic faith. Undermined over the centuries and decades by feminism, materialism, pragmatism, and cynicism, it has been eclipsed, in our own day, by an assembly of inferior idols. Stripped of its lyrical charge, it has become as convenient and tasteless as fast food. It has become fast love. Or rather, it has become non-love.

★   ★   ★

IN THE following pages I will draw on the history of western love—from Plato and Ovid to the medieval troubadors, from Dante and Shakespeare to Emily Dickinson and Simone de Beauvoir—in an attempt to identify alternative models and arresting new visions of romantic behavior for the twenty-first century. I will juxtapose, in every chapter, examples from literature, folklore, and philosophy with stories from the lives of pioneering women artists. I will also be overtly polemical. This is not an unopinionated book. I argue by provocation. I embrace generalization. We live in an age of emotional correctness. Writers take out insurance policies lest they offend. My intention is not, in every assertion, to be statistically or sociologically bulletproof. My aim is to awaken, to interrogate, to inspire, and sometimes to anger.

The point, ultimately, is both simple and not so simple:

Romantic love needs to be reinvented for our time. For those of us as bored by the cult of safe love as we are repelled by the man-hating clichés of old-style feminism, it needs to be formulated afresh. The purpose is by no means to beatify romantic love, or to reclaim it as a fine hallmark sentiment suitable for swooning schoolgirls. The goal is to embrace its dangers and darknesses as well as the light it sheds so amply, so sometimes piercingly. We must confront the role of transgression, the effect of power inequalities, the place for obsession, the reality of strife, the seduction of chastity, the necessity of heroism, the draw, sometimes, of death. Love is a volatile play of shadow and light. It is a brush with the sublime.

ONE

Cupid Doffs His Blindfold:
Love as Wisdom

DRINK TO ME ONLY WITH THINE EYES,
AND I WILL PLEDGE WITH MINE.

—Ben Jonson, "Song: To Celia" [1]

FOR CENTURIES PHILOSOPHERS and poets have insisted that love is blind. It is an expedient maxim, allowing one to extricate oneself from a liaison that has soured. It's rather like saying in the good old days of excessive alcohol intake: "I was drunk; I'm not responsible. I was in love; I didn't see what a cad he was." Or: "I was infatuated: all those good things I saw in Mr. X were in my imagination." Ovid champions this line of self-defense in "Remedies for Love." Dwell upon her negative qualities, he urges the man fighting to reclaim his heart from an ungrateful mistress. "Try to remember her deeds, her wicked, wanton behavior, / Itemize if you can, all she has cost you to date . . . Call those attractions of hers defects. . . ." [2] Assume, in other words, that you were blind when you fell in love with her and now, at last, you can see her true colors and flee.

But the excuse of blindness is a tired excuse, and, in the majority of cases, disingenuous.

One could equally well make the opposite case: Love, far from being blind, is the very emotion that allows us to *see*. It is the only state of mind in which one is entirely and uncompromisingly open to another person. Most of our adult life we are preoccupied with our own projects, our own schemes small or large; we move through the world as ships move past the villages of Potemkin—seeing only façades, satisfied with colored surfaces, seeking nothing beyond. Random persons on one's path receive, at best, a cursory and absentminded look. Only when one falls in love does one seize the liberty for a long and serious look.

Only in love does one take the time to puncture one's neighbors' masks, to consider them in the kaleidoscopic fullness of their psychology, to refrain from dismissing them when they say or do something embarrassing or something that—worse—falls into a category, a stereotype we recognize from elsewhere. Categories are the end of thought and, in many real ways, the end of sight. With most people we have firm habits of categorization: If they exhibit a certain behavior, we put them in a certain category; if they say a word, betray an accent, wear their hair or their tie in a certain way that we recognize from our tired life experience, on goes the label.

Too often it is only love that strengthens us to see intensely, immediately, and individually—to see, as St. Paul says, "face to face" rather than "through a glass darkly."³ Too often it is only love that makes us engaged enough, alert enough, alive enough to see.

★   ★   ★

WHY, THEN, have so many of the great artists of western civilization invested their careers in the opposite argument? Why do Renaissance love poets in England incessantly imply that while they love their ladies, these ladies are not, in fact, deserving of their love? Why does a sudden insult in Shakespeare's satiric sonnet "My mistress's eyes are nothing like the sun" surprise us so *little*?⁴ Sonneteers routinely swear that their mistresses' eyes are *like* the sun, but it is understood (and it is meant to be understood) that they are not. Shakespeare simply underscores a point that is implicit in all the love poems of his contemporaries: It is the lover's heated imagination that endows his mistress with solar power—not her own gifts.

"Love looks not with the eyes, but with the mind," as Helena declares in *A Midsummer Night's Dream*,

> And therefore is winged Cupid painted blind
> . . . Wings, and no eyes, figure unheedy haste,
> And therefore is Love said to be a child,
> Because in choice he is so oft beguiled.
> (1.1.235–9)⁵

Wherever Cupid turns, he is tricked. This is the recurring lament of Shakespeare's sonnets:

"Thou blind fool, Love," Shakespeare's speaker demands in Sonnet 137,

> *what dost thou to mine eyes,*
> *That they behold, and see not what they see?* [6]

The complaint is the same in Sonnet 148:

> *O me! what eyes hath Love put in my head,*
> *Which have no correspondence with true sight!*
> *. . . how can Love's eye be true,*
> *that is so vex'd with watching and with tears?* [7]

Weepy as he often is, Cupid cannot see straight. Even the "eye of heaven" can't see on rainy days:

> *The sun itself sees not 'till heaven clears.*
> *O cunning love! with tears thou keep'st me blind,*
> *Lest eyes well-seeing thy foul faults do find.* [8]

Why is it that poets write such repetitive complaints to unseeing love; why is it they insist their mistresses are not as good as they (the poets) themselves say that they are? One answer: Poets are as vain and self-protective as the rest of us, and they like to hedge their bets—to claim that they control an affair in which (to all appearances) they are enslaved. If it ends badly, the girl was never all she was cracked up to be: "I have sworn thee fair and thought thee bright, / Who art as black as hell, as dark as night," they can say with the speaker of Shakespeare's Sonnet 147.[9] If, on the other hand, the affair ends well, they can take credit: They are the reason for its success; it is their own fine and lyrical sensibility, their own generous imagination that has bestowed upon the lady her apparent charms. Under the guise of humility, they commit an act of supreme arrogance. They take credit for all that goes well in a love story, while cutting their losses in the case it goes ill.

This strategy for saving face—this theory of love as projection, illusion, and distortion—receives its most systematic formulation not by Shakespeare but by the famous French novelist of the nineteenth century, Stendhal. Successful as a literary figure, Stendhal was rejected on a regular basis as a lover. It is not for that reason, however, that posterity has ignored the ambitious philosophical treatise he penned on love: quite the opposite. Published in 1822, *On Love* was Stendhal's favorite of his own works; he preferred it to his classic novels *The Red and the Black* and *The Charterhouse of Parma*.[10] So did others. By the beginning of the twentieth century there was hardly an upper-class French household that did not have a copy of it on its coffee table. For many a well-born European gentlewoman, Stendhal's book became a sort of fashion accessory—a sign of good breeding and romantic aspiration.

It is only when one looks between the covers of Stendhal's work that the irony of its bourgeois success becomes evident. Stripped of a certain veneer of poetical prettiness, Stendhal's argument in *On Love* is sad indeed. He wrote it as he was recovering from an early romantic disaster: Mathilde Countess Dembowska, the twenty-eight-year-old widow he adored, had gone from being mildly tolerant to his propositions to being violently repulsed by them, and the book portrays romantic love as a single spectacular mistake. Its central theory—"crystallization"—posits that a woman who is loved by a man resembles a bare stick that is thrown into a crystal salt mine: She is covered, in his imagination, with bright sparkles. In reality, however, she remains the dry wood she was before.

"At the salt mines of Salzburg," he explains,

> *they throw a leafless wintry bough into one of the abandoned workings. Two or three months later they haul it out covered with a shining deposit of crystals. The smallest twig, no larger than a [bird's] claw, is studded with a galaxy of scintillating diamonds. The original branch is no longer recognizable.*[11]

Like twigs, like women. The tiniest specimen—no larger than a small-town housewife, for example—looks ravishing to the great-souled male. Throw her into the "abandoned workings" of his grand imagination and she emerges "studded with a galaxy of scintillating diamonds." No longer discernable as her dull old self, she is "covered with . . . crystals."[12] Flattering? To the girl, hardly. To the man who loves her, tremendously.

Stendhal returns to this theory throughout his 300-some page treatise. There is a "first crystallization," he tells his readers, a "second crystallization," a "long-term continuous crystallization," and—it would appear—a *de*crystallization. Only the very first crystallization is the fruit of what one would normally call romantic success: "If you are sure that a woman loves you, it is a pleasure to endow her with a thousand perfections . . ." Stendhal says. "In the end you overrate wildly, and regard her as something fallen from Heaven. . . ." This, he declares, is the "first crystallization."[13]

The second crystallization already has gloomier sources and occurs at the moment you begin to question whether the object of your love actually loves you as you had imagined. It occurs when "doubt creeps in" to your heart, when you "ask for more positive proofs of affection"—and are "met with indifference, coldness, or even anger" instead. As a result you are "seized by the dread of a frightful calamity" and "thus begins . . . the second crystallization, which deposits diamond layers" still thicker on your object than did the first crystallization. Suspended between "doubt and delight, the poor lover convinces himself that his enamoured could give him such pleasure as he could find nowhere else on earth. It is the . . . fearsome precipice on one hand and a view of perfect happiness on the other which set the second crystallization so far above the first."[14]

Panic, in other words, drives this crystallization, and all subsequent ones. If "crystallization goes on throughout love almost without a break," as Stendhal claims, it is *fear and trembling* that fires it. Indeed, if there is one thing that can stop the process in its sparkling tracks, it is *comfort*; it is your companion's unwavering affections: "If your beloved gives way to her passion and commits the cardinal error of removing your fear [of losing her] by the intensity of her response then crystallization stops," Stendhal tells us soberingly. The best recipe for restoring things to order in this case is for her to jilt you: "If she leaves you crystallization begins again. . . ."[15]

The fact that so perverse a theory gained as widespread a currency as it did at the time is testimony to the deficit of strong theoretical writing on love. Not only does the notion of crystallization insult the *objects* of human love by suggesting that their every grace is fabricated, but it also condemns the *agents* of this love to enduring misery. In order to keep up the diamond production, lovers must be forever unhappy. If women, as Stendhal interestingly claims at one point in the book, sometimes crystallize more strongly than men, it is for a simple reason: Women have a greater capacity for unhappiness.

A lady who has permitted a sexual liberty to her suitor feels, according to Stendhal, that "she has demeaned herself from queen to slave." Vulnerable as she is in this state, she trembles lest the person to whom she has granted so much power discard or dislike her. This fear is that much more powerful in women than it ever becomes in men because women, says Stendhal, have so much more time to indulge it: "A woman at her embroidery—an insipid pastime that occupies only her hands—thinks of nothing but her lover; while he, galloping across the plains with his squadron, would be placed under arrest if he muffed a maneuver."[16] Greater leisure, for Stendhal, equals greater suffering. Greater suffering equals greater crystallization. Greater crystallization equals greater love.

★ ★ ★

BUT IF women are greater lovers than men, they get no honor for it. For if crystallization—or the art of projecting virtues onto the person you love—is difficult business for either sex, it is ultimately *creative* business for men, and *pathetic* business for women.

The girl who "crystallizes over her embroidery" is a target for pity. The man who crystallizes on the back of his arching horse is an object of admiration. The girl a fool; the man a tragic hero.

Nor is this Stendhal's prejudice alone. It is an assumption shared by the larger society of his day as well as by our own; an understanding implicit in Hollywood movies as much as in Victorian novels, in twenty-first-century literary biographies as often as in seventeenth-century sonnets. A man who falls in love with a simple girl and sees in her all manner of secret refinement is a fine and noble spirit: He is the Richard Gere character in *Pretty Woman*; the idealistic professor in *My Fair Lady*; the prince who falls for Cinderella; the great Doctor Faustus who loves Gretchen; a many-splendored marvel, a fertile and fertilizing spirit. Cut to a woman falling in love with a man whose virtues are not evident to her neighbors. She is the butt of local comedy, the antiheroine of films like *Shirley Valentine*. She is the weak-willed and exploited Emma Bovary, the dupe who falls prey to her senses or her stupidity, or to male subterfuge.

One need only compare the discussion of famous women who have made unconventional amorous choices with that of famous men who have done the same thing. The first is embarrassed or contemptuous; the second reverential and poignant. What a man is that! we incline to think, when an artist of the male persuasion dotes upon an apparently undistinguished woman: How lustrous his soul must be to lend a sheen to this dull coin! Don't worry, Ralph Waldo Emerson enjoins us, if your bright spirit gives sparkle to an unworthy object: You are "enlarged by [your] own shining."[17]

These are bold words. They are also easy words to say for

Ralph Waldo Emerson. As a nineteenth-century gentleman, he could indeed have adored anyone he wished—from his maidservant to the queen of England—without being diminished in the eyes of his contemporaries. The woman who was perhaps his most important intellectual companion had no such luck. Margaret Fuller was the leading member of the Transcendentalist Movement, a fearless war reporter, history-making journal editor, and possibly the first woman in American history to make her living writing. Yet she died an ignominious death because of her choices in love. If her survivors forgave her the passionate flirtation she conducted for many years with Emerson, they did not forgive her the consummated love she had for a dodgy Italian aristocrat whose wealth had disappeared and whose years were substantially fewer than Fuller's own. Because of Giovanni Ossoli, Fuller's tragic death in a shipwreck on the way back from Italy to her home in Massachusetts in 1850 was welcomed by many who considered themselves her friends.

"If Margaret had lived, there would have been a thousand cares for her to encounter," said her brother. Grief for the young woman was "tinctured with selfishness," therefore. "Margaret's euthanasia," was what an old friend called the catastrophe at sea: "It was manifest that she was not to come back to . . . chilled affections. There was no position for her" in the world any longer.[18] Her reputation had been destroyed by her last year's association with a man some took for a gigolo. It did not help that she and Ossoli had an infant boy on board with them when the ship capsized, whose birth—in or out of wedlock—was disputed.

But it was not the child who caused Fuller's shame: It was the man himself. Eleven years her junior (unheard of in nineteenth-century Boston), he was not, as Fuller was, an intellectual; he had fallen, moreover, on hard times. He lacked cash. It was an embarrassing match by any New England standard and a staggering number of onlookers esteemed Fuller's drowning in the Atlantic Ocean at age forty as a tender mercy.

Compare this to the drowning, only twenty-eight years earlier, of another literary figure: Percy Shelley. The Romantic poet had lived a life of considerably greater debauchery than had Margaret Fuller—and had made visibly more disastrous romantic choices. Before he became the husband of Mary Shelley (whom he betrayed and who did not attend his funeral), Percy had already married a sixteen-year-old called Harriet Westbrook, a sweet and unsophisticated girl whom he abandoned (along with his infant child) by the time she turned nineteen and who committed suicide immediately afterward. Shelley and his friend Byron went through inappropriate young girls as though they were tarot cards on a deck. Constantly they found themselves holding the crossbones of death. Wives, girlfriends, and illegitimate children died in droves. The hangers-on of the Shelley and Byron show as they traveled through Italy together were almost always unequal to their male protectors—and unprotected by them.

Yet Percy's death when it occurred—like Fuller's on the water —was full throatedly lamented in his native England: The entire populace mourned the death of "the best and least selfish man." Shelley's fatal infatuation with the Harriets of his life was chalked up to his imaginative soul as it always is when great men make unexpected romantic choices. His irresponsibility was forgotten first and forgiven after. Meanwhile, Margaret Fuller was the object of calumny for many decades, deemed an idiot, a false

feminist idol, a sorry pool of hormones. This, because of an amorous choice that her contemporaries did not understand—a single
love that they considered blind.

* * *

WAS MARGARET Fuller's love really blind? Was Shelley's? Is it really
the case, as we read in Stendhal, that "from the moment he loves,
even the wisest man no longer sees anything as it is?"[19] Stendhal's
position has become the cliché of our time. Its consoling proper-
ties are beyond dispute. Since all too many of us spend more time
spurned by ideal mates than celebrated, it is a relief to believe that
our perception of them is usually wrong.

But what if it were actually right? What if love was not irrational but astute? Not myopic but clairvoyant? Would it make
the world a worse or a better place? Would it make us more dis-
traught about our losses, or more ecstatic in our (sometimes just
ephemeral) gains?

There is a vitally important countermovement in western
literature that is routinely overlooked, and that we need to reclaim today. The countermovement says: *Love is wise.* Love is
discerning. What we see when we are in love is not a chimera
through rose-tinted glasses or an optical or emotional illusion. It
is as close as we get to perfect sight, as close as we ever come to
grasping the essence of another human being. It is not when we
fall in love that we err, but when we fall out of love. It is when
we drop the magnifying glass that is the tool of each lover that
our vision blurs and our understanding dims. It is the person who

has never loved who misjudges reality—not the one who loves perpetually.

*   *   *

THE NOTION of love as vision and the lover as visionary goes back to the Greek philosopher, Plato. But alas, whoever turns to Plato for romantic insight runs flush into a problem, and that is: A majority of modern scholars has decided romantic love did not exist until nearly fifteen centuries *after* Plato's birth in 423 BC. They have decided that romantic love comes from "courtly love," and courtly love leapt full grown from the heads of eleventh-century troubadors in the obscurer regions of France—the same troubadors who invented the Tristan myth.

"Every one," contends C.S. Lewis in his seminal 1936 study, *The Allegory of Love*, "has heard of courtly love, and every one knows that it appears quite suddenly at the end of the eleventh century in the Languedoc."[20] Before the eleventh century, according to this view, romance, such as we know it today, did not exist. There may have been animal lust, there may have been amiable companionship, there may have been boisterous sex play, but there was not that spiritualized sort of euphoria, that combination of sexual and metaphysical transport that we, in our day, associate with romantic love. To those who would counter that love is in our nature, Lewis attributes historical ignorance: "We are so familiar with the erotic tradition of modern Europe that we mistake it for something natural and universal," he says. "It is only when we imagine ourselves trying to explain this doctrine [of love] to Aristotle, Virgil, St. Paul, or the author of *Beowulf* that we become aware how far from natural it is."[21] His conclusion: "There can be no mistake about the novelty of romantic love: our only difficulty is to imagine in all its bareness the mental world that existed before its coming. . . ."[22]

Lewis's thesis has been the consensus of modern scholars since the early decades of the twentieth century. Stephanie Coontz upholds it in her 2005 title, *Marriage, a History.*[23] Morton Hunt pushes it in his popular *The Natural History of Love* (1994). When romantic feeling appeared at the courts of French warlords, Hunt says, it "had only the faintest of precedents in Western culture . . . Ovid, and St. Augustine . . . would all have been astonished and even mystified by it."[24]

Astonished and mystified? It is an odd reader, indeed, who can examine an ancient Greek work like Plato's *Phaedrus* and imagine that its writer—or its ostensible subject, Socrates—had no knowledge of romantic passion. To be sure, Socrates did things differently from C.S. Lewis. He was, for one thing, at least a part-time homosexual, and much of his discourse on romantic love takes place in the company of men. It takes place in the company of students and teachers. Whereas in our own time sex in academia is demonized, in antique Athens sex in the classroom—or rather in the *agora*, where philosophers perambulated with their disciples—was more or less the norm. Then, as now, sex was different things to different people at different moments. But where Lewis and Hunt and the majority of other modern specialists on the subject pretend that for the men of the *agora* it was chiefly a good-natured romp on the order of wrestling—the reality is far wider, far deeper, and emphatically more interesting.

Witness one of the descriptions Socrates offers, in *Phaedrus*, of what happens when one encounters a human being by whom one is especially affected:

> . . . *when he sees anyone having a godlike face or body . . . at first a shudder runs through him . . . looking upon the face of the beautiful one, as if of a god, he reveres him and if he were not afraid of being thought a downright madman, he would sacrifice to his beloved as to the image of a god. Then while he gazes on him there is a sort of reaction, and the shudder passes into an unusual heat and perspiration, for, as he receives the effluence of beauty through the eyes . . . he warms.*[25]

Shuddering, perspiring, reverence, sacrifice, and fevers—if it's not sunstroke Socrates is describing here, it may as well be the pangs of romantic love. The entire understudied dialogue of *Phaedrus* is about romantic love. Much of the perhaps overstudied dialogue *Symposium* is about romantic love. It is a peculiar form of cultural narcissism to imagine that only we, in the modern day, are capable of such refined and transformative emotions; that only we, in our post-Christian enlightenment, have discovered the combination of physical arousal with spiritual, intellectual, and sentimental elevation. As long as human beings have possessed both sense and sensibility, they have been more or less bound to stumble at least occasionally into the throes of romantic love.

The dialogues of Plato bear living testimony to this.

Composed toward the end of Plato's career around 370 BC, *Phaedrus* is a typical Socratic dialogue in that it features a Socrates who toys with his students, who jokes with the young men in his company, slyly teasing out their prejudices in order to puncture them. The prejudice Socrates is teasing out of his student, Phaedrus, at the beginning of the dialogue that bears his name is one familiar to anyone who has recently browsed through the relationship section of a Barnes & Noble bookstore. It is the prejudice that boyfriends are trouble; that *men suck*—or, rather, that men as *lovers* suck.

Much better to have a friend than a boyfriend, swears Phaedrus. Boyfriends are unreliable; boyfriends are dangerous; boyfriends go hot and cold on you. One day they butter you up, the next day they break your heart. "For when their passion ceases, lovers repent of the kindnesses which they have shown," Phaedrus intones; they "consider how by reason of their love they have neglected their own concerns" and punish you accordingly.[26] A simple friend, on the other hand, "has no such tormenting recollections; he has never neglected his affairs or quarreled with his relations" on your account and, therefore, won't give you a hard time later. Where a lover's "judgment is weakened by passion," the judgment of a friend is sound and steady. Where a lover is blind, a buddy is clear eyed and sane, safe and sober.[27]

The rap is as familiar to Socrates as it is to the readers of *Smart Women/Foolish Choices* today.[28] Indeed, it's not just Phaedrus who's making this argument at the start of Plato's dialogue, it is a famous Athenian orator named Lysias. Phaedrus has just come from a speech of Lysias, and is eager to repeat it to Socrates. For a long while Socrates listens with seeming admiration. When Phaedrus asks, "Isn't the speech great?" Socrates responds effusively: "Yes," he says, "the effect on me was ravishing."[29] So impressed does Socrates pretend to be by Lysias's speech that he offers to give a similar one himself, taking for his premise that "the lover is more disordered in his wits than the non-lover."[30]

The performance that ensues is a masterpiece of Socratic irony. Socrates pronounces with eloquence on the idiocy of lovers, outdoing Lysias at every turn, and stopping only long enough to demand of Phaedrus "if you do not think me, as I appear to myself, divinely inspired?"[31] "You have a very unusual flow of words," affirms the compliant young man. And on Socrates goes, railing against the ignorance of persons infatuated and warning all who will hear of the dangers of associating with "a demented lover instead of a sensible non-lover. . . ."[32] To spend time with an individual in love is to spend time, he declares, with a "faithless, morose, envious, disagreeable being [who is] hurtful to his [own] estate, hurtful to his bodily health, and still more hurtful to the cultivation of his mind. . . ."[33]

At the height of this tirade, however, Socrates pauses. He stares hard at Phaedrus. "That was a horrible speech that you brought with you," he says, "and you made me utter one as bad."

Phaedrus is dumbstruck. "How so?" he asks at length.

"It was foolish," proclaims Socrates. Worse, it was "impious— can anything be more dreadful?"[34]

For the rest of the dialogue Socrates delivers himself with dazzling intensity to the praise of passionate love. He explains his reversal, moreover, with an anecdote from antique history about blindness.

There was a man, he begins, by the name of Stesichorus. He was a poet of the sixth century BC, and—like that other great Greek poet, Homer—he was struck suddenly blind. Unlike Homer, however, who "never had the wit to discover why he was blind," Stesichorus had wit to spare and immediately grasped the reasons for his blindness. "He was deprived of his sight," Socrates attests, "for reviling lovely Helen."[35] He had lost his eyes because he had refused to fall in love with the most exquisite woman in Greece, the woman over whom Troy had been lost and won, the woman whose face had "launched a thousand ships."[36] Not only had he failed to adore her, he had even written a dismissive verse about her—and the gods, reeling at such emotional insipidness, smote him soundly with blindness. And blind he remained, the unhappy Stesichorus, until he made amends for his criminal inability to love. Blind he remained until he cursed the poem he had composed and began to write a new one: "When he had completed his [new] poem, which is called 'The Recantation,' immediately his sight returned to him."[37]

Socrates has learned from Stesichorus: "I will be wiser," he declares, "than either Stesichorus or Homer in that I am going to make my recantation for reviling love before I suffer." He will renounce his attack on love before the gods have the chance to strike him blind. ". . . [A]nd this," he adds, "I will attempt, not as before veiled and ashamed, but with forehead bold and bare."[38]

Bold and bare is the face of the lover. Veiled and blind is the eye of the non-lover. In the philosophical imagination of ancient Greece, love is sight. Indeed, it is more than *sight*, as Socrates proceeds to explain; it is divine clairvoyance.

Not that the clairvoyance of love is always understood as such by outsiders. Philistines disdain a lover, Socrates warns; more often than not, he is "castigated for being mad."[39] The truth is, the lover does behave differently from his peers; often he behaves wildly. This wildness is not a symptom of disturbance though, but a sign of revelation. For this reason, the Greek word *manike*—madness—so closely resembles the Greek word *mantike*—prophecy—or so Socrates speculates. Prophecy and madness are of a piece.

It is not wrong, therefore, to call a lover mad: "It might be so if madness were simply an evil; but there is also a madness which is a divine gift, and the source of the chiefest blessings granted to men." What *is* wrong is to think the lover's madness a vice. The lover's madness is a precious virtue, a sort of genius that puts him on a footing with visionaries and oracles, sages and saints. To look into the future, the great seers of Greece have always had to go into a trance, a sort of frenzy. Without such a frenzy or trance, they were no more able to discern the future than the average Athenian burgher in a bathhouse. "When out of their senses, the prophetess at Delphi and the priestesses of Dodona have conferred great benefits on Greece," Socrates points out, but "when *in* their senses they have conferred none."[40]

Sensible people are not inspired people. Sensible people, in fact, are often shortsighted people. They cannot penetrate into the secrets of the universe: "He who comes to the door having no touch of the Muses' madness and thinks he will get into the temple . . . is not admitted," Socrates says. To see into the core of things, you have to be transported. You have to be in love. ". . . [T]he sane man is utterly eclipsed by . . . the inspired madman."[41] The sane man's gaze falters at the first obstacle in its way—whether it be a wall of marble around an altar or a wall of timidity around a soul. Compared to the wild-eyed and wide-eyed lover, the prudent friend blunders around in the dark. For this reason, Socrates proclaims, we must *never* be persuaded by "an argument which says that the temperate friend is to be chosen rather than the driven one."[42] The sanity of friendship may be reassuring, but the madness of love is "the gift of the gods most conducive to our benefit."[43] It is a chance we have, trapped as we are in the prison of our private preoccupations, to see into the heart of the person at our side.

*   *   *

SOCRATES WAS extraordinarily good at seeing into the heart of the person at his side. It was a part of his modus operandi as a philosopher. He made his points not by writing in isolation or lecturing to an unseen crowd, but by talking with another human being, by spotting that human being's secret thoughts, and bending them to his own purpose. Rarely did Socrates advance his arguments in his own voice; far more often, he manipulated his conversation partners in such a way that they themselves articulated the arguments he wanted to make. He did this by looking into their souls, by loving them. And he did this, at least sometimes, by seducing them.

Perhaps it is no surprise, then, that Socrates has recently been called "the most erotic of our philosophers." [44] The very manner in which he conducted his teaching was erotic. What may come as even a greater surprise is that Socrates himself—modest as he unfailingly was—would probably have welcomed such a title. A banquet in Athens around 416 BC finds him announcing to the cream of Athenian society that love is his special area of expertise. The assertion is the more astonishing for the fact that Socrates is perhaps best known for his denial of expertise in any subject whatever. "I know that I don't know" is what he routinely told his students.

And yet at the august gathering billed as the *Symposium*, Socrates dramatically contradicts this assertion. I know that I *know*, he says on that night: I know that I know *one* topic—if no other. Standing before many of the most prominent citizens of Greece (before the playwright, Aristophanes, for example, and the general, Alcibiades), Socrates speaks loud and clear: "I declare that love is the only subject that I understand."[45]

And he proceeds to prove it. He proceeds to prove, in any case, that love is the only subject for which he has unlimited esteem.

If Socrates makes grand claims for love in *Phaedrus*, he makes still grander claims in the *Symposium*. Where in *Phaedrus* he gave love credit for allowing us to see another person, in the later dialogue he gives it credit for allowing us to see eternal truth.

Socrates' oration on love in the *Symposium* comes in the wake of several others. In the interest of not drinking themselves into comas (as was their custom), the dinner guests have decided to stage a sort of speech contest. "Let us have a conversation instead . . ." someone proposes, "I can assure you that I feel severely the effects of yesterday's drinks, and need a respite . . ."[46] When it comes Socrates' turn to speak, he delivers a disquisition dictated to him—or so he claims—by a wise woman named Diotima. Studied ad infinitum by the Neoplatonist philosophers in the third and fourth centuries AD, revered by religious thinkers in the Renaissance, the disquisition has provoked both adulation and alienation in our own day.

For all the sound and fury it has generated over the millennia, its argument is rather simple: Love, Socrates says, is a ladder on which one climbs from base physical obsession over higher-minded mental admiration, all the way up, in time, to an appreciation of the good not just in one person, nor even in several persons, but in all of mankind. Finally, on the highest rung, one arrives at a "notion of beauty absolute."[47] The goal, says Socrates, is to "begin from the beauties of earth and mount ever upward for the sake of that other beauty, using these [initial beauties] as steps only."[48] It is love as self-improvement; love as a multistep program for enlightenment.

Socrates is winningly explicit about how the program should work:

> *For he who would proceed aright in this matter should begin in his youth to visit beautiful bodies; and first, if he is guided by his instructor aright, to love one such body only, and in it he should engender beautiful thoughts; and soon he will of himself perceive that the beauty of one body is akin to the beauty of another; and then, if beauty . . . is his pursuit, how foolish would he be not to recognize that the beauty present in all bodily forms is one and the same! And when he perceives this, he will abate his violent love of the one . . . and will become a lover of all beautiful bodily forms; in the next stage he will consider that the beauty of the soul is more honorable than the beauty of the body so that someone even of slight beauty, but virtuous in soul satisfies him, and he loves and cares for him . . . until he is compelled to contemplate and see the beauty of institutions and laws, and to understand that the beauty of them all is of one family, and . . . contemplating the vast sea of beauty, he will create many fair and noble thoughts and notions in boundless love of wisdom. . . .[49]*

It is by loving our fallen mortal neighbor in our fallen mortal way that we rise, in time, to a vision of the eternal. It is by seeing first the outer beauties of our beloved, and then the inner beauties, that we eventually train our "eyes to see the true beauty—the divine beauty . . . pure and clear and unalloyed, not clogged with the pollutions of mortality. . . ."

Critics have objected that this is, in fact, a cold speech—antagonistic to romantic love as we know it, for it seems to propound that we "use" our partner as a ticket to eternity, a free ride to universal truth—and then discard him. "The original object of human love . . . has simply fallen out of sight before the soul arrives at the spiritual object," complains C.S. Lewis. "Those who call themselves Platonists at the Renaissance may imagine a love which reaches the divine without abandoning the carnal, but they do not find this in Plato."[50]

It is easy to understand where Lewis's complaint comes from. Socrates' account of the ladder of love is hardly dressed in the language of love songs. Socrates is far more interested in the pursuit of abstract truth than he is in the praise of a particular person. And yet Lewis's objection seems pedantic nevertheless; indeed, it seems willfully blind. What is vital about Socrates' argument in *Symposium*—what is new and essential in it—is not the abandonment of the beloved but his eye-opening and elevating effect on the lover.

For when in love we are not simply alive to the beauties of our beloved; we are—in *general*—more alive. We are more alert to the beauties of the world around us, more inquisitive, more anxious, more observant. We read books we otherwise would not read; we contemplate questions we otherwise would not contemplate; we consider moving to new places, learning new languages, acquiring new lifestyles, picking up *The Sonnets of Shakespeare* for the first time.

In order to be inflamed intellectually, we need to be enlisted emotionally. In the absence of emotional engagement, most people do not interrogate themselves about topics for which there is no immediate or pragmatic urgency. When neither our jobs nor our self-interest require us to reexamine a knotty subject, chances are we won't. The laws of inertia militate against it. To consider afresh our views of capitalism, of patriarchy, of propriety, we have, in most cases, to be rattled. We have, at least, to be stirred. And what more stirring incident is there in human life than to fall in love?

Socrates identifies an essential point in *Symposium*: To fall in love is first to study the person who has awakened your affections, second to study yourself, and third to study the world around you. Were you right to imagine it better to live in California than Berlin? Were you justified in assuming marriage was the best way to live with a partner? Was it a mistake to resist the study of Judaica or modern Greek? It is no accident that so many potent love relationships—Socrates' with his students, Heloise's with Abelard, Hannah Arendt's with Martin Heidegger—are relationships centered in some way around learning. The thirst for knowledge about another human being leads almost inevitably to the thirst for knowledge about other things. Sometimes they are things your lover likes or needs. Mostly they are things you simply did not notice before your senses were stirred by affection.

What Socrates is saying above all else in *Symposium* is that *love makes us think*. Love makes us explore. Love makes us blaze through new subjects and new cultures; it makes us hatch new visions. And in that way it does, in fact, transcend its human object.

Sometimes that object *is* just a rung on the ladder—a stepping-stone to higher places. At other times it is the altar itself.

* * *

SOCRATES' TROPE of love-as-vision resonates throughout the millennia. It finds medieval literary resonance in the heavenly pilgrimage of Dante and Beatrice to the face of God; it finds a worldlier parallel in the twentieth-century philosophical crusade of Simone de Beauvoir and Jean-Paul Sartre. Unlike their ethereal Italian predecessors, Beauvoir and Sartre were anything but a pair of angels. The distance they strayed from conventional moral ideals emerges more starkly with every new study that comes out on them. What the French thinkers share with Dante and Beatrice is only this—but it is much: They fell in love at once with a human being and with high truth.

Their passion helped make them two of the leading truth-seekers of the last century. Between them, they produced two of the most important philosophical tomes of their time—*Being and Nothingness* and *The Second Sex.*[51] They popularized existentialism on one hand and feminism on the other. Sartre's essays, plays, disquisitions, and biographies, and Beauvoir's polemics, memoirs, novels, and reviews, formed a literature unto themselves.

When they began their fifty-odd-year relationship, both were faulted for their choice of partner. They were accused by contemporaries—as Beauvoir is still accused today—of compromising intellectual credibility for the love of a human being who was unworthy. "Why," demands Angela Carter, "is a nice girl like Simone wasting her time sucking up to a boring old fart like

Jean-Paul?"[52] They *were* improbable together: the willowy, regal Simone de Beauvoir next to the wall-eyed, prematurely wizened, pasty little Sartre. And yet Beauvoir called him her "sweet little face," her "dear little being," as though the cranky intellectual was an Adonis, a boy toy.[53] Feminists, in particular, have recoiled at such cloying language from the hard-nosed French champion of women's rights, the author of the twentieth century's most exhaustive and indignant book about sexual equality.

Yet the apparently idolatrous way Beauvoir addressed Sartre in her letters and life captured something far more fundamental about him than did the writings of the experts. Beauvoir's passion for Sartre permitted her to see into him deeper and earlier than anyone else. Sartre was only twenty-three when the twenty-one-year-old Simone identified him as the genius of his age. He had just failed his philosophy exams at the *École Normale Supérieure*, and she had to put a lot of effort into preparing him for the next round lest he flunk again the following year. If his examination was finally awarded top honors while hers was only offered second place, it is chiefly because the judges hoped—as one of them later specified—to reward Sartre's harder work and older age. Perhaps they also found it easier to reward his gender.

One wonders whether Sartre would have become Sartre without a person like Beauvoir to reflect his brilliance back to him on a regular basis—without someone to see through his antic exterior and identify his genius. Sartre needed Beauvoir as a mirror even more than he needed her as a lover. After Beauvoir told Sartre a thousand times how trenchant he was, he came to believe it—and to be trenchant. This is one of the services lovers provide to each other: not to invent virtues in the other, but to identify those that are incipient and to drive them to fruition.

History has vindicated Beauvoir's sight to a spectacular degree —even if Sartre's reputation has taken some knocks in recent years. History has vindicated Sartre's vision of Beauvoir even more dramatically. From the beginning of their acquaintance, he knew that the eager little bourgeoise, whose industriousness prompted him to call her "le castor" (the beaver), would change the world.[54] It is for this reason that he told her that it must be she—and no one else—who writes a book about womankind. "Look," he told her, "why don't you put *yourself* into your writing? You're more interesting than all these Renées and Lisas that you put into your novels."[55] He saw her as a pioneering feminist—as well as a pioneering autobiographer—long before she became one. It is the fact that Sartre *saw* Beauvoir that enabled her to *be* Beauvoir.

The two philosophers began by identifying the truths about each other and ended by identifying the truths about their time. These activities went together for them—as they did for Socrates and his students. In the last decades of her life, Beauvoir pondered how her readers would judge her after her death. Ever the realist, she knew they would think she had often stumbled. She had often fallen. She had made many mistakes. *But*, she also believed, they would think *"there wasn't much she didn't see!"*[56] She was right.

* * *

IF LOVE has such an enlightening effect on students and writers, feminists and philosophers, why is it that we so often feel duped when a romance ends? Why is it that we so often see people differently—and more darkly—after passion has passed? Could it be not because our vision improves after the fog of infatuation clears, but—for the opposite reason—because it deteriorates?

The stories collected by the Brothers Grimm in the nineteenth century abound with characters whose eyes are destroyed. More often than not, these characters are the ones who are either finished loving or could never have loved in the first place. The evil stepsisters in "Cinderella," for example, are blinded at the end of the story. Their eyes are pecked out by the doves who befriended Cinderella as she sat in the ashes. They are pecked out of the girls who made Cinderella's life miserable and who faked love for the prince when he came searching for her. It is the love*less* members of the story who lose their sight; the loving figures are graced with acute perception. The prince sees instantly through Cinderella's disguise as a serving girl. Through her ash-covered clothes, her awkward manners, and the studied deceit of her stepfamily, he sees the noble young lady she actually is. It is because of his uncanny sight that he loves her. Or rather: It is because he loves her that he *possesses* this uncanny sight.

The story of "Rapunzel" offers a similar reading of blindness. A king's son has been climbing up the side of a tower to visit his beloved; he has been climbing up her long blond braids, because the witch who holds her captive inside has omitted to equip the tower with stairs. One day, alas, the witch catches the young man and puts an abrupt end to his love. "You want to fetch your darling wife," she sneers, "but . . . the cat has got her, and it will also scratch out your eyes." And sure enough, the king's son loses his sight at the very moment that he loses his love. Jumping from the tower window in terror, he plunges into the brambles: "He escaped with his life, but the thorns he fell into pierced his eyes, so he became blind."[57]

It is not until many years later when he rediscovers Rapunzel and the two begin their love afresh that his vision miraculously returns: ". . . as two of her tears dropped on [the prince's] eyes, they became clear, and he could see again."[58] The return of love is the return of sight. The loss of love is the loss of sight.

*   *   *

WHAT HAPPENS when we cease to love is that we return to the world of surfaces and stereotypes. It is as though we wrapped a set of eccentric canvases in homogenous manila packing paper and labeled them "Oil on Silk" or "Charcoal on Paper." Henceforth, we see a category, but we no longer see a reality. We may remember our lover as a "neurotic intellectual," an "angry alcoholic," a "spoiled beauty," or a "compulsive seductress"—much as we remember the character in a novel we read a long time ago.

When we fall out of love, we reclaim the blinders with which we trot horse-like through so much of our lives. We replace the rich realities on the roadside with sparse signposts, abstract catchwords—always reductive and usually disparaging. Where once we saw many-splendored marvels, we now see one-dimensional caricatures. "Commitment-phobic male," we think wearily, or "tourist looking for a fling." Ulysses on the island of Aeaea stands before an assembly of glittering individuals and can see only swine.[59]

When love dies "the whole world is depopulated" says the

nineteenth-century French poet, Alphonse de Lamartine. We might as well live on an abandoned island.[60] Nothing anyone says seems interesting; nothing anyone does looks meaningful. But it is not the world that has changed—it is the quality of our own vision.

We must steel ourselves for the loss of love as we steel ourselves for age and infirmity. We know that our senses will one day be feeble—but it is not for this reason that we condemn them while they are still sound and strong. We do not curse the sun-flooded vista because we know the night will come and the shadows engulf it.

Human eyes can only bear so much light. Were we constantly in love, the skyline would be too bright for us, the landscape too various. We would blink like an animal in the headlights—like Dante in the fluorescent face of Eternal Truth.

Perhaps charitably, it has not been granted us to love at equal intensity at all times. Passion fluctuates. That does not mean it lies. "Let not my love be called idolatry," Shakespeare pleads in one of his fiercest sonnets.[61] Let us not apologize for greatness just because it fades. Let us not curse the vision just because it flees. We would do better to cherish the vision more warmly, to detain it as long as we can, to plumb it for all the wisdom it can yield—for all the poetry, for all the joy—and to praise it when it has gone.

To speak with Edna St. Vincent Millay:

After all, my erstwhile dear,
My no longer cherished,

Need we say it was not love,
Now that love is perished?
("Passer Mortuus Est," 9–12)[62]

We need not. We need not say "it was not love"—nor even "he was no prince," simply because he appears to us now a frog.

The happiest and wisest persons are those who, like Socrates, prize the frenzy of transcendent sight even when it is past, even when the reds and oranges have faded and the world has returned to a lighter shade of gray.

We must be grateful for the visions we are offered be they never so brief. "Human kind cannot bear very much reality," says T.S. Eliot.[63] But that reality can make all of life worth living, worth remembering, worth honoring, and worth recording.

TWO

✧

The Power of Power Differentials: Love as Inequality

TO FALL IN LOVE IS TO CREATE . . . A FALLIBLE GOD.
—Jorge Luis Borges[1]

POWER DIFFERENTIALS: the buzzword of our day. Or rather, the bad word of our day.

Is there a "power differential" between two people? Is one a student, the other a teacher? One a junior and the other a senior staff member? One a patient and the other a doctor? Relationship doomed. Mission impossible.

A student "cannot engage in genuinely consensual interactions" with a professor, says the mainstream. Such a relationship can, at best, be "submissive."[2] A twenty-one-year-old English major not only should not but also *can*not agree to a love affair with a thirty-one-year-old English professor, we are told—no matter what she may think about the matter herself. Such a relationship will always be imposed on her from above. She will always (so the story goes) be the child victim of an adult predator.

Most people outside the academy suspect this is nonsense. We know college students can initiate relationships with college teachers; interns can seduce presidents. And yet the stigma remains: Such relationships are, we vaguely feel, unfair, unhealthy, and perhaps abusive. They work to the disadvantage of the person with less power; they deepen, we imagine, that person's sense of inferiority. No matter that there is little evidence for this argument—beyond the fact that when relationships end there is often an aggrieved party. Love hurts. Being left hurts. But it does not hurt any more—nor is it likelier to occur—in the context of an asymmetrical relationship.

Our society's infatuation with symmetry ranges from the quixotic to the ridiculous. The enemies of student-professor relationships imagine a symmetry between ideal lovers that all but cannot exist. They imagine a love affair between identical twins, Cabbage Patch dolls, that is as uncommon as it is undesirable. They imagine that the only differences between lovers are differences of academic rank—or standing within an institution. They ignore the fact that there are as many kinds of power as there are psychological or physical traits. Youth and beauty is a form of power—as anyone knows who has read a Philip Roth novel in which the decrepit celebrity intellectual is awestruck by an unknown young shiksa whom he perceives as omnipotent; as anyone knows who has ever loved a person of lesser years or greater physical attractiveness. To have time on your side is to have the scales tipped in your favor. Potential itself is a form of power; unlived life is a form of power. So is street wisdom; so is liveliness, good breeding, local savvy, or muscular force. In the ghetto, a ghetto-kid has more clout than a CEO. In the streets of Athens, a local waiter wields more authority than a famous foreign writer. On a university campus, a beautiful young woman may well possess more power than her bespectacled advisor. Power is as various as the color bars of the rainbow. Most pundits who pronounce on it today treat it as though it had a single hue.

So perverse is our faith in symmetry that we find specialists who should know better extending its attractions from interpersonal relations to facial characteristics: "Women," claims a 2001 study on sex, "even report more orgasms when having sex with symmetrical men"—i.e., men whose ears are the same size and whose nose is well centered.[3]

Whence comes this puerile adulation of symmetry? It would seem that any examination of the fantasy life of our contemporaries as well as of the literary legacy of our predecessors would suggest that far from being sexy, symmetry in a relationship is the kiss of death. What fills the sex shops? French maid costumes and slave shackles. The storybooks? Tales of Beauties who fall in love with Beasts; of princesses who lose their virginity to reptiles, of kings who court orphans, and princes who wed girls cast into the woods by their wicked stepmothers. It would seem that the public imagination is at odds with the public consensus.

Not only are power differentials tolerated in these archetypal relationships, but they are emphasized, and—whenever possible—increased. They are essential to the tension of the relationship. It is in fiction as in physics: The energy between two objects (romantic or material objects) comes from the vertical distance between them. Two objects at the same level of elevation have no potential energy between them. Left to themselves, they will not move toward each other. Two objects on different levels, on the other hand, will, by definition, have potential energy between them. There is a gravitational pull that draws them close. When their potential energy turns into kinetic energy, they spring violently and dramatically together.

Thus it is with people. Power discrepancies—so far from damaging a relationship—often prove its magnetic force. Even when partners are equal they do well to invent these discrepancies; they do well to role play power inequities. They may exaggerate the other's status or severity, chastity, or authority. "Most great and severe mistress!" exclaim medieval knights to their girlfriends.[4] "Oh Mister Rochester, my dear Master," says Jane Eyre to her fiancé, ignoring his invitation to call him "Charles."[5] Power differentials are electric. They are exciting. If sex—as has been observed—is a great "leveler," it works better when there is something there to level in the first place. It works better among mountains and valleys than it does in flatlands.

Adult erotic relationships—in contrast to the toddler loves often depicted on nostalgic black-and-white photo Valentines (read: three-year-olds in oversize trench coats with roses taller than they are)—thrive on inequalities of almost every ilk. Heterosexuality itself is an attraction of opposites—an attraction to inequality. Where love, historically, has *not* been heterosexual, it has often compensated for this dearth of otherness by insisting the more dramatically on alternative sources of difference. The ancient Greeks, for example, took for granted that liaisons between male lovers involve age differences that would be considered shocking in our own day.

Erotic love in Plato's and Socrates' day is a phenomenon that occurs almost exclusively between a "youth" and an older man. Ideally—as set forth in the opening speech of Plato's *Symposium*—it occurs between boys whose "beards begin to grow" and their graying instructors.[6] Thus matched (or mismatched, by today's standards), the lovers gain maximal benefit from their passion: "I know not any greater blessing to a young man who is beginning life than a virtuous lover [many years his senior], or to the [senior] lover than a beloved youth," intones the first speaker in *Symposium*.[7] It is not merely a matter of the older person's physical attraction to the younger person, it is a matter of mutual mental chemistry; the fascination of a "mind yet unformed" for a mind ripened by experience—and vice versa.[8]

One of the earliest seduction scenes in occidental literature is, arguably, the fourth-century BC attempted seduction of Socrates by his student Alcibiades—the seduction, that is, of an aging philosopher by the boisterous young man whom he teaches. It is Alcibiades himself who tells us the tale in *Symposium*—and it proves one of the most amusing, liberating, engaging, and power-imbalanced love stories of all time.

Coming after Socrates' high-minded lecture about the "ladder of love," Alcibiades' high-spirited account of how he tried to get his teacher to bed with him provides the most robust comic relief of the dialogue. Alcibiades is a latecomer at the Symposium; he has been off drinking on his own—and drinking deep. He arrives on the doorstep of his hosts with an outlandish crown of violets and ivy on his head. "Hail friends!" he hollers over to them, "Will you have a very drunken man as a companion to your revels?"[9]

Having been invited to join the company and address the sub-

ject of the day—love—Alcibiades launches into an impromptu oration about a painfully specific love affair: his own with Socrates.
Socrates may look like a man who appreciates the male anatomy,
Alcibiades informs his audience—he possesses the "outer mask"
of a guy who craves bodily beauty—"but, oh my companions in
drink," he exclaims in frustration, "when he is opened, what tem-
perance there is residing within!"[10] Socrates only *seems* lustful. In
fact, he is distinctly and tragically moderate in his appetites. No
matter. Alcibiades is prepared to sharpen those appetites. Forti-
fied by a "wonderful opinion of the attractions of my youth," he
sets off on the seduction trail.[11]

"When I next went to [Socrates] . . . I sent away the attendant
who usually accompanied me," he reports. In so doing, he hoped
that "I should hear him speak the language which lovers use to
their loves when they are by themselves, and I was delighted."
But alas, "nothing of the sort" happened. Instead of murmuring
torrid secrets into Alcibiades' ear, Socrates "conversed as usual,
and spent the day with me and then went away."[12]

Fazed only for a moment, Alcibiades conceives a fresh plan:
He invites his instructor to the local gym. "I challenged him to
the *palestra*," he tells us (a full-body wrestling competition), "and
he wrestled and closed with me several times when there was no
one else present; I fancied that I might succeed in this manner."
But no, "not a bit; I made no way with him," Alcibiades laments.
Superior strategies were needed: ". . . I thought that I must take
stronger measures and attack him boldly. . . . So I invited him
to sup with me, just as if he were a fair youth, and I a designing
lover. He was not easily persuaded to come," Alcibiades admits.

But what is far worse is that when he finally *did* come, Socrates
failed to commit even the smallest sexual impropriety.[13]

Frustrated but not vanquished, Alcibiades invites Socrates for
still another dinner. But on this occasion he maneuvers to keep
him at his home longer:

> *The second time . . . after we had supped, I went to conversing far
> into the night, and when he wanted to go away, I pretended the
> hour was late and he had much better remain. So he lay down on
> the couch next to me . . . and there was no one but ourselves sleep-
> ing in the apartment. All this may be told without shame*[14]

—or ego damage—"to anyone," Alcibiades says, "but what
follows I could hardly tell you if I were sober. Yet as the proverb
says, '*In vino veritas*' . . . and therefore I must speak." And with a
large swig from his wineglass, Alcibiades recounts the tale of his
ultimate humiliation:

> *When the lamp was put out and the servants had gone away, I
> thought that I must be plain with [Socrates] and have no more
> ambiguity. So I gave him a shake, and I said: "Socrates, are you
> asleep?" "No," he said. "Do you know what I am meditating?"
> "What are you meditating?" he said.*[15]

You are the noblest man in Greece, Alcibiades tells him in so
many words. And flexing his muscles seductively, he begs permission to "lay at your feet all that I have."[16] Socrates amiably agrees
to give the matter some thought. Whereupon Alcibiades

fancied that [Socrates] was smitten, and that the words I ut-
tered like arrows had wounded him, and so without waiting to
hear more I got up, and throwing my coat about him crept under
his threadbare cloak, as the time was winter, and there I lay
during the whole night having this wonderful monster in my
arms. . . .[17]

Yet even under a single coat with the sensual young man, Socrates

was so superior to my solicitations, so contemptuous and derisive
and disdainful of my beauty—which really, I fancied had some
attractions—that hear, O judges; for judges you shall be of the
haughty virtue of Socrates—nothing more happened, but in
the morning . . . I arose as from the couch of a father. . . .[18]

The tale is over. The teacher has repulsed his student. The
powerful party has cruelly jilted the weaker party. "No one," Alcibiades attests, was "ever more hopelessly enslaved by another"
human being than he was to Socrates.[19]

But is this really a story of enslavement? Is it not, more accurately, a story of empowerment? For all the vanity of his efforts to
seduce Socrates, Alcibiades shows exemplary enterprise, imagination, and chutzpah in the pursuit of his venerated idol. Even in the
throes of rejection, he is rich with faith in his own talents ("I had
a wonderful opinion of the attractions of my youth"[20]). He never
wants for fresh strategies. Far from fueling a sense of inferiority,
moreover, these strategies exercise his initiative and ingenuity.

And herein lies one of the many problems with our contemporary critique of asymmetrical relationships: It is far too simple. For if Alcibiades is enamored of his teacher's wisdom and eloquence, he is equally impressed with his own virility, his own strength, his own beauty, and his own will power. Negligible assets? Hardly. A few years later they would win him widespread fame and fortune as a Greek general—and a proud place in classical history. No doubt, Alcibiades was aware of his own upward-arching career as he was of Socrates' downward-sloping one—even as he held the "wonderful monster" in his arms. The lively co-ed who seduces her middle-aged college dean has a similar awareness.

It is only in the tunnel vision of sexual harassment officers and their like that the dizzying *diversity* of power gets lost. It is only in the one-sided victim rhetoric of our day that youth and beauty and indeed femininity become sources of subjugation and never of strength. In reality, it is frequently student and teacher who are equally awed by each other (or starving artist and wealthy collector, emerging writer and established editor, and so on). Intimidation in romantic relationships is most often mutual. More importantly, it is productive. "Love . . . ceases to live as soon as it ceases to hope or fear," wrote the French aphorist, La Rochefoucauld.[21] Power differentials do a great deal to fire both hope *and* fear. They do a great deal to fire love.

* * *

IT IS no wonder, therefore, that the landscape of western love is littered with power-imbalanced liaisons. Eleventh- and twelfth-century troubadors to whom scholars point as the progenitors of modern romance pursued asymmetrical passions to the exclusion of all others. The typical troubador consistently chose for the lady of his heart a woman of higher rank than his own—generally the wife of his lord or king. If he himself was a fighter, his beloved was a princess. If he himself was a young man, she was a woman of mature years. Queen Guenevere had already been married to King Arthur for several years at the time of the birth of Sir Lancelot. We can assume, therefore, that she was at least nineteen or twenty years the senior of her lover, and possibly far more.

One of the most dramatic—as well as prolific—knights of the Middle Ages was a German by the name of Ulrich von Liechtenstein. The author of a 30,000-line verse autobiography called *The Service of Ladies (Frauendienst)*, Ulrich habitually chose mistresses who had many years on him—and more ranks.[22] A boy from the provinces, he was only twelve years old when he identified the love of his life—a married princess living in the Austrian capital and well known for her haughtiness. He applied to work in her court in Vienna as a page and adored her from afar.

If his station was far below hers to begin with, he went to extraordinary lengths to diminish it still further. Even while rising to greater and greater accomplishment as a knight, he groveled lower and lower as a suitor. It is, in fact, as though both Ulrich and the princess conspired not merely to *maintain* but to *multiply* the power differential that split them.

As related by Ulrich, after six years of silent devotion and stalwart military achievement, he resolved one day to introduce himself to his lady. Rather than appear before her in person, however, he sent a smaller version of himself—his little niece—to represent him. He taught the child to sing a song and to plead that he might become her distant admirer. The princess, however, spat upon the girl and told her to inform her uncle that whatever might be his value as a knight, he was much too ugly to aspire to her acknowledgment. He had, for one thing, a harelip that displeased her. Hearing this reply, Ulrich immediately traveled across the country to command that the harelip be chopped off by a surgeon, who, true to the practices of his day, more closely resembled a butcher.

His next exchange with the princess took place more directly. He attempted to greet her at a horse riding party but was struck dumb with reverence. Annoyed by his ineloquence, and unsatisfied, perhaps, with his having merely removed his harelip and nothing else, the princess stepped down from her horse and ripped out Ulrich's forelock. Thrilling to the sacrifice by this time of *two* body parts for his princess, Ulrich begged the privilege to fight battles on her behalf—and soon sacrificed a third body part. This time it was a finger. In a duel over his lady, he had suffered an injury, and she had received the false report that he had lost a digit for her. When she realized that his injury had healed, she was insulted. Ulrich's response was to seize a sharp knife, command a friend to hack off a healthy finger, and mail it (affixed with gold clasps on green velvet) to the princess.

Now thrice mangled for the lady of his heart, Ulrich finally earned a thank you, which he received, as was his custom, on bended knee as though praying to a goddess. The history continues. Ulrich performs acts of valiance for the princess, but always in such a manner as to make himself somewhat ridiculous; always in such a way as to renew, refresh, and redouble the distance between their stations. Thus, for example, he sets off on an armed tour of the countryside, challenging every knight he encounters to joust with him, and breaking (by his own contention) 307 lances in five weeks of travel. But he goes on this tour-de-force dressed, not as one might expect, as a brave young nobleman, but as a woman—rather unflatteringly and unwieldily, as the goddess Venus. For all the awe he struck into the breasts of the knights he conquered, he struck laughter into the breasts of all other onlookers.

When Ulrich was not dressing up in the garb of pagan mythology, he was dressing up even worse—as a leper. Such was the princess's condition for his entrance into her castle after the jousting victories: that he disguise himself in the rags of the lowest members of medieval society—in the rags, that is, of the diseased, exiled, and impoverished class of lepers. Not only this but he must also, she added, join hands with some *actual* lepers and beg her for alms. Such was the price of admission into her presence.

But it's not over until it's over. Having climbed, in leper rags, all the way up to the castle window of his princess, Ulrich had to suffer her to throw him back down again by releasing the rope on which he hung and tossing him into the muddy castle moat. Only after this supreme embarrassment—and an additional night of wading around in freezing cold water—did the princess vouchsafe Ulrich her affection. Only when every last shred of dignity had been shorn from him did she offer him an hour of love. It had been fifteen years since the beginning of his "service" to her.

What is most surprising about such tales is not the courage, stamina, and sacrifice demanded of the knight by his lady (superhuman as these may seem)—but the ritual *humiliation* imposed on him. For it is no accident that Ulrich's princess subjects him to such demeaning treatment. The diminishment and ridicule are not side effects; they are part of the purpose. Guenevere, too, imposes humiliation on Lancelot. When she has finished, it is the story's other characters who pick up where she left off.

The most important original narrative that has come down to us about Lancelot is a story from twelfth-century France known as *Le Chevalier de la Charrette* (*The Knight of the Cart*).[23] Far from the sparkling dignity of his later Hollywood incarnations, this Lancelot is made to suffer the deepest degradation known to criminals of his period—the twelfth-century equivalent of putting your head into the stocks and having fruit flung into your face. To save Guenevere from an evil abductor, Lancelot is forced by a spiteful dwarf *to ride in the back of a wooden cart.*

For those of us unable to imagine the indignity associated with such an action for a medieval knight (known to his peers by his elegant horsemanship and earnest pride), suffice it to say that after Lancelot's tenure in the dirty cart he is mocked uniformly by his country people—both nobles and peasants, women and men. Not until he has completed countless further feats of daring is he partially redeemed in their eyes. And even then, he is still shunned by Guenevere. Escorted into her prison by the warriors he has vanquished in order to obtain her freedom, Lancelot finds himself dismissed. I have no interest in seeing him, Guenevere declares. Why? She does not say. Lancelot can only assume it is because she has heard of his humiliation in the cart.

In fact, it ends up being for the opposite reason: not that he climbed into the cart on her behalf, but that he hesitated for a second before doing so. The effect, however, is the same: Lancelot is twice shamed. He is twice made to grovel for—and *before*—the object of his passions. The power differential between lover and beloved, queen and "criminal" is doubly reinforced, doubly magnified.

*   *   *

WHAT HOLDS true in the flashing fields of medieval knights holds just as true at the homely hearth of nineteenth-century woodchoppers. It can be found as pervasively in the fairy tales of the Brothers Grimm as in the medieval French fantasies of Chrétien de Troyes. What more forceful evidence of the aphrodisiac effects of inequality is there than that it captures the erotic imagination of spinning housewives and lumberjacks as despotically as the imagination of conquerors and courtiers centuries before?

It is hard to find a love story collected by the German brothers, Jacob and Wilhelm Grimm, that does not rely for a good part of its tension on a larger-than-life power disparity between its protagonists. Sometimes this difference is simple as in "Snow White": spurned stepchild working as housecleaner for seven dwarves weds prince.[24] Or "Rumpelstiltskin": miller's daughter normally confined to spinning wheel tricks gnome and marries king.[25]

Often, though, the tales are more complex, marked by one or more spectacular metamorphoses. What makes these stories so compelling is that while the power differential shifts back and forth, *it is always retained*. The idea, in other words, is not that a particular sex, or a particular party, has power over the other, but that one party, *either* party, be stronger. And the relationship can flip, with the woman, for example, starting with less clout than her partner and finishing with more. The point is not *"who* is the fairest of them all," but that *someone* be fairest at any given moment. The only indispensable quality is *in*equality.

Take the story of Beauty and the Beast, known as "The Winter Rose" in the brief Grimm tale that inspired the better-known modern tale.[26] The story begins with a merchant who asks his three daughters what gift he may bring them from his travels. The two older girls demand expensive clothes; the youngest requests a rose. But nothing is ever simple in fairyland, and the rose proves unusually difficult to secure. Winter falls, and it proves impossible. Just as the father is running out of hope, he stumbles across an enchanted garden in which it is only half winter—and half summer. Here he steals a gorgeous rose, only to be caught in the act by the garden's owner, a ghastly monster, who demands in payment the hand of his youngest daughter. Thus we have, in the beginning of the story, a couple consisting of an exemplary human being and an amoral animal—an asymmetrical pair if ever there was one. And yet love is born.

The proof? Before the forced wedding of Beauty and the Beast can take place, Beauty's father falls ill, and she begs leave of her fiancé to go to his sickbed. The Beast assents, but asks her to return in a week's time. We have every reason to expect that the girl will seize the opportunity and flee. But no, she returns to the monster's home of her own free will and, in the instant of her return, the power pendulum swings from one side to the other. The Beast suddenly turns into a handsome prince. Where a week before we had a merchant girl in love with a horrible monster, we now have a splendid monarch in love with a (mere) merchant girl. The power differential has been reversed—and yet the relationship's inequality has been deliberately maintained—and with it, the chemistry between the partners. They lose no time in celebrating their wedding.

A similar power trajectory appears in the lesser-known "Snow White and Red Rose" (not to be confused with "Snow White and the Seven Dwarves"; a different Snow White!).[27] The heroines of the story are two sisters who live with their poor but virtuous mother in a cottage in the woods. One night they are surprised at their front door by a great black bear. At first they recoil in horror, but before long they realize the bear is kindly disposed toward them, so much so that they let him into their home to warm himself by the fire. They begin to tease him. "They tugged his fur with their hands, planted their feet upon his back and rolled him over. . . ." Before long their play becomes rather rough—"they took a hazel switch, and hit him"—and their companion eroticizes it: "Would you beat *your suitor* dead?"[28] asks the bear. His word choice is prescient, for in short order his absences from the cottage are lamented like those of a boyfriend.

At night the girls never "bolted the door until their black playmate had arrived."[29] And when he leaves in the morning to fight battles with evil dwarves, they are bereft. They respond to their grief by developing an animosity for dwarves themselves. Indeed, the tale ends with the bear surprising Snow White and Red Rose in a fight with an especially vicious member of the midget race—and knocking him dead with a blow of his paw. But at the moment the dwarf falls, the bear's fur peels off and underneath is a man of pure gold. "I am the son of a king," explains the golden man, "and I had been cast under a spell by the wicked dwarf who stole my treasures. He forced me to run around the forest as a wild bear, and only his death could release me from the spell."[30]

True to his established identity as the girls' "suitor," the bear now asks the sisters to marry him—or rather, he asks the hand of Red Rose for his twin brother and the hand of Snow White for himself. For all the differences between "Beauty and the Beast" and "Snow White and Red Rose," the power pattern in the stories is the same: Inferior Male (e.g., Beast, Bear) meets Superior Female (e.g., Merchant's Daughter, Cottage Girl), transforms into Superior Male (Prince, Golden Boy), and weds her. The power shuttles back and forth, but the asymmetry is preserved at all costs.

*   *   *

WHAT IS it that makes these skewed and slanted, top-heavy and side-veering relationships so potent?

Certainly one factor is that power differentials encourage theatrics—and theatrics are at the very heart of romance. It is far sexier and more challenging to feel simultaneously connected to an individual and divided by a consideration of status than it is to be presented from the beginning as "two peas in a pod." It is more stimulating to be forced into a role in which one does not quite believe ("beast" or butler or juvenile delinquent; "princess" or priest or parole officer) than it is to be offered to each other as bare fraternal twins, naked and equal. There is an intrinsic suspense and ceremony in power-imbalanced relationships that—if not the same as the suspense and ceremony of romance—are easily confounded with them, and notoriously conducive to them. Much as there is no tennis without a net, there is no courtship without a barrier—and what more immediate barrier than a conspicuous difference in class or experience, age or employment?

There is hardly a sexier moment in the history of opera than the scene in which the truant gypsy, Carmen, lies in the chains of her police captor, Don José—ostensibly in his power—and begins to sing into his ear.[31] Shut up, he snarls at her; you are not allowed to talk to me. No? But I am allowed to talk to myself, she says: *"Je chante que pour moi-meme."*[32] I sing only to myself. And *how* she sings. Within moments, the power has shifted and Don José is ready to sign off his life for her (as indeed he does later in the opera). By reeling him swiftly into the spool of her imagination, by evoking for him the life she might lead if she were with "someone like him," she changes the antagonistic tension of their encounter into the balled tension of desire. Hostility becomes hunger. Hierarchy becomes an occasion to tease and provoke, bait and flirt. The exchange of chilly formalities evolves into a rally of increasingly heated innuendoes and *sous-entendus*. At the end, Don José tears the shackles off his beguiling captive and flees the land with her. Henceforth it is Carmen who is the captor.

Which brings us to the next reason why power differentials are as compulsively interesting as they are: One moment you are in control; the next moment you are not. One moment you are on top; the next moment you are underfoot. The to-and-fro movement of power mimics the to-and-fro movement of sex itself. The give-and-take, the back-and-forth between two persons is by its very nature intimate, by its very nature rousing. A liaison in which power is constantly being renegotiated is a force field alive as the ocean tides, bittersweet as the mermaid's song.

Finally—and perhaps most controversially—power discrepancies help us to recognize the divine in the human being at our side. They allow us to see god in another and to play god *for* another. At the end of the day, few of us want to feel that our passion is simply fair exchange, even-steven remuneration for favors performed, charms displayed. We long to be generous in love; we yearn to give every last drop of blood and sweat—as long as we feel we are giving it to someone who is, in at least some sense, our superior. It is to gods that human beings make their most lavish sacrifices, not to siblings.

To maintain a perceived power inequality need not be a cynical enterprise. It is not a cynical *need*. The urge to admire our partners as much as we like them is a noble impulse. In a recent essay, the novelist Siri Hustvedt describes the charge she gets seeing her husband—the even better-known novelist, Paul Auster—give public appearances.[33] She knows that he is the same man who will be taking out her garbage an hour later, and she loves both men. She loves the famous writer more for dealing with her garbage. But sometimes it is necessary for her to see the stranger again, the man at the podium, the man to whom she might have written a fan letter if she weren't already married to him. It is not always enough to feel tenderness for our beloved. At times we must also feel awe.

For all the egalitarian rhetoric about searching for one's "other half" (rhetoric that dates back to a speech in the *Symposium*, for that matter), it is not ultimately another half we seek. We do not want something that is part of us. We want something bigger—someone intriguingly greater. The surprise is that this person need not make us feel smaller.

★ ★ ★

CONSIDER THE evidence of the greatest English love novels by women: Jane Austen's *Pride and Prejudice*, Charlotte Brontë's *Jane Eyre*, and Emily Brontë's *Wuthering Heights*.[34] Written within thirty-some years in the first half of the nineteenth century, all three of these classic love stories foreground a relationship that is conspicuously unbalanced. *Pride and Prejudice* (1813) features the impoverished Elizabeth Bennet with the high-handed aristocrat, Fitzwilliam Darcy. *Jane Eyre* (1847) presents us with a disinherited young governess (who is not, we are told, even *pretty*) in the employment of the wealthy and dashing Edward Rochester. In *Wuthering Heights* (1847), we see the rich and beautiful Catherine, called Cathy, in love with the dirty street-orphan, Heathcliff, who becomes her family's stable hand.

Yet, in all three of these novels the "weaker" party is empowered by the relationship to the stronger one. In the company of the condescending Mr. Darcy (who loves her against his "will, against [his] reason, and even against [his] character,") Austen's silver-tongued heroine hones her wit, multiplies her pride, and learns to say some eloquent "no's."[35] If she says yes to Mr. Darcy in the end, it is only because she has reconstructed him from the ground up.

Jane Eyre similarly discovers her self-assurance in the house and heart of a social superior. So does Heathcliff, who has been picked out of the slums by Cathy's father and taken to live in the family's country home. For all Cathy's abrasive effects on Heathcliff (she frequently slights him and ultimately marries another man), it is through her that he comes to believe that his "father was Emperor of China and [my] mother an Indian queen" and to behave accordingly.[36] It is through the love of a woman he considers his superior that he discovers his own worth. Through his love of Cathy, Heathcliff acquires the courage to leave Wuthering Heights, conquer the world, and return to conquer his detractors.

What happens in the works of women artists also happens in their lives. Not much is known about the love relations of Jane Austen or of the Brontë sisters—few of their letters survive—but a fair amount is known about the love relations, say, of their near-contemporary, the greatest female poet America has created, Emily Dickinson. Dickinson's verse betrays a good deal of interest in imbalanced relationships. Poems like "He put the belt around my life / I heard the buckle snap" are hard to forget.[37] For some feminist critics they are hard to forgive. But what has been held against Dickinson most vehemently is not her poetry but her personal correspondence—in particular a set of three mysterious epistles that have become known as the "Master Letters."

The Master Letters were found in Dickinson's possession at the time of her death in 1886; it is not clear whether she mailed them. Nor is it clear for whom they were intended since the only term of address in them is "Master." What *is* clear—at least to the moral majority among Dickinson experts—is that they show the towering artist at her most groveling and pathetic, her most shockingly unfeminist. She writes "in abject humility," according to her biographer, Richard B. Sewall: Her "tone is almost entirely self-abasing and apologetic."[38]

Many of Dickinson's admirers wish these letters did not exist. The next-best scenario would be if they were not really letters, but merely literary exercises. Perhaps Dickinson's Master is a god to whom she is addressing an artistic prayer; perhaps he is a character in a novel she is imagining; perhaps he is the Personification of Art. The evidence, however, speaks against these theories. Dickinson asks the Master to visit her home in Amherst; she worries about his health; she seems to share private terms of endearment with him (she is his "Daisy," for example). He bears an uncanny resemblance, moreover, to not one, not two, but three of the men Dickinson loved in her lifetime—from the newspaper editor, Samuel Bowles (whose ill health often troubled her), to the charismatic New England preacher, Charles Wadsworth, to the prominent poetry critic, Thomas Wentworth Higginson. All three were influential figures in their day, movers and shakers. When the fragile little recluse that was Dickinson addressed them, she addressed them with deference.

The Master Letters show Dickinson pushing this deference into high performance. They show her raising humility and timidity into an art form. Indeed, they exhibit the same elliptical expressions, abundant em-dashes, intense images, interpretational difficulty, and emotional explosiveness that distinguish her poetry. The letters *look* like her poetry. And they show her reimagining her love relationships exactly as she, the poet, prefers them: as religious epiphanies.

They also reveal something else, and that is: Dickinson is finding a foothold on the steep slopes she has helped create. In the landscape of power differentials, they show her digging her heel into the incline. They unmask her eccentrically but effectively asserting her own worth, her own prerogative, her own genius, and even—yes—her superiority to the person she calls "Master."

Let us take a look at the first letter—the lightest and lowest key of the trio.

"Dear Master," it begins,

I am ill, but grieving more that you are ill . . . I thought perhaps you were in heaven, and when you spoke again, it seemed quite sweet, and wonderful, and surprised me so—I wish that you were well.[39]

On one hand, Dickinson is setting herself up as solicitous here: She calls the man she addresses "Master" and declares his illness more important than her own. On the other hand, the solicitousness is immediately undercut since she goes on to suggest that she imagined he was dead—a fact to which she appears to have resigned herself rather quickly. At the same time she suggests a pun on "heaven": "I thought perhaps you were in heaven" could mean she thought him dead—or it could mean she thought him too lofty for her, too virtuous, too consumed by his vocation (of minister—if the Master is Charles Wadsworth).[40] It could mean, even, that she thought him too *happy*. It's worth noting that all three men nominated as Dickinson's Master were married. Were they too happy in their marriages, too much "in heaven" with their families, to pay attention to their strange correspondent?

Dickinson proceeds to apologize to the Master for gifts she has sent him—poems, probably—that he did not understand: "You ask me what my flowers said—then they were disobedient—I gave them messages."[41] She had not intended to be unclear. She wishes she did not have to rely on words to express herself to him: "I wish that I was great, like Michael Angelo, and could paint for you." [42] She is not great. She misspells Michelangelo. She apologizes. And then the tone suddenly shifts.

"Listen again, Master." [43] She employs the imperative. She seizes control of the situation. The child raises the gavel and calls for order. She knows her Master will listen. She knows the relationship is not as asymmetrical as she has made it out to be—or not in the *way* she has made it out to be. Her childish voice can silence the room.

The letter ends on a further command, however girlish: "Tell me," she says, "please to tell me, soon as you are well." [44] The repetition of "tell me" gives the line an air of urgency, of authority. The distribution of power in this pair is not as simple as Dickinson's self-deprecation would have us believe.

The second Master letter starts on a tragic note. It is a more dramatic letter than the first, and worth quoting at some length: "Master," says Dickinson,

> *If you saw a bullet hit a Bird—and he told you he wasn't shot— you might weep at his courtesy, but you would certainly doubt his word.*

> *One drop more from your Daisy's bosom—then would you believe? Thomas's faith in Anatomy was stronger than his faith in faith. God made me—Master—* . . . *He built the heart in me—By and by it outgrew me—and like the little mother—with the big child—I got tired holding him . . .* [45]

> *Have you the heart in your breast—Sir—is it set like mine—a little to the left? . . .* [46]

Daisy's arm is small—and you have felt the horizon haven't you—and did the sea never come so close as to make you dance? . . .[47]

I want to see you more—Sir—than all I wish for in this world—and the wish—altered a little—will be my only one— for the skies

Could you come to New England—would you come to Amherst—Would you like to come—Master?[48]

Would Daisy disappoint you—no—she wouldn't—sir— it were comfort forever—just to look in your face, while you looked in mine—then I could play in the woods till Dark— till you take me where the Sundown cannot find us—[49]

On the surface this letter is indeed abject. From start to finish, Dickinson emphasizes her "smallness" in relation to her great, grand lover. First she is a bird, then she is a frail flower (a Daisy), next she draws attention to her "small arm," and in the end she is a child who "could play in the woods till Dark." And yet, for all the apparent subservience of the missive—for all the stops and starts and childish hesitations, for all the excesses of politeness—it is fundamentally a letter about self-assurance. It is the letter of a powerful and confident woman—a woman who employs saccharine formulations, to be sure, and harbors the odd obsequious impulse, but a woman who ultimately knows exactly who she is and how vast is her worth.

One need only look at the first paragraph. Dickinson smarts from the pain of rejection: She compares herself to a bird that has been shot. Even this comparison, though—when considered closely—is a proud one. Dickinson is mortally injured, but she is urbane and "courteous"; she swears she was not struck.

Were it not for the blood bursting from her bosom, the Master would not believe in her wound. Were it not for the nail holes in Christ's hands and feet, his disciple Thomas would not believe he had climbed down from the cross. (Thomas's "faith in Anatomy was stronger than his faith in faith"). Already so soon in the letter, Dickinson is reversing the power dynamic she set up in her salutation. No longer is her "Master" *the* Master; he is already being likened to a mere *disciple* (and a bad one at that). In the meantime Dickinson herself is being compared to Jesus.

The next lines find her reasserting her divine construction— "God made me . . . He built the heart in me"—and casting doubt on the construction of the Master: "Have you the heart in your breast—Sir—is it set like mine—a little to the left?" Or did somebody get it wrong? *Did they mess up when they made you—Master?* [50]

Dickinson's childlike demeanor allows her to get away with murder. It allows her to make harsh insinuations, deliver troubling truths, and assert both her pain and her worth with a candor that would ordinarily get her into great trouble. Like the jester in the courts of Renaissance kings, Dickinson uses her strangeness, her whimsy, her defiance of adult convention, to speak Truth to Power. Her obvious vulnerability allows her to avoid giving punishable offense. Or so she hopes.

Having suggested that her Master's heart may be defective, Dickinson calmly describes her own as oversized. The metaphor she evokes of the heart as a child that outgrows its mother is striking and surreal, but it is to the point. Dickinson may be a fragile creature—a bird, a bee—but her heart is larger than life. Her heart is larger than *she* is. "I got tired holding him," she explains.[51]

It would be hard not to recognize the implicit pride in such a statement. The Master may be a man of the world; his broad arm may embrace the entire "horizon," but it is not for this reason that he grasps as much as the "small-armed" woman who loves him.[52]

His experience is exterior; hers interior. Though she may never lay eyes on the sea, she dances with it. The Master does not. For all his great life experience, he seems oddly paralyzed.

Perhaps this is why she asks him to move, to come to her in Amherst. "Would Daisy disappoint you?" she asks in her little girl voice, and instantly answers:

> *no—she wouldn't—sir—it were comfort forever—just to look in your face, while you looked in mine—then I could play in the woods till Dark—till you take me where the Sundown cannot find us—*[53]

Is this abjection or assertiveness? The two melt into each other. If Dickinson did not make herself so small, she could not talk so big; she could not *feel* so big, or risk so much. In the end, she has great confidence both in the reciprocity of her love and (paradoxically) in her own independence. She assumes that her Master wants to look in her face as much she wants to look in his. She invites him to take her "where the Sundown cannot find us"—into eternity.[54] No small matter.

"Master," she says in her final letter—abruptly embracing the imperative (as she had in the first letter)—*"Open your life wide—and take me in forever—."*[55] Dickinson demands "forever." She demands sacred permanence. Having found union with her beloved, "I shall not want anymore." Even Paradise can no longer tempt her; "Heaven itself will not seem as dear" as what she has with him: "Heaven only will disappoint me," she says, ". . . because it's not so dear."[56] Thus ends the infamous series of Master Letters.

These letters do not close on a note of renunciation. They do not close on a note of humility. They close on a note of triumph. Dickinson thrives in her position of weakness; she comes into her own when she casts (or indeed *mis*casts) her partner—as the superior in the liaison. She could never reach the level of lyric or emotional intensity we see in the Master Letters in a liaison with a person she construed as an equal. To hit the highest marks, she has to look upward.

Even if Dickinson knows she is "no Rose," as she writes in a couplet inserted into the letters, "yet still" she "felt myself a'bloom" in her exchange with the Master; even if she's "No bird—yet—[she] rode on Ether."[57] Critics have argued about where these two lines of poetry precisely fit in the correspondence—there are some confusing asterisks indicating where Dickinson intended them—but ultimately it barely matters. Dickinson flew in "Ether" throughout. For all her groveling, she soared in this liaison. Passions like these inspired her loftiest verse.

Not so for another great American poet, Edna St. Vincent Millay, born half a century after Dickinson, in 1892—and equally castigated for her relations with men. Where Dickinson was an insistent recluse, Millay was a notorious flirt. Where Dickinson cast herself as a sort of servant, Millay cast herself as a diva-monarch. Where Dickinson focused obsessively on one person, Millay was distracted by dozens of men and women at a time.

"What lips my lips have kissed, and where, and why, / I have forgotten," she declares in one of her most incantatory sonnets,

> and what arms have lain
> Under my head till morning; but the rain
> Is full of ghosts tonight, that tap and sigh
> Upon the glass and listen for reply,
> And in my heart there stirs a quiet pain
> For unremembered lads that not again
> Will turn to me at midnight with a cry . . .[58]

"Unremembered lads" are a major motif in Millay's verse—unremembered lads who are hardly untroubled—who have cried and bled for her. The chemistry in Millay's rapports is a chemistry of queenship: She lords over her subjects, they strain to be worthy of her attention, of her conviction, of her rabid adventures, of her savage beauty. Millay lived wildly and bravely; she expended herself; she tossed herself into the fire like a moth. She is perhaps best known for her defiant autobiographical quatrain:

> My candle burns at both ends;
> It will not last the night;
> But ah, my foes, and oh, my friends—
> It gives a lovely light![59]

The poem is a metaphor for Millay's life: fiery and wasteful, gorgeous, dangerous, brief. She died too soon; she died from smoke and drink and drugs and overexertion; she died by plunging down a staircase and breaking her neck. But the poem may also be read (as has been pointed out by critics) as an anatomically precise description of a night she spent in her twenties with the most celebrated literary critic of her time, Edmund Wilson, and with his friend and fellow editor at *Vanity Fair*, John Peale Bishop. Having flirted with these two writers for some time, having dined with them and toyed with them and fought with them and drunk with them, Millay decided, also, to sleep with them—at the same time. So, like an empress, she apportioned her territories. She divided her body between her subjects: Bishop attended to the top half of Edna St. Vincent Millay, Wilson to the bottom. The night was successful. (Both men eventually proposed marriage.) And her candle did indeed burn at both ends.

If Dickinson sometimes likened herself to a fragile bird, Millay could be compared to a queen bee—a queen bee making honeyed verse and reclining among her male workers while they minister to her. Millay rarely allowed a man to get the upper hand; what provoked her to her greatest flights of poetry and sentiment was precisely the experience of being above the men (and women) with whom she kept company. It is in part for this reason that her most important love affair was with the twenty-two-year-old boy poet, George Dillon (she was thirty-six at the time). It was for this reason that she never had fewer than a minion of men courting her at any one point. It is for this reason, finally, that she married an unknown Dutch businessman at the height of her fame, a man who happily told reporters that "It is so obvious to anyone that [Edna St.] Vincent is more important than I am."[60]

Millay courted superiority in her relations: "I shall forget you presently my dear," she would tell her suitors in verse and conversation,

> So make the most of this, your little day,
> Your little month, your little half a year,
> Ere I forget, or die, or move away. . . .
>
> I would indeed that love were longer-lived,
>
> And oaths were not as brittle as they are,
> But so it is . . .[61]

By keeping her boys on alert, she kept herself on pitch. She kept the decibel of her relationships at a crescendo.

In one sense, at least, Millay may be a model. It is the rare lover who genuinely thrives on the egalitarian, suspense-less brand of love touted today by our media and institutions of higher learning. The heart craves adventure—and adventure more often involves princes and paupers than twins and teammates. The day that there are as many women as men in positions of power there will be as many men "sleeping up" as "sleeping down." Perhaps the most difficult situation in romance is the one we are striving so officially and noisily to achieve today: equality. It is precisely equality that destroys our libidos, equality that bores men and women alike, *equality* that Maureen Dowd yawns over in *Are Men Necessary?*[62]

The statistics are misleading. The finding is not—as is often assumed—that men do not want partners who are more successful than they are. They do not want partners who are exactly *as* successful as they are. They prefer—as women do—dating *either* down or up. Sideways is dull. Sideways is painful. The man and woman who dash to open the door at the same pace bang their heads. A man wants what a woman wants: someone compellingly different. Only where there is sharply etched disunity can there be ecstatically earned unity. It is with the enigmatic Other, the strange superior that we dream to join, not with a brother, not with a familiar, and not—for all our fair-mindedness—with an equal.

◇

THREE

The Blade Between Us:
Love as Transgression

TELL ME THE RULES, THAT I MAY BREAK THEM.
—Silesian proverb[1]

EROS IS A MISCHIEVOUS CHILD. It does not take orders. It does not jump where it is bid; nor does it shoot where someone marks an "X." No wonder that all the classic tales of love potions—from *Tristan and Iseult* to *A Midsummer Night's Dream*—involve love potions misapplied.[2] Love potions served to the wrong person, love potions that drive you toward the opposite partner than you intended. Iseult is supposed to fall in love with King Mark—it is for him that her doting mother has prepared an aphrodisiac brew—but the brew is dispensed in error and Iseult falls instead for Tristan, the king's most trusted knight.

Lysander in *A Midsummer Night's Dream* is intended to adore his fiancée, the gentle Hermia, but Puck confuses his liquids and makes him fall for Helena, the mistress of his friend Demetrius.[3]

A few scenes later the Fairy Queen succumbs to an ass. It is the inappropriate party to whom we are overwhelmingly pulled. It is the transgressive choice—not the intended choice, not the choice we are *applauded* to make by parents and guardians, authorities and well-wishers—that viscerally draws us. We may, at various points, embrace matches of convenience and reason, but our instincts draw us irresistibly to the inconvenient, the unreasonable, the unsanctioned. "Love," sings Carmen, "is a rebel bird." Cupid is a career contrarian.[4]

With the decline of taboos in the last few decades has come a decline in feeling. There are no more Hester Prynnes among us—no more women with an "A" for adultery slapped onto their breastcoats—and this is a blessing.[5] But it's also, paradoxically, a curse. For obstacles create obstacle-jumpers; fences create passionate trespassers. What are Pyramus and Thisbe, Romeo and Juliet, Rapunzel and the Prince without the wall between them?[6] But today we have the opposite of walls: We have banged open doors with signs imploring us to enter. Come through, they say, and take possession of the girl in the tower! Rapunzel is yours for the asking. Indeed, here's a sex manual to consult on your second date. Follow the diagrams.

There was a time when sex—even in marriage—had the whiff of transgression about it. Today it smacks almost of duty. We understand from the armies of Kinsey and *Cosmopolitan* that we are supposed to have it so and so many times a week, a day, a month. We understand that we are supposed to have it alone if not with partners; alone as *well* as with partners. We know that we are supposed to demand certain numbers and types of physiological responses—and dole them out symmetrically. Should we stir from this ideal, we are inhibited. Frigid. Repressed. (Far more crippling insults than "wicked" probably ever was to our ancestors. People would much rather be thought wicked than dull.)

Healthy Americans are urged to have sex the way they eat Special K cereal and go to the gym. Our love lives have become something we "work on," much like our bodies, or CVs. Countless books prescribe countless exercises for better bedroom performance. *Atlantic Monthly* columnists compare erotic overtures to "get(ting) the canoe out in the water" and urge their sisters to *be brave about it!*[7] The "paddling" gets easier once you're in the open sea! Desirelessness at any point in our lives or relationships is treated as an illness no less medically legitimate than cancer. Even the denizens of some nursing homes are urged to get with the program and explore their "right" to sexual pleasure. Where some generations were offended by lust, we are offended only by lustlessness. Result: The single genuinely transgressive sexual behavior left today might well be *no* sexual behavior.

Perhaps this accounts for the surprise success, some years back, of an otherwise undistinguished film like Sofia Coppola's *Lost in Translation*, in which a restless young newlywed and an attractive older actor distinguish themselves by *not sleeping together* when they meet and fall in love during an extended residence in a Tokyo hotel.[8] Perhaps it accounts for the renewed fascination for novels like Edith Wharton's *The Age of Innocence* in which the romantic leads spend a lifetime deferring their physical passion, or, indeed, for the unexpected curiosity about the "modesty movement" as spearheaded by writers like Wendy Shalit.[9] Promiscuity has become untransgressive—and therefore dull.

The preservation of transgressive relationships has a long

and illustrious history in literary myth. We could speak as readily of Heloise and Abelard as of Lancelot and Guenevere, of Shakespeare's *Romeo and Juliet*, his *Antony and Cleopatra*, or his Angelo and Isabella in *Measure for Measure*. We could evoke the co-conspirators in *Liaisons dangereuses,* or the Marquis de Sade; *Madame Bovary* or *Anna Karenina*, Casanova or Pauline Réage, the author of the *Story of O*.[10]

For each of these figures, love is something that arises—at least in part—out of obstruction and illegitimacy. The medieval Abelard may have adored his brilliant student Heloise for all sorts of sober reasons, but he also gloried in being able to ravish her in the holiest spots of a nunnery.[11] Nor was it inconsequential to Heloise that the man she loved was not merely the most magnetic philosopher of the twelfth century but also a clergyman with a reputation—until then—for unblemished chastity. (Abelard was thirty-eight when he met the teenaged Heloise; she was, as far as we can glean, his first lover.) When he proposes to marry her, she protests. Duty and legitimacy, she says, may not enter their free love. Straight up to the moment of Abelard's brutal castration, their relationship crackles with the fire and rambunctious delight of transgression.

Less obviously, so does Romeo and Juliet's. For even while Shakespeare's best-known lovers express their dismay at the feud between their families and the misfortune of their names, all their rhetoric serves to emphasize and fondle it. "*Romeo, Romeo* wherefore art thou *Romeo?*" Juliet laments over and over again.[12] "Deny thy father and refuse thy *name* . . .'Tis but the *name* that is mine enemy; O be some other *name!*"[13] At the time she says this, the only thing she really *knows* about Romeo is his name. She has barely yet cast eyes on the man. Visiting Juliet's balcony long before any indiscretion has taken place between them, Romeo, for his part, hungrily envisions the hostile armies that he hopes stand in wait for him: "There lies more peril in thine eye," he boasts to Juliet, "than twenty of their swords!"[14] Twenty swords? On a sleepy summer night the first time he visits her?

If Shakespeare's most attractive romantic hero gets a certain charge from the prospect of being assaulted by a midnight military, his least attractive romantic hero—the hypocritical governor Angelo in *Measure for Measure*—gets a far more sinister charge from the fact that the woman he desires is not only the sister of a man he has just condemned to death for premarital indiscretions—but also a starch-collared nun-in-training. Never, Angelo vows, could a less pious girl have had the same effect on him: "Never could a strumpet, / With all her double vigour, art, and nature, once stir my temper, / But this virtuous maid subdues me quite. . . . / O cunning enemy," he accosts Satan, "that to catch a saint with saints dost bait thy hook!"[15] A more permissible woman could not have heated the governor's chill blood; but this untouchable angel, this paragon of purity whose brother he stands ready to execute is sufficiently out of bounds to be irresistible.

What family feuds and clerical clout do for some lovers, plain old adultery does for others. "Without adultery, what would happen to imaginative writing?" asks Denis de Rougemont, author of *Love in the Western World*.[16] Probably the earliest and most high-spirited champion of recreational adultery is the Roman poet Ovid. His first-century "self-help book," *The Art of Love*, essentially *assumes* that any woman his readers might woo is married. The trick, for Ovid, is not simply to seduce a married woman, but to seduce a married woman whose husband is particularly vigilant, violent, dangerous, and jealous: "Fool," he upbraids a hypothetical husband,

> *if you feel no need to guard your girl for your own sake*
>   *See that you guard her for mine, so I may want her the more.*
>   *Easy things nobody wants, but what is*
>   *forbidden is tempting. . . .[17]*

The consent of authority is the kiss of death for a lover longing to prove his mettle. "Give me the chance to prove that I am resourceful in love," Ovid implores. "Anyone who can love the wife of an indolent cuckold . . . would steal buckets of sand from the shore."[18] To prevent the impression of indolence, Ovid instructs his women readers in the art of faking the existence of a dangerous spouse where none is conveniently available:

"Though you are perfectly free," he charges the ladies,

> *. . . act scared.*
>   *When you might let [your lover] in by*
> *the door, let him in by the window,*
>   *Let your features assume every expression of fright,*
>   *Have your maid rush in (she will have to be clever about it)*
>   *Crying "My God, we're caught!" Hide*
> *the poor frightened young man.[19]*

Lest we wonder why it is necessary to stage such exhausting dramas, Ovid explains his theory of love:

Gifts too easily made encourage no permanent passion.
  Often a boat goes down sunk by a favoring wind. This
  is what keeps some wives from being loved by their husbands.
  It's all too easy for him, coming whenever he will.
  Put a door in his way, and have a doorkeeper tell him
  "No admittance: keep out!"—then he will burn with desire.[20]

Transgression has rarely had so exuberant a defender.

It is not, however, the amiable Ovid to whom modern scholars trace the rule-breaking fervor of Western love literature, but to a group of far graver young men who lived 1000-plus years after him. The troubadors—as they became known—were essentially knights in shining armor who emerged in eleventh-century Provence and invented—according to current critical opinion—what our collective culture has ever afterward recognized as "romance." Love, in the company of these knights, revolved around "humility, courtesy . . . and the religion of love."[21] It also revolved around adultery.

A representative troubador was a warrior infatuated with the wife of his lord or king. Sometimes, as C.S. Lewis has pointed out, she was the only woman in his vicinity; his own wife—if he had one—was typically far away raising his children. The troubador himself lived alone with his gallant colleagues waiting to go to battle.[22] And, as increasingly occurred, writing seductive verses to the Lady of the House, performing feats of valor on her behalf, and waiting with impeccable courtesy and apparently endless patience for some small sign of favor. When this kind of courtship remained within limits, it seems to have been taken rather as a compliment by the lord—a tribute to his good taste and fortune. When, however, it stepped out of bounds, it could be ruthlessly punished by execution—not only of the offending courtier, but also of the lady.

Certainly the most iconic and influential myth that arose out of troubador culture is the myth of Tristan and Iseult.[23] Degraded or deformed, rehabilitated, renounced, or renewed—it has yielded, argues Denis de Rougemont who studied it at length, the love triangles of French comedy, the happy endings of Hollywood romance, as well as the suicidal love quests of countless German Werthers.[24] If it is the founding myth of western passion, it could also be said to be the founding myth of western transgression. For that reason—and because it will resonate for the rest of this book—it is worth pausing over here.

* * *

THE STORY, as it has come down to us in five "original" manuscripts from the eleventh and twelfth centuries, is roughly this: The perfect knight Tristan is sent by his valiant lord and uncle, King Mark of Cornwall, to find him a wife. Now Mark has recently received a golden hair from the beak of a swallow, and it is his idea that the owner of the hair—she and only she—should be the woman he weds. Tristan sets out, and before long a storm has washed him onto the shores of Ireland.

It must be said that Tristan is a bit nervous in Ireland. Some years earlier, he had killed the Irish queen's brother, a villain called Morhold, who had come to carry away Cornish boys in collection for a debt. Tristan's slaying of him had made Tristan a local hero. It had also given him a wound that never altogether healed. Wandering around Ireland, for the second time Tristan learns that a dragon is preying upon the people and that the Irish king has offered the hand of his daughter Iseult to the man who succeeds in killing it. Being, as we have said, the perfect knight, Tristan does just this. Being a gruesome medieval warrior as well, he cuts out the dragon's tongue and puts it in his stocking. This backfires. The dragon's poisonous blood seeps into Tristan's veins, and he collapses into a dead faint.

Enter the king's cowardly seneschal who chops off the dead dragon's head and rushes to announce that it is he who has killed it. Unconvinced by the seneschal's tale, Iseult sets out to examine the dragon for herself, stumbles upon the unconscious Tristan, and brings him back to her castle for medical attention. All looks well until Iseult notices a gash on Tristan's sword and realizes that it is he who delivered the fatal blow to her Uncle Morhold's cranium (a piece of which—being a gruesome medieval princess—she has carefully preserved). Horrorstruck, she seizes Tristan's sword and determines to murder him.

Tristan, luckily, is not merely brave but also eloquent. Within moments, he has convinced Iseult that if she does away with him she will have to marry the lowly seneschal, since only he, Tristan, can prove that the dragon was killed by someone else. The argument seems convincing. Tristan produces the dragon's tongue and is awarded Iseult, who he whisks onto his ship and carries to Cornwall to offer King Mark for a wife. (It is assumed that Iseult has golden hair and therefore satisfies the king's single marital requirement.)

Alas, the trip to Cornwall is long and Tristan and Iseult are handsome people. Worse, Iseult's mother has prepared a love potion for her daughter to give to Mark. Iseult's maid accidentally gives it to Tristan. The two fall violently and deeply in love. By the time Iseult arrives on Cornish shores, her virginity is history, and her hapless maid is enlisted to replace her on her wedding night. From that time forth, Tristan and Iseult meet in secret. They succeed, for some time, in deceiving Mark, but they do not succeed in deceiving his counselors. Warned, on one occasion, of an upcoming tryst between his wife and nephew, Mark hides in a tree to spy on them. Luckily, Iseult spots him in time to invent an innocuous dialogue with Tristan that convinces the king of their innocence.

Another occasion is less propitious. Wounded by a wild boar, Tristan leaps into the queen's bed one night and bleeds all over the sheets. Our twelfth-century French narrator Béroul (author of the most cited of the "original" manuscripts) is aghast: "God, what a pity the queen did not take the sheets off the bed!" he exclaims. "If she had thought of it, she could easily have protected her honor."[25] But she did not, and she and Tristan are both sentenced to burn at the stake.

Tristan is a hero, however, so, as expected, he contrives to escape. Moments before his execution he leaps out of the window of a cliffside chapel in which he has been allowed to murmur a final prayer. Meanwhile, King Mark is persuaded to consign his wife to a leper colony rather than to the flames. Presumably this is worse punishment for a lady of Iseult's stature. Fortunately, it is also punishment from which it is easier to be freed. Tristan frees his beloved accordingly, and the two go into hiding in the forest where they hunt for food, live in a bower of leaves, and love each other voraciously.

The king, ostensibly furious at their escape, is clued in to their whereabouts and arrives to assassinate them. At the moment when he arrives to wreak his vengeance, however, they are sleeping with Tristan's sword carefully poised between them. Touched by the apparent chastity of his subjects, the king seizes Tristan's sword, replaces it gracefully with his own, and returns to his castle.

For a while Tristan and Iseult inhabit a Garden of Eden-like idyll. But a surprise awaits. The love potion wears off; it was only supposed to last, we abruptly learn, for three years. The couple determines they must repent for their adultery. Tristan pens a letter to the king, declaring that it has all been a huge misunderstanding, that he only ever loved Iseult as a gentleman, and offering to bring her back home to her husband. The lovers pledge to adore each other only "honourably" forever after.[26] Tristan bequeaths Iseult his favorite dog as a memento and leaves her in the castle of Mark. Only in the moment of parting does he hesitate: Iseult, he tells a friend, is "a lovely woman," and he knows "that he would one day have her with him again, although the king would not allow this."[27]

Reader, he *does* have her with him again. For love potion or no love potion, Tristan and Iseult's passion proceeds apace. Though Tristan lives at varying distances from Mark's castle and even ultimately marries another woman called "Iseult," he continues to long for, cherish, and tryst with *his* Iseult. The new wife, "Iseult of the White Hands," can't hold a candle to his original "Iseult the Fair" and, before long, King Mark is suspicious again. To appease him once and for all, Iseult proposes to invite all the nobles of the country (including the legendary King Arthur) and to publicly swear fidelity to him. The convention is called, but to attend Iseult must cross a swamp. Rather than soil her clothes, she sweetly asks a nearby leper to carry her. Then she takes her oath: "So help me God . . . I swear that no man ever came between my thighs except the leper who carried me on his back across the ford and my husband, King Mark."[28] The leper—who the assembled dignitaries had seen Iseult straddle moments before—is Tristan in disguise.

All might now continue calmly if Tristan did not miss Iseult so painfully, suffer a bout of madness, shear off his wavy long hair, and visit Mark's castle dressed up as a court fool. Mark, as it happens, is on a fishing trip. But the scars of Tristan's illness and the skill of his disguise prove too much for Iseult; she fails to recognize him. It takes the word of her maid and the welcome of his old dog to convince her of his identity. Once convinced, she "kisse[s] his eyes and nose and face countless times." Tristan, for his part, "slipped under the sheets without another word and held the queen in his arms."[29]

It was the last time he would do so alive. For the next event recorded by our faithful narrators is Tristan's death. Injured in an ambush in Brittany, he realizes that the wound he received from Morhold so long ago has reopened. Only Iseult, he knows in his heart, can heal him. He calls for her in Cornwall, and she leaps aboard a ship immediately. But Tristan has asked his messengers to raise white sails if she is coming, black sails if she is not. And his new wife is jealous of his old mistress—and so when he asks her the color of the sails moving over the water toward Brittany, she lies. Tristan, imagining himself abandoned by the one true love of his life, leans back in his sickbed and dies. Iseult arrives too late. She runs past the mourning Britons to her beloved, clasps him to her heart, and dies in his arms.

King Mark has both their bodies returned to Cornwall and buried on either side of the nave of his church. Two trees grow on their two tombs—one on Iseult's and the other on Tristan's. Try as the church authorities may to prune them, they continue, for many centuries, to intertwine their branches over the apse.

*   *   *

ON THE surface this is a tale of tragic love, of noble heroes doing all they can to unite and legitimize their relationship, but failing because of cruel social structures, hard fates, and malicious kings. In reality, it is a tale of ecstatic love, whose success is ensured or at least encouraged by the heroes' canny efforts to delegitimize their relationship, artificially impose and strenuously maintain a transgressive edge, and regularly reinvent reasons for separation.[30]

Let us begin with Tristan's mission: to find a wife for King Mark. Does King Mark want a wife? The story tells us he sends Tristan out on the insistence of his counselors who fear he will die without an heir. It is safe to assume that Mark is advanced in age or his nephew would not already have such a lengthy *curriculum vita* in heroism—and his counselors would not be so anxious. But the instruction he gives Tristan—that he wants to marry the woman who owns a golden hair obtained from a swallow *and no other*—seems like another way of saying "Search forever." How is Tristan to make such an identification? There are innumerable blondes on the British Isles today and there were then! It is a hopeless proposition and Mark knows it.

Tristan knows it too—and therefore immediately forgets it.

At no point is Iseult asked for a hair sample. She who matched the chip from her uncle's cranium to the notch on Tristan's sword is not required to submit to the slightest reciprocal experiment. Tristan never even produces the golden hair to see if it resembles Iseult's. He simply assumes she is the proper girl and brings her to Mark; he knows there is no other way.

A further suggestion that something is not as it should be with King Mark: the love potion. Love potions are not, after all, *that* common in medieval romances. Why, if Iseult is the most beautiful and best-loved girl in the entire countryside (as the narrator repeatedly assures us), is Iseult's mother convinced Mark needs an aphrodisiac to fancy her? The seneschal didn't need an aphrodisiac. Iseult's father didn't think a single man in his kingdom needed an aphrodisiac to brave dragons for his daughter. Could it be that Iseult's mother makes the love potion because she knows what Mark's counselors know also: that *the Cornish King has no interest in young women*? That if King Mark were not pushed and shoved, bribed and drugged, he would go to the grave without taking a wife—and without loving one if she were thrust upon him?

Were we assessing this tale from the sort of modern psychological perspective despised by serious scholars, it would not be amiss to say: King Mark is gay. Or: King Mark is asexual. Or simply: King Mark hasn't the stomach for love. All of his behavior before and after he acquires the beautiful Iseult suggests indifference to her. He only acts jealous when endlessly needled to do so by his advisors. Even when Iseult's guilt has been proved beyond a shadow of a doubt, he loses no opportunity to be repersuaded of her innocence—and of his own right to ignore the whole matter.

Are Tristan and Iseult hiding under a tree at three in the morning? It's harmless. Iseult *said* it was harmless, didn't she, after all? Is there blood on the bed? Blood on the floor between Tristan's quarters and Iseult's? a gushing wound in Tristan's side? Ah well, Mark tells himself before too long, they weren't sleeping together when I saw them in the *woods* the other day, were they? There was a sword between them. Surely Tristan was just . . . retrieving something from Iseult's bed that night. A Band-Aid, perhaps?

All Mark's efforts to demand sexual fidelity from his wife are undertaken in response to the insistence of other people. Left to his own instincts, Mark is happily rid of his wife. This becomes shockingly clear on at least two occasions: first, when (in one of the myth's "minor" incidents) he bequeaths her to a harp-player in payment for a song (it is only his nephew who captures her back for him), and, the more important one, when he finds her in the forest with Tristan, determines that she is innocent, and then *leaves her there*. Why ever would a king leave his much-loved queen cowering in the cold woods when she has been cleared of all blame? Shouldn't he be bearing her triumphantly home? Doesn't he want his loyal wife back?

The answer, of course, is *no*. He never wanted her in the first place. That's why he keeps "losing" her. When she is returned to him a final time, it is Mark himself who runs for the woods. This, in any case, is the impression we get. The single time Tristan pays a visit to the conjugal castle after returning Iseult, Mark is off on an extended fishing trip. May he "not come back for a week!" exclaims Iseult.[31] Clearly this is Mark's wish, too.

Final scene: Iseult dies on the breast of Tristan. What more damning proof of guilt could Mark want? Not only have his nephew and wife lived in sin, they have now died in sin. They have died in each other's arms, entangled. And what does Mark do? Does he toss Tristan's guilty corpse into the sea, send Iseult's to the leper colony? *Au contraire*: He ships them reverentially back to Cornwall; *it is the first time in the entire tale that he has taken the initiative to bring his wife home*—and the reason is that she is *dead*! He gives her and her lover a noble burial in the church he himself attends. To be sure, they are separated by a narrow nave, but that—we are by now certain—is for the sake of the counselors. It is for the sake of appearances. Or indeed, it is for the sake of Tristan and Iseult themselves. Because if Mark hasn't realized much in the course of the tale, perhaps he has realized this: Tristan and Iseult *require* the transgressive separation between them in order to love. They cannot be too close. They need a sword between them, or they need a nave. Only then can their hands clasp and the trees on their tombs embrace.

*   *   *

IF MARK never wanted Iseult, why does Tristan bring her to him as a bride? Why does he not simply do what her father expects, what Iseult herself expects, and what propriety would dictate: namely *marry the girl himself*? It is Tristan, after all, who killed the dragon—and the man who killed the dragon was supposed to be the man to wed the girl. That was the edict of the Irish king. That is what Iseult believed would happen—or she would not have tried so hard to disprove that the low-born seneschal had slain the monster. Had she imagined the seneschal would simply pass her along to a nice local king "Tristan-style," she might have been content to go along with his tale.

It isn't as though Tristan weren't emphatically, charismatically, even compulsively marriageable. He has a five-star record of chivalric accomplishment behind him; at the same time, he is still young and handsome like Iseult—and unlike Mark. Moreover, Iseult evidently adores him. If she discovers the notch in his sword, it is because she is *cleaning* it one day as he reclines in the bath beside her—surely a familiar—even a compromising—position for a princess to be in with a strange knight. Moreover, Tristan *owes* Iseult. This is not the first but the second time that she has nursed him back from near-death to health. (There is a prehistory to the tale as summarized above: Iseult, in fact, treated Tristan once before when he washed up on Irish shores.) Iseult already half *feels* like his wife. Perhaps that is the problem.

Well before the two of them set out for Cornwall, routine has already reared its ugly head. And Tristan senses that Iseult is too good for routine. He senses that their intimacy can't last—it can't retain its "hard, gemlike flame"—if Iseult is forever cleaning his sword and he is forever lounging around in the soap suds.[32] So he decides to put someone else in the suds by her side; to marry her to someone else—not in order to give her away but precisely in order to keep her. To keep her in the way that he has begun to love her and she has begun to love him—ardently.

Everything else follows from this. The love potion, upon which so many critics have lavished attention, is secondary. It only reinforces what Tristan and Iseult already feel. They are in love and the potion gives them the excuse to act on this love—

while retaining their moral high ground. It is not they, but the *drink* that makes them act recklessly: *"In vino veritas."* Tristan and Iseult believed that what they were drinking when they took the potion was wine. In any case, it unleashed the *veritas* in them. It allowed them to live this *veritas*, this truth, according to its own rules—as opposed to subordinating it to a social system as elaborate and anaesthetizing as medieval marriage.

For the rest of the story, Tristan and Iseult fight for their love by doing battle for its continued transgressiveness. Whenever it threatens to lapse into social tolerability or sentimental calm—as even illicit love affairs do!—they jerk it back abruptly, as though away from a dangerous precipice. In light of King Mark's reluctance to play the role of possessive husband, they have to do a lot of jerking.

They have, for starters, to take mad and deliberate risks. What else is Tristan's bloody leap into Iseult's bed on a night that Mark is within castle walls? What else is Iseult's refusal to change the blood-drenched sheets afterward—a refusal about which even our narrator, Béroul, marvels? It is as though the lovers wanted to be caught. There is a great deal of evidence that they do.

When there is nobody to catch them, they catch themselves. Free as birds in their forest exile, they place a sword between their two bodies. This detail is given no explanation or elaboration in any of the five original narratives. It makes no sense in any conventional way. Surely they cannot be observing a perfunctory piety—their relationship has been consummated over and over and over again by this time. And the story is clear: They are not expecting the king when they do this (though he arrives and duly absolves them of all blame, as is his wont). The only plausible explanation is the psychological one: They are not doing this for the sake of propriety or protection; they are not doing it for Mark, or for God. They are doing it for themselves. They are doing it because their passion demands it; because their passion demands constant reminders that it is prohibited—and what better proof of prohibition than a sharpened blade between their pulsating bodies.

Some of this transgressive energy is sapped, of course, when Mark replaces Tristan's sword with his own and trundles off again. On one hand, the king's gesture can be read to reinforce the lovers' separateness; on another, more important hand, it validates their togetherness. I have been here, says the sword; I have witnessed you together and elected to let you live. What you are doing is all right. I give you permission to continue. Which, of course, is the last thing the rebels want to hear, the last—perhaps the only—thing their radical love cannot bear.

So they turn themselves in. They turn themselves in to King Mark (who has so perversely refused to claim them himself), and they start their love up again on a riskier footing. Iseult moves back in again with Mark and declares to Tristan that "their physical intercourse is over." And then, just as he turns on his heel, desire resurges. Tristan will have Iseult in his arms again, he tells a friend, "though Mark will not allow it."[33] *Though*? "Because" would be more accurate.

Tristan and Iseult do numerous other things to render their relationship more dangerous, illegitimate, and offensive. Iseult publicly straddles Tristan—then tells the assembled authorities that he has "come between her thighs"![34] To be sure, her confessions are formulated in such a way as to deceive her listeners—but they are formulated at least as much to provoke fate. Tristan, after all, is standing just around the corner ready to be recognized in his leper costume. Iseult's words are a gamble. They are a way to up the ante—not, as she pretends—to crank down suspicion.

The same holds true for the fool costume Tristan dons to meet Iseult in her castle —and retains even after he learns that Mark is away. By dressing up as someone other than himself, the familiar lover, he makes the encounter both more uncertain—Iseult might not recognize him, as indeed for a considerable time she does not—and more transgressive; to the degree that she *does* embrace him in his costume she is committing a second adultery.

Most puzzling of all, Tristan marries a woman called Iseult! What harder slap at social decency—and what better way to ensure that the wife in question is insulted from the outset and that her marriage to Tristan will not, therefore, prove as lenient as the original Iseult's alliance with King Mark? Tristan's marriage is the blackest thing to happen to the lovers—and thereby, in some sense, the most incandescent. It is Iseult Number Two who assures that Tristan does not live to see Iseult Number One again. By telling him that the sails on the arriving ship are dark—i.e., that his beloved is not aboard—Tristan's wife deals him his death blow.

Death plays the same role in Tristan and Iseult's final embrace that the sword played in the forest. It allows the lovers to be at once separate and together, at once united and poised sexily apart. Death allows Tristan and Iseult to lie peaceful in each other's arms at the same time that they strain, as always, against authority. In this case it is the authority of nature rather than the authority of society, the clout of the grave rather than the clout of the castle, the power of Hades rather than the power of Cornwall.

*   *   *

WHAT DO we make of all this *straining*? What do we make of all this searching for authority in order to flout it? Is it—as it often seems in Ovid—a purely cynical affair, a manner of artificially inflaming feelings that otherwise would be too tame and tepid? Once we have realized what Tristan and Iseult are up to, it is easy to see their actions as a perverse game—a puerile, narcissistic, and destructive sport that has little to do with love and a lot to do with the lovers' efforts to entertain themselves. This, ultimately, is the position of the most original twentieth-century interpreter of their myth, Denis de Rougemont: "Tristan and Iseult do not love one another," he declares at the climax of his almost legendary 1939 analysis: They only love their "passionate dream."[35]

Like Denis de Rougemont, I believe Tristan and Iseult make life unnecessarily hard for themselves and that they do so on purpose. But where Rougemont has argued that they seek obstructions of any kind, I believe they pointedly seek *transgressive* ones. Most important, where Rougemont judges this impulse as negative—and as ultimately antithetical to love—I would like to propose that it is *positive* and altogether of a piece with love.

It is of a piece because love, like war, opens untapped founts of energy in its recruits. Love, like war, mobilizes forces in the heart that ache to be enlisted. They ache to be enlisted in the subduing of some dragon. When there is no dragon available they search for a watchdog—or a husband, or an inanimate object that stands in the way to fulfillment. Love inspires heroism. And where there is no illegitimate power to overcome, it will settle for a legitimate power. The point is to flex its adrenaline-filled muscles.

For at its core, love is about breaking boundaries. It is about breaking boundaries between people and about breaking boundaries of propriety. Arrogant and intense, it disdains to exist in the narrow playpen of bourgeois convention. It feels it is bigger than the world it inhabits—bigger than the categories we assign it, the narrow paths we instruct it to walk. So it continually breaks out of those paths. It bursts out of those categories. In transgressing, it transcends.

Denis de Rougemont has said that death is the ultimate goal of passion and that passion is therefore, by definition, destructive, and, by definition, the opposite of love. Tristan and Iseult have passion for each other, according to Rougemont, but not love. At the risk of disagreeing again with the man from whom I've learned most on the subject, I must disagree with him again. Death is neither a fetishized goal of passion nor even a necessary one; it is simply *one* authority among others, one referee among others, *one* boundary against which passion—being as despotic as it is, as eager for activity, and as contemptuous of barriers—naturally strains. And in straining against death, of course passion simultaneously longs for death. You cannot prove yourself against a champion unless you have that champion in the ring with you. You cannot prove yourself superior to death unless you wrestle with him arm to arm.

This is *not* the same as to say that passion is a death-drive. Tristan and Iseult spend far more time averting a romantic love-death than courting it. Their passion is often disconcertingly pragmatic. Tied to the stake and ready to burn, Iseult urges Tristan to escape without her—and without further ado, he does. Only quite independently of him—and much later—does Iseult escape also. This is only one of many occasions on which the lovers aggressively decline the invitation to die in each other's arms. Which does not mean that they decline it always; which does not mean that they do not wish also to love each other *against death* as they love each other against morality, against reason, and against moderation. Love is always *against* some*thing* as ardently as it is *for* some*body*. Such contrarianism is part and parcel of its warlike spirit, its combative constitution, its hungry impatience for excess.

*   *   *

ALL THIS does not mean that to be at war is to be in love. Nor does it mean that to break a rule is to groom a passion. Transgression can be gimmicky and superficial as readily as it can be profound and necessary. The couples who buy silken whips and use forbidden words in bed are no closer to the amorous sublime than others—and there is a case to be made that they are farther. Rougemont is right when he says that the legacy of Tristan and Iseult has been systematically cheapened and trivialized over the centuries. We want their transgression, today, without wanting to pay its price: "The tragic element in our period has been diffused into mediocrity," he wrote roughly seventy years ago.[36] What would he say today? Self-help authors instruct us to act "ruthless" in bed, to rage and roar, even while we are increasingly unwilling to take the slightest real risk for—or with—our partners.[37] Magazines encourage role playing various sorts of white-collar crime—doctor seducing patient, president seducing intern—even while many of our real lives are models of safety and careerish practicality.

Real transgression takes guts. Real transgression comes at a price. "Few are capable of the thirst that would cause them to drink the love-potion," says Rougemont.[38] It is baby sips we want to take, plastic chains we want to bind us, fake rebellion in which we revel. We want transgression in a can—as contained and symbolic as those "cows in a can" you can buy in rural American gift shops and which moo when you tip them over—but alas, it is not to be purchased in that form.

What form *can* transgressive love take in the modern age? Many have experimented with it and only a few have made an unmitigated success of it. Adultery, of course, is alive and well. Many of the more interesting lovers of the last century have averted marriage altogether. Simone de Beauvoir and Jean-Paul Sartre were together longer and more intimately, uncompromisingly, and intensely than the overwhelming majority of married couples, but they pointedly refused legal vows. They pointedly rejected fidelity. And yet fifty years after they made a pact of "essential love" with each other, they still told each other secrets and snuck behind the backs of new partners in order to spend time together.[39] On vacation with Beauvoir, Sartre would place calls to other women, swearing his devotion and disguising the importance of Beauvoir at his side. During World War II, he had scheduled hotel dates with Beauvoir in Paris at times he'd told other lovers that he was still stuck at a military base preparing to fight the Germans. Beauvoir's and Sartre's greatest courage lay in their attempt to be totally open with each other—often, it must be admitted, at the expense of others—but clearly to the advantage of their own relationship.

The letters they wrote each other throughout their lives have the quality of clandestine trysts, of excited sleepovers: "I have a very keen taste for her body," Beauvoir would write Sartre after a night with a particularly fetching female student.[40] "I am devoting all of my energy to my love life but absolutely nothing is coming of it," Sartre would write back.[41] Such unconventional honesty—even more than their erotic experimentation—made the liaison not merely unusual but authentically transgressive. The people around them could not help being jealous of it. It is for this reason that even long after Beauvoir's and Sartre's sexuality was no longer the burning center of their relationship they still had often to convene quietly. *Transgressive sharing* was the center of the Sartre-Beauvoir couple—though its margins certainly contained all manner of other transgressions too.

On and off throughout their lives they were lovers; at the same time they courted and even proposed to other people; attempted the odd *ménage à trois*, ended marriages, shared partners, and swapped them. This, one might argue, was the least successful part of their experiment in transgression. It produced a potent sense of betrayal among third parties (notably on the part of Beauvoir's lover, the Chicago novelist Nelson Algren), a couple of cases of insanity (one of Beauvoir's students, Wanda Kosakiewicz, and one of Sartre's nurses, a Brazilian), and at least one suicide (the brilliant Evelyne Rey, sister of filmmaker Claude Lanzmann).[42] Had they kept only the core of their radical relationship—the transgressive sharing—and cut away some of the rind, they might have done less damage to others and greater good (even) to themselves. The forbidden fruit that was their love might have poisoned fewer passersby and sweetened more of the days they called their own.

The poet Edna St. Vincent Millay—in contrast to Simone de Beauvoir, her contemporary—did marry. She married a few months after becoming the first woman to win the Pulitzer Prize; she married at twenty-nine years of age, and she married a successful Dutch businesssman by the name of Eugen Boissevain. The union, though, was at least as unconventional as Beauvoir's. "A completely faithful marriage is like an icebox with always some cold chicken in it," Boissevain proclaimed brightly—and neither Millay nor he seemed to care much for poultry sandwiches.[43] Millay had countless affairs with women as well as men, most of them passionately sanctioned by Boissevain: "Go to it, Scaramoodles!" he would charge her when she took off with a lover. "And no feeling sorry for *anyone!*" [44] Her most important love affair ended when the dashing twenty-three-year-old poet she was living with in Paris got so jealous of the fifty-odd-year-old stay-at-home husband in New England that she could no longer stand him. George Dillon couldn't bear the epistolary intimacy Millay maintained with Boissevain (over thousands of kilometers though it may have been), and the relationship that inspired her most famous sonnet sequence, *Fatal Interview*, collapsed.[45] Her relationship with Boissevain, on the other hand, retained its erotic and emotional charge for the rest of her life—this in spite of a Tristan-like poem Millay wrote after her first night of love with Dillon:

> *The memory of this encounter like a sword*
> *Shall lie between me and my troubled lord.*[46]

There is nothing like a sword, apparently, to promote enduring love.

Still more transgressive, though, than Millay's and Boissevain's amorous adventures was their willingness to risk death and
disease for the other. When, toward the end of her life, Millay
fell victim to a debilitating morphine addiction, Boissevain coolly
and deliberately provoked the same addiction in himself in order
to show Millay how to shake it. A healthy man, he made himself
sick so he could help his beloved get well. Slowly but steadily,
he self-administered morphine until he depended on it. He did
not, he explained, want to preach to Millay from a position of ignorance and sanctimony; he needed to know—and suffer—what
she suffered. To guide her out of hell, he had to be there himself.
In our disease-frighted and safety-besotted culture, this is a far
more defiant and magnanimous gesture than any sexual liberty
he could have allowed her—or she him.

Boissevain had gone even farther in the past. Before he met
Millay he had been married to a passionate young women's rights
advocate, Inez Milholland. When Milholland fell suddenly and
mortally ill at age twenty-eight, the thirty-something-year-old
Boissevain offered, in all soberness and seriousness, to die with
her.[47] It is only because Milholland implored him to live—as Iseult
once implored Tristan at the stake!—that Boissevain was still
around two decades later to make a comparably courageous gesture to Millay. Within a year of Boissevain's artificially induced
morphine addiction he had shown Millay how to rid herself of
the drug.

Transgression can be many things: It can involve behavior
that is *medically* incorrect as well as politically incorrect; it can
mean radical confidences or sexual experiments, the flouting of
convention or convenience, expectation or morality. It can be

more successful or less successful. What is consistent is the price: a preparedness for sacrifice. Real sacrifice. Not synthetic sacrifice, nor the imitation of sacrifice.

It is this preparedness, this courage to renounce not only inconvenient rules but convenient ones that bears rediscovery in our day. We must transgress against our own fears—against the narrowness of our vistas, the modesty of our wishes, the slightness of our altruism. Because at the end of the day, transgression—for Tristan and Iseult, for Romeo and Juliet, and even for the small-town Casanova down the street—is ever a prayer for transcendence.

FOUR

☙

There Must Be Two Before There Can Be One: Love as Absence[1]

ALTHOUGH MY NEIGHBORS ARE ALL BARBARIANS,
AND YOU, YOU ARE A THOUSAND MILES AWAY, THERE ARE
ALWAYS TWO CUPS ON MY TABLE.

—John Fowles, *The Magus*[2]

WE LIVE IN AN AGE that idolizes access. Internet access, access to up-to-the-minute news stories, real-time highway chases, twenty-four-hour-a-day pizza delivery, instant erotic gratification, access to acquaintances and co-workers and friends wherever they may be in the world and at whatever time. The new technologies put everything at our fingertips. The new liberties make us bold enough to grasp. Click here for a dozen romantic partners between twenty-nine and thirty-six who live within two miles of your zip code and are online *now*. Quick-dial "4" to get your ex-boyfriend at a monastery in Tibet. Scroll up on your remote control and you're in the bedroom of a bachelorette on a blind date.

But access has rarely been the road to intensity. In matters of the heart, it is often the very reverse of access—it is unavailability and absence, scarcity and omission—that sharpen the passions and refine them. "It is in the love that vainly yearns from behind prison bars that we have, perchance, the love supreme," says Antoine de Saint-Exupéry.[3] If the myth of Tristan and Iseult is a tale of transgression, it is almost equally a tale of separation—both geographic and sexual. Why are the lovers forever saying farewell to each other? Why, in the phrase of Denis de Rougemont, do they "never miss a chance of getting parted?"[4] It is as though they knew that to yearn for each other they cannot always *have* each other. Do they sense that without the salt of self-induced separation, their love might well go bland?

By the time the story of Tristan and Iseult officially begins, their knack for loving and leaving each other is well established. Tristan has already slain the evil Morhold and had his wounds treated by the dead man's niece, Iseult. The two have already spent a great deal of intimate time together. And yet once Tristan's wounds improve, he turns on his heel and disappears. He also comes back, instantly gets injured all over again, and returns to the care of his princess-cum-doctor.

But does Tristan stay with her? If the first time he was deterred by timidity, there can be no such excuse this time: He has just slaughtered a beast whose death the Irish king will reward with Iseult's hand in marriage. But instead of seizing her hand and settling into marital bliss, Tristan gratuitously decides that Iseult must be the owner of the lock of hair that his lord, Mark, has claimed belongs to his future wife. *You will marry Mark*, he therefore tells Iseult—thus provoking another rupture. The two set sail for Cornwall in the knowledge that upon arrival Iseult will disappear forever into Mark's bedroom, while Tristan will continue to travel the globe in search of slayable dragons. There is no greater aphrodisiac.

By the time the boat trip is under way, Tristan and Iseult are openly intoxicated with each other. A few days later, Iseult marries Mark, and they begin their clandestine trysts. Meeting, parting, meeting, parting, until finally they make a big mistake: Tristan and Iseult get caught, narrowly escape execution, and end up in the woods together *permanently*. If there was any hope of violent separation, this hope is extinguished when King Mark discovers his wife's forest hideout, observes her sleeping next to Tristan, takes her wedding ring off her finger, and *leaves her with him*. It is at this juncture that Tristan and Iseult fall abruptly out of love.

For the rest of their lives they reunite and separate. Whenever the reasons for separation become too feeble, they strengthen them; i.e., Tristan moves far away from Mark's castle. Then he marries a woman who militates against his visits with Iseult. When this woman prevents Tristan's seeing her after his injury, he sickens and dies and Iseult—more moved than ever by this final break—expires of love in his arms.

As though acting on the lovers' cue, King Mark inters them together but separate: He buries their bodies in the same church but places a nave between them, as they themselves once placed a sword. United but riven. Pulling together but pushing apart. The eternal motion of love. The endless seesaw of passion.

But if *Tristan and Iseult* dramatizes the aphrodisiac effects of absence, there is a second founding legend of Western romance that does so with still greater aplomb: the story of Dante and Beatrice.

* * *

OFTEN ALLUDED to reverentially, rarely read as a whole, and still more rarely approached with any critical aggression, the tale of Dante and Beatrice reserves a veritable host of surprises. It is related, for the most part, in Dante's 1294–95 work, *Vita Nuova* (*New Life*), a volume of mingled poems and prose that has long been considered "the masterpiece of Dante's youth," a "work of crystalline beauty and fascinating complexity,"[5] in short (in the words of an Amazon.com reviewer) "the most romantic thing ever." *Vita Nuova* forms a preamble to one of the two or three most important literary works of all time, the *Divine Comedy*.[6] This accounts, in part, for the sanctimony with which it is often handled. But where the *Divine Comedy* offers Dante's vision of the afterlife, *Vita Nuova* offers his vision of *this* life—or at least of his own multiyear relationship with the lady who will become his imaginative guide to Paradise.

He met her when they were each roughly nine years old—if one may take the word of a man who attributes superstitious significance to the number nine: She was a little younger and he a little older. Beatrice "was dressed in a noble, but subdued and modest, crimson."[7] Her effects on Dante were instantaneous: ". . . My vital spirit, which lives in the most secret chamber of the heart, began to tremble so violently that its pulsations were felt with terrifying force in the most remote parts of my body."[8] Critics have made much of the supposedly sexless character of Dante's response to young Beatrice Portinari; the author of the foreword to a recent British edition marvels at length about the "complete absence of any allusion [in *New Life*] to the visceral and extreme sexual longing that is invariably a part of the experience of being in love." But this sexlessness is a fiction. It is a function of the naïveté of the critic, not the naïveté of Dante—or more accurately: It is a function of the critic's desire to find in Dante a more "ethereal" and "pure" version of love than the one Dante in fact offers.[9]

We can rest assured that when a thirteenth-century Christian gentleman refers to "violent . . . pulsations" in "remote parts of his body" upon observing a beautiful girl he is not referring to cramps in his leg. Nor is the most famous image in all of *Vita Nuova*—a vision Dante has of Beatrice chewing and eating his burning heart—sexless. It could hardly be more jarringly, more hallucinogenically sexual.

Let us take a closer look at the passage in which it appears. Dante has just met Beatrice for the first time and he tells us that

> *I fell into a pleasant dream in which I saw a marvelous vision. I seemed to see a cloud of fire in my room, in which I could make out the figure of a lord. . . . I seemed to see someone sleeping in his arms, naked except that she seemed to be wrapped lightly in a crimson cloth. When I looked at her attentively I saw that she was the lady that had condescended to greet me the day before [Beatrice]. And it seemed to me that in one of his hands he held something that was on fire, while he said these words "Vide cor tuum" ["Look, this is your heart"]. And when he had been there a while, it seemed to me that he awakened the sleeping figure. And he persuaded her to eat that object that was burning in his hand. She ate it fearfully. . . . Shortly afterwards his joy turned to bitter weeping . . .[10]*

There is no more arresting a picture of whole-body sexuality in medieval literature; no more explicit, intense, and daring vision of the synesthesia-like confusion of heart and head and loins; the melting into each other of pleasure and pain that typifies erotic love.

Dante proposes some pages later that the man (or "lord") he sees in this dream is a personified figure of Love, a kind of grown-up Cupid. Perhaps he is; on the other hand, he may as well be a stand-in for Dante himself—a projection of the dream's author. It is common to view oneself from the outside in dreams. If this were the case, then it would be Dante himself who clasps the naked Beatrice in his arms, Dante himself who is consumed in a "cloud of fire," Dante himself who bears "in his hand" a "burning" object and enjoins the reclining Beatrice to "eat" it. Were it not for Dante's Latin voice-over reminding us that the object he holds is, in fact, a *heart*, ("vide cor tuum"), there would be little question as to how we would identify it.

But we are discoursing pedantically about what is, after all, a dream—an adolescent's wish dream, on one hand, and, on the other, a dream of sacrificial surrender to an almost divine human being. It is not useful in such dreams to distinguish nicely between parts of the anatomy. In the grip of awe, one says that one's heart is "in one's mouth"; in the grip of passion, it can be between one's legs—or, indeed, in one's hand. The longing that ignites one's temples also pulses in one's extremities. Synesthesia is among the most vital features of erotic love—it is only Dante's vivid and unsqueamish formulation of it that catches us by surprise; the fact itself is known. It is an egregious irony that in return for the very boldness of his sexual vision, Dante is dubbed asexual.

It is an irony as so *many* conventional readings of *Vita Nuova* are ironies. Critics wish to see a pristine and idealized love in this venerable text, but what they have instead is a chaotic and lustful, vain and fallible, human and all-too-human passion. The latter is far more interesting—and far more valuable as a guide to emotions with which we still contend today—but it is also far more unsettling.

How many among Dante and Beatrice's high-minded admirers discuss, for example (or even acknowledge), that in the midst of Dante's romantic throes for Beatrice he falls in love with another woman? Leaving aside, for a moment, that he is married for most of his adult life to someone never mentioned in *Vita Nuova*, he in fact admits in *Vita Nuova*'s very pages that a pretty girl he spots in a window one day causes him to *forget* Beatrice: "My eyes started to take too much pleasure in seeing this lady . . . I cursed my eyes' inconstancy . . . I liked her too much."[11] This, the perfect lover, Dante? Unfaithful? To be sure, he eventually jolts himself back into place—swearing off the temptress in the window and rededicating himself sternly to Beatrice—but it is not for this reason that the incident is trivial. Along with the searing (not the missing!) sexuality witnessed earlier, it is evidence of the deep and often dark humanity of Dante's passion.

It is *more* reason—not less—to read his book seriously rather than just deferentially—to read it as though it had something to say about our fallen selves rather than only about the lives of saints. For if Beatrice has, in fact, become an angel by the time she appears in the "Paradise" section of the *Divine Comedy*, her suitor in *Vita Nuova* is just the opposite.

For one thing—and here we return to the central argument of

this chapter—Dante is forever pushing Beatrice away. Under the guise of straining to be at her side, he exerts extraordinary effort to keep her at bay. For all the fires ignited in Dante by Beatrice's presence, her absence ignites him still more. Let's make no mistake: Even under the "best" of circumstances, Dante does not see Beatrice often; he watches her chiefly from afar, and on the rare occasions that she offers him a greeting, or an exchange of civilities, one might as well proclaim a national holiday. And yet, the reader has the distinct suspicion that even this minimal contact is too much contact for Dante. Why else would he continually envision Beatrice's disappearance and hasten her departures?

For if Tristan and Iseult "never miss a chance of getting parted," Dante never misses a chance to imagine Beatrice far from him.[12] He has no sooner met the young beauty but he labors to increase the distance that divides him from her. He effects this in a series of less or more ingenious ways—the first being quite simply to interject a "screen" between the two of them—a screen in the form of another woman. Witness his account of the matter:

> One day it happened that this most gracious lady was sitting in a place where people were praising the [Virgin Mary] . . . Between her and me, in a direct line, sat a noble lady of very pleasing appearance, who kept looking at me, surprised at my gaze which seemed to be directed to her. Many people noticed she was looking at me, and this attracted so much attention that, as I left that place, I heard people saying behind me: "You see how that lady is destroying him." . . . And I immediately thought of using that

noble lady as a screen for the truth. And I made such a show of
it that soon most people who spoke about me believed they knew
my secret. I hid behind this lady for several years and months,
and, to make it the more convincing, I wrote certain little things
in rhyme for her. . . .[13]

Even allowing for the sometimes bizarre conventions of courtly love—the cult of secrecy, for example—Dante's behavior is remarkable. Both physically and psychologically, his "fake love" separates him from his true love: Physically, she blocks his view of Beatrice; emotionally, she takes his energy from her. Instead of exerting his imaginative powers to write love poems for Beatrice, Dante is now exerting these powers to write love poems for another woman. In doing as much he minimizes Beatrice's chances of realizing his love of her—much less responding to it. He is, in effect, minimizing her proximity to him.

This is merely the beginning. Not long after his acquaintance with his "fake love," Dante learns that this woman has left town, and, having decided that to keep up his pose of loving her he must write despondent poems about her loss, he begins—strenuously— to envision *Beatrice's* departure.

"O you who come along Love's road," he pines,
"Pause awhile and decide:
Is any grief as heavy as mine is?"[14]

He tells the reader that he only quotes this poem because "my lady [Beatrice] was the immediate cause" of it—i.e., he has managed to imagine Beatrice's absence so perfectly that he is writing about her rather than about the woman who is in *fact* absent.[15]

As if it weren't bad enough to imagine the departure of your true love, Dante next imagines her death. Another young lady in the community has suddenly died—a lady of whom Dante knows no more than that he "had sometimes seen her with my lady"— and he can think of no better response to the tragedy than to pretend it has happened to Beatrice, to pretend, in other words, that Beatrice is dead.

> "Weep lovers," he therefore cries,
> "Since you see that Love is weeping,
> All because brutal death has seized upon a
> Noble Heart . . ."[16]

This theme gives him so much mileage he writes about it in not only one poem, but two. The second ends triumphantly on an evocation not merely of never seeing Beatrice again in this life but of never seeing her again in the *next* life either.

"Who fails to save his soul," Dante announces, "has no hope of seeing her again."[17] Whoever, in other words, is not as virtuous as Beatrice, has no chance of meeting her in the high ranks of heaven she will inhabit after death. And there are not many, we may be certain, who are as virtuous as Beatrice.

But imaginary distances only work for so long. Eventually one must install a genuine distance. The reader will not, therefore, be shocked to hear that "a few days after the death of this lady something happened which meant that I had to leave the city . . . to travel. . . ."[18] Wandering around the countryside far away from

Beatrice, Dante's passion breathes deeply. But all good things must have an end—even Dante's travels—and when they do, one must come up with alternatives. Upon his return to Beatrice's hometown, Dante dreams up a new pretext for distance between Beatrice and himself.

He invents a second "screen" for his love. Having lost the old stand-in (because she left town), he finds a new stand-in on whom to focus his amorous attentions and through whom to preempt any suspicion that he loves Beatrice. The only difference? This time he applies himself to the task so well—he courts this second stand-in so insistently and extravagantly—that his public reputation takes a nose dive, the whole city finds him disgraceful and even Beatrice herself—who never spoke to him much in the first place—ceases to speak with him altogether. One has to read it to believe it:

> I had in so short time made [the other lady] so thoroughly my defense that too many people spoke of it beyond the bounds of courtesy . . . And for this reason—that is, the excessive gossip which was apparently defaming me out of malice—the most gracious Beatrice, who was the destroyer of all vices . . . denied me that sweet salutation in which all my bliss consisted.[19]

One has to give the man credit. Not only does he fail to expand on Beatrice's reasons for addressing him, but he eliminates them altogether: He makes her ashamed to so much as squint in his direction.

And *were* this not enough? Dante addends that at about this time he also locked himself away—"shut myself in my room where I could make laments without being heard."[20] If a man wanted to keep the Black Plague away from his door, he could not do a better job than Dante does with Beatrice.

Nor is it only cynical modern readers who may notice this; some of Dante's contemporaries did too. *"Why do you love your lady when you cannot bear her presence?"* asks a woman at a party. He gives no good answer.[21]

He simply pursues his course of absolute avoidance, imagined absence, and self-induced separation. Is it any surprise that he imagines Beatrice's demise a *second* time before it actually occurs? If Beatrice's untimely death did not exist, Dante would have to invent it—and indeed he *does* invent it. He invents it several times in the first thirty-odd pages of *Vita Nuova*. Witness the level of detail to which he delivers himself the second time around—and the flimsiness of his excuse for doing so:

> *A few days later I happened to be afflicted by a painful illness in a certain part of my body, and I suffered from it for nine days continuously . . . On the ninth day . . . I began to think of my lady . . . with a deep sigh, I said to myself: "My most gracious Beatrice must die sooner or later." . . . I imagined that some friends came to me and said: "Do you not know? Your wonderful lady has left this world." Then I began to weep piteously, and not only in my imagination, for my eyes were bathed in tears, I imagined myself looking up to heaven, and I seemed to see a multitude of angels . . . singing gloriously . . . And then I thought that my heart, the home of so much love, said to me: "It is true that our lady lies dead." And so I imagined I went to see the body in which that most noble and blessed soul had once lived. And my erring*

fantasy was so strong that it showed me this lady dead. Ladies
seemed to be covering her head with a white veil, and it appeared
to me that her face had such an appearance of humility that it
was saying: "Now I behold the fountainhead of peace." [22]

For all Dante's intention that we understand this as a nightmare, it bears many of the marks of a wish dream. No detail goes
unvisualized, no loving brushstroke is neglected. We witness the
death veil and we hear the mourners. We listen to the singing
angels and we obtain an interpretation of the corpse's beauteous
facial expression. And why this flight of fancy? Why this five-star
production? Because Dante had a pain "in a certain part of his
body" on one day. Or rather on "nine days" (recall his superstitious commitment to the number nine).[23] An earache? Whatever
the pain is, it gives Dante a pretext to meditate at length upon the
death of his twenty-something-year-old love. The soul creates its
occasions.

By the time Beatrice actually and historically dies, Dante has
killed her off so many times in the privacy of his imagination that
we, as readers, are overprepared. Indeed, it almost feels like Dante
himself has little left to say on the matter. His treatment of Beatrice's real death after so many false alarms and phony auditions
is sparse. He was, he says, "still in the process of writing" a poem
about Beatrice, when the news arrived that

the Lord of Justice called this most gracious lady to glory under
the banner of the Queen of Heaven, the Blessed Virgin Mary,
whose name was always spoken with the utmost reverence by the
blessed Beatrice. [24]

Perhaps at this point some explanation of her departure would be welcome

but it is not my intention to give any. . . .[25]

This is the full account that Dante provides of the tragic and wholly unexpected death of the twenty-four-year-old woman dearest to him in all the world. The next paragraph finds him deliberating once again over the meaning of the number nine. ". . . Because the number nine has occurred frequently in the preceding account . . . it is appropriate to discuss it now. . . ."[26] With that he launches into an elaborate exposition of numerology: "There are," we learn, "nine moving heavens." Beatrice, moreover,

> *was herself this number, by analogy. What I mean is this. Three is the square root of nine. Therefore since three is the only factor of nine, and the only factor of miracles is three, that is the Father, the Son, and the Holy Spirit, who are three and one, then this lady was accompanied by the number nine to indicate that she was a nine, that is, a miracle, a miracle whose square root is nothing more than the miraculous Trinity itself.*[27]

Should readers (God help them) desire more detail on this subject, Dante admits that "someone more subtle might perhaps find a more subtle explanation. . . ." But the present account, he concludes, "is the one I see, and the one which pleases me most." It is remarkable that after so many chapters of anguish and tears, Dante finally declares himself "pleased"—now that Beatrice is six feet under.[28]

Not that he doesn't resume his weeping later; he does. But one has the impression that the high point of Dante's love, its greatest joy and its ultimate consummation is not the conquest of Beatrice but her loss; it is not her embrace but her departure; not her presence at his side but her absence from him forever.

The book continues for many more pages with rapturous poems to Beatrice, complete with the poet's own explications of them. In fact, this is one of the weirder aspects of *Vita Nuova*. It offers not only prose that advances the plot of the love story and poetry that evokes its sentiment, but also very elaborate prose *explanations* of the poetry. These explications are often as cumbersome as they are unnecessary—a fact that Dante himself seems to realize as he delivers them. That is why he will start, for example, by saying

> *This sonnet begins: Your bitter weeping. It is divided into two parts. . . .*

—but finish by confessing that

> *The sonnet might well be analyzed further, but that would be pointless, since its meaning is quite clear. . . .*[29]

As indeed the sonnet invariably is. What is less clear is why Dante saw fit to include these painfully self-regarding passages at all. His best-known translator, the nineteenth-century poet Dante Gabriel Rossetti, found them so excruciating he refused to look at them and requested, instead, that a sibling translate them after he himself had left *Vita Nuova* behind.[30]

Literary scholars often pretend that works of great authors are perfect. They are not. Dante's book is stock full of *faux pas*. It fairly bristles with blunders of tone, style, and emotion. But it is precisely for this reason that it is so precious. Far from resembling the well-pitched, well-turned, and well-moralized *Divine Comedy*, *Vita Nuova* is a document of raw human passion—its lapses and lethargies, its vanities and frailties, its poor consolations and its artificial stimulants.

Dante knows this: He ends his book with an injunction to himself "not to say anything further about this blessed lady *until I could do so more worthily*."[31] He sees as clearly as any critic that he is a vain and inconstant man attempting, rather unsuccesfully, to live an ideal and eternal love. He wishes that he may do better in the future; he hopes (in the *Divine Comedy*) to do Beatrice greater honor; to write of her again at such a time as the years, sufferings, and humilities will have multiplied his wisdom. Then and only then, "I hope to write of her," he says, "what has never been written of any woman."[32] But for now he writes of her what *has* been written—and felt—about many women. He writes of the synesthesia-like effects of sexuality, of the disturbing distraction of other loves. He also writes—and writes best—about the indispensable aphrodisiac that is *absence*.

* * *

WHY *is* absence such an aphrodisiac—in the life of Dante, of Tristan and Iseult, and of the rest of us? For were it anything less, there would be no folksy maxims like "absence makes the heart

grow fonder" or "familiarity breeds contempt." There would be
no bestselling seduction manuals like *The Rules* that instruct us
to make ourselves scarce to capture the mate we want.[33] There
would be no notion of "playing hard to get." As much as the Beatrice portrayed in *Vita Nuova* can be pitied (her lover fails to do her
any visible good, he murders her mentally without cease . . .), she
may also be envied: Just think of all the heavy lifting Dante takes
off her hands! She has no need to artfully avoid his calls; she has
no need to invent pressing appointments in order to be the first
to say good-bye. Dante plays hard to get on her behalf. He makes
her hard to get by the power of his own imagination; she needn't
move a muscle or plot a rebuff. Were all men like Dante, *The Rules*
would not exist.

Let us reformulate the question then: Rather than ask "why
is absence an aphrodisiac?" let us ask "are there any *good* reasons
why absence is an aphrodisiac?" Bad reasons spring to mind without effort: If we don't want to see too much of our romantic partners, it is because we don't *like* them as much as we hoped we
would. It is because we are easily bored. It is because our pleasure
lies in conquest, not coexistence. Like the well-fed cat who tires of
the mouse the moment it stops moving between its claws, we tire
of our partners in the instant that we have obtained them.

One would be a fool to insist that these reasons are never
viable. They are. And yet there are also nobler motives at work.
For if the human heart is lazy and distractable, it is also ambitious
and generous. It is eager, for example, to extend its largesse to
objects that are different from itself. It does not crave its double;
it does not seek sycophantic imitation but rather contact with an

authentic Other, a stranger. The irony is that the more closely we live together with another human being—the less often we are separated from her or him—the more twin-like that human being becomes. It has been much observed that the members of long-married couples grow to resemble each other—in mannerisms, dress, posture, habits, and sometimes even looks. (Even pets and pet-owners come to resemble each other. Who has not seen a man who is the spitting image of his pit bull, or a woman who puts one in mind of her poodle?) This extraordinary phenomenon may, in fact, increase compatibility—but it almost inevitably decreases passion.

"There must be very two before there can be very one," writes Ralph Waldo Emerson in an essay entitled "Friendship," which deserves far more attention from apostles of Eros than it receives. When people consult Emerson on the life of the affections at all, they understandably turn to his essay on "Love." But "Love" is a poor and paltry piece of work compared to "Friendship." Perhaps because the long-married Emerson did not permit himself to admit he was in love with the persons most important in his life— Margaret Fuller and Caroline Sturgis—he explored his responses to them not in his writings on romance (replete as they are with hokey caricatures of "divine madmen" rushing through forests carving the names of their blushing maidens into tree bark), but rather in his deeply felt meditation on friendship.[34]

In "Friendship" Emerson formulates in so many words what Dante and Tristan and Iseult perform in so many actions. Do not go *too close* to your friend too often! he enjoins us. "Guard him as thy counterpart. Let him be to thee forever a sort of beautiful enemy, untameable, devoutly revered, and not a trivial conveniency"—an accessible sidekick.[35] True friends are too precious for casual companionship. We easily forget their nobility when we see them too constantly: "The hues of the opal, the light of the diamond are not to be seen, if the eye is too near," Emerson declares. "To my [ideal] friend I write a letter, and from him I receive a letter."[36]

Who would Tristan and Iseult be without the urgent clandestine messages conveyed (and sometimes misconveyed) between them? We will consider more deeply the role of letters in love affairs in the final chapter of this book. It is enough now to say that they embody almost to perfection the at once intimate and distant exchanges of the successfully infatuated. Nor must we worry lest these exchanges become too distant, Emerson reassures us: "It is foolish to be afraid of making our ties too spiritual," he claims; foolish to fear that because we do not have enough physical contact our ties may loosen.[37] It is almost the opposite. A few words separated by significant silences, a few gestures, are far more potent than floods of words and orgies-ful of activity.

Sex may be a riveting means of communication—but only when it is often adjourned and awaited does it retain its power to bind. Sex-on-tap attenuates rather than inflames passion. It is for this reason that the relentless emphasis on sexual climax that distinguishes our day from most others in historical memory has a largely depleting effect on the life of the emotions. When erotic intimacy is available at the tap of a mouse or, indeed, at the amiable request of one's household partner ("what about a quickie before lunch, dear?"); when magazines nudge us to "claim" orgasms as we do receipts at the end of our transactions at Starbucks; when Broadway hits like Eve Ensler's The Vagina Monologues have women hollering the names of their genitals and baking cakes in their shape, then sex has simply become too available.[38] The natural distances between people have been diminished so radically as to make romance—which depends on the retention of other-ness, tension, and reserve—impossible.

Emerson takes this point so far as to appear—in a culture of access like ours—almost absurd. Why, he demands, must we know our "friend's" family members? "Why insist on rash personal relations with your friend? Why go to his house, or know his mother and brother and sisters? Why be visited by him at your own?" There is no rush for such familiarities, according to Emerson. They may even diminish the real "covenant" between lovers—which is one of searching honesty rather than casual chit-chat. The presence of the inessential weakens the power of the essential. Love is not about micromanaging your partner's quotidian concerns; her noisy co-workers and his irksome aunt; her brassiere sizes and his starched shirts. "Leave this touching and clawing," exclaims Emerson. Forget this petty detail! Let your love be to you "a spirit. A message, a thought, a sincerity, a glance . . . not news, not pottage. I can get politics and chat and neighbourly conveniences from cheaper companions."[39]

If there is something severe about Emerson's vision of intimacy here, there is also something powerful. The kind of love he describes is not the cozy and practical kind; it is, rather, the kind that allows for continued smoldering admiration, curiosity, respect, and obsession—which may, at the end of the day, be worth more than the "neighbourly conveniences" of more inclusive couplings.

Many of history's greatest lovers have acted—either consciously or subconsciously—to insert distances into their rapports. Think passionate pairs and you almost automatically think distance; you almost automatically think break-ups and make-ups, separations and reunions, displacement and desire.

Never a proponent of either cohabitation or marriage, the eighteenth-century feminist Mary Wollstonecraft compromised on the second, but hardly on the first. Thirty-seven years old and pregnant for the second time, she consented to marry the political philosopher William Godwin, but she did not consent to move in with him. "I wish you . . . riveted in my heart; but I do not desire to have you always at my elbow," she declared.[40] They rented separate flats—hers at No. 29 Polygon; his twenty doors down at No. 17 Evesham Buildings—passing notes to each other through messengers and arranging dinner dates and amorous trysts the way courting teenagers might do. Far from rendering their relationship adolescent, however, this elective distance kept it intensely engaged: ". . . You haunt me . . . ," Wollstonecraft wrote her husband.[41]

The two also led separate social lives, seeing the persons they valued individually more often than they did together. This created frictions now and then—as when Godwin showed up at the theater with a certain Mrs. Inchmore and sat in conspicuously better seats than Wollstonecraft—but, more often, it kept these two free spirits aware of each other as free spirits. It kept them alive to the philosopher and the lover in their spouse—rather than the household prop. Wollstonecraft never forgot that her cerebral husband was capable of seducing others; he never forgot she was an amorous entrepreneur and had directed many a cinematic love affair before his arrival on her screen.

At a time when husband and wife were expected to be joined at the hip—and head—even more tightly than they are today,

Wollstonecraft and Godwin championed each other's separate lives. They revered each other's separate thoughts. Their love resembles nothing so much, in fact, as the ideal communion Emerson evokes in "Friendship"; it was—in the words of the essayist—"an alliance of two large, formidable natures, mutually beheld, mutually feared, before yet they recognized the deep identity which beneath these disparities unites them." [42]

What writers such as Wollstonecraft and Godwin did for love in the eighteenth century, artists like Frida Kahlo and Diego Rivera did for love in the twentieth. A renowned muralist by the time Kahlo was a little girl, Rivera was more influential in bringing Mexican painting to the outside world than any artist of his age. His third wife, the portraitist Frida Kahlo, became a byword for tempestuous genius.

The relationship between the two painters was explosive, ardent, bracing, enduring—and riddled with distances. Married in 1929, they were divorced in 1939—only to remarry in 1940. For much of their conjugal life, they maintained separate houses—Kahlo's blue, Rivera's pink—connected only whimsically by a walking bridge and divided by dozens of animal cages, fruit trees, and patches of desert. Their relationship was punctuated by extensive independent trips and entanglements with other people. Indeed, after they married each other for the second time, one of Kahlo's rules was "no sexual intercourse." [43] Whether or not they obeyed this commandment matters less than that they made it. Enforced absences and abstinences were as vital to the continuation of their bond as fire, art, and brimstone had been to its creation.

But if Frida Kahlo commanded sexual ceasefires and Mary

Wollstonecraft ordained individual residences, there is one woman who trumps them all when it comes to the defense of distances between lovers at once geographic and erotic. That woman is Emily Dickinson. If her Master Letters (discussed in Chapter 2) may be called paeans to inequality, her verses may be called songs of absence. Her life was a life of reclusiveness and chastity. What is so remarkable about it in this light—the life as well as the art—is that it is defined by desire. Sharp, blood-letting desire such as America's other great nineteenth-century poet, the cheerfully omnisexual Walt Whitman, could not even approximate. Whitman, the man who loved men and women, and mud and meadows, and blades and fire, is a magnetic character and a highly original voice—but the oft-discussed desire in his poetry is the weaker for being spread all over the place so lavishly. Dickinson's is like a laser beam—thin, circumscribed, ethereal; you can do surgery with it. You can cut through membranes and mountains with it.

Emily Dickinson spent her life sequestered away in her family home. From the late 1850s—when she was in her late twenties—to her death in 1886, she lived in self-imposed isolation in Amherst, Massachusetts, rarely going out of doors, uniformly dressing in white, never marrying, dating, or having—so far as one can tell—a consummated romantic relationship. With rare exceptions, she saw no one but her sister and sister-in-law who lived a few hundred feet away. There is a certain part of myth to this story—but a great part of reality also. To be sure, Dickinson had nephews and nieces who visited once in a while; she also (as we have seen) had consuming epistolary intimacies. Perhaps she went out for groceries more than her mythologizers like to admit (much as Henry David Thoreau, her contemporary, who apparently abandoned his *Survivor*-style isolation at Walden Pond to wolf down weekly meals in adjacent Concord). Overwhelmingly, however, Dickinson was alone with the daisies in her garden, the ribbons on her dress, the larks in her little spot of sky—and the tigers in her brain.

For tigers there were. Dickinson was full of tigers, "red in tooth and claw." Witness a mere shred of the sort of verse she was writing in the first few years of her bucolic house-arrest:

As the vulture teased . . .
As the tiger eased

By but a Crumb of Blood, fasts Scarlet

Till he meet a Man
Dainty adorned with Veins and Tissues
. . . his Tongue

Cooled by the Morsel for a moment

Grows a fiercer thing . . .[44]

It is a poetry of bottomless hunger, of stinging appetite, an altogether unladylike poetry that has nothing to do with the virginal vision of whiteness that Dickinson presented to the outside world.

Where did it come from? As Whitman's genial eroticism came from embracing life, Dickinson's carnivorous want came from holding life at arm's length. It came—like Dante's synesthe-

siac, blood-and-guts sensuality—from envisioning and enforc-
ing absences. Unlike Dante, Dickinson had no real-life spouse to
take the edge off of her fantasy love. What she had instead was
high-voltage correspondences with low-access men. She had a
weakness for devout clergymen. (A minister like the charismatic
Charles Wadsworth could rivet her imagination from the day she
first heard him preach in 1855 until his death in 1882.) She also
had a vivid vulnerability to married editors with no grasp of her
genius and no courage to fight for it if they'd had it (men like
Samuel Bowles, who ran the *Springfield Republican*, or Thomas
Wentworth Higginson, who edited poetry).

One has the strong sense, though, that Dickinson, like Dante,
relished the very distance of these magnetic poles. Consider the
opening of a poem inspired, at least in part, by Charles Wadsworth:

I cannot live with you,
It would be Life
And Life is over there—
Behind the Shelf . . .

The Sexton keeps the key to—

Putting up
Our Life—His Porcelain—
Like a Cup

Discarded of the Housewife[45]

Morality and propriety stand guard over their love in the figure of the Christian sexton—preventing them from removing it from its hiding place, preventing them from living it, consummating it, seizing it from where it sits immobile and pristine as porcelain. And yet one has the nagging suspicion that if it weren't the "sexton" getting in the way of romantic realization, it would be Dickinson herself.

She is far too quick to resign herself to the necessity of distance:

So We must meet apart—
You there—I—here—
With just the Door ajar
That oceans are—[46]

There is an idolatry of renunciation in this poem—as there is in all of Dickinson's work. *"We must meet apart."* We can gaze at each other only across the abyss, only—like Madame Butterfly and her paramour—across an ocean.

Some of the men to whom Dickinson wrote wanted more than only to write her. She made it very difficult. At once excited and apprehensive, she estranged them with odd excuses for being unavailable—or with the violence of her anxiety when she finally consented to see them. After meeting Dickinson for the first time after a charged eight years of letter writing, Thomas Higginson told his wife that "I am glad I do not live near her." Nobody, he swore, had ever "drained his nerve power so much." Her step when she came down the stairs to him was "like a pattering child's"; she was "breathless" and said "Forgive me if I am frightened." In so doing, she frightened *him*. Her intensity, her gratitude: it was like holding a fluttering butterfly in one's large, clumsy hand; a chaos of fragile movement. Higginson was not equal to it.[47]

Nobody much *was*. Dickinson's editor friends failed with superhuman regularity to see that they were dealing with the most original and intense poetic talent of their period—and a great number of other periods as well. Her poems went almost uniformly unpublished in her lifetime—not entirely, as is sometimes thought, because of her seclusion and unwillingness to show her work—but as much for the resilient stupidity of her literary allies. There was hardly a moment in her adult life that she was not vigorously exchanging poems and letters with a man who might have published her verse as easily as he tied his shoe in the morning. If she initiated contact with Thomas Higginson to begin with, it is because he had written an *Atlantic Monthly* article imploring new poets to step into the limelight and assuring them that editors like himself were "always hungering and thirsting for novelties."[48] Dickinson's repeated efforts to entrust her poetry to intelligent editors brought her nothing. The intelligentsia failed her. And yet failure—perhaps as a result—became her expertise, her art, her honey. She sucked its bitters as though they were sweets:

> *Success is counted sweetest*
> *By those who ne'er succeed.*
> *To comprehend a nectar*
> *Requires sorest need.*

Not one of all the purple Host

Who took the flag today
Can tell the definition
So clear of Victory

As he defeated—dying—

On whose forbidden ear
The distant strains of triumph
Burst agonized and clear.[49]

Success is ecstatic only when you know defeat. Presence is bewitching only when you know absence—only (one is tempted to say) when it is a *form* of absence. A lover on the other side of the world is often more preoccupying than a lover on the other side of the room.

On the occasions that the man whom Dickinson loved made himself genuinely accessible to her—as did the final major love of her life, a celebrated judge called Otis Phillips Lord who had recently lost his wife—it is Dickinson who became inaccessible. When Lord begged Dickinson to live with him, to kiss him, to (editors suppose) marry him, she demurred: "Don't you know," she asked, "that you are happiest while I withhold and not confer? *Don't you know that 'No' is the wildest word we consign to language?*"[50] In this one question lies the key to all her poetry and all her life.

It was not an easy life, in the bland Disneyland way that we sometimes imagine lives should be. But it was a life of rare, fine feeling and charged communication from which much can be learned. With a minimum of entertainment, Dickinson lived an abundance of drama and desire, high lyricism and disconcerting passion.

She continued her ardent exchange with Otis Lord until his death in 1884. Only two years earlier, in 1882, it had been her other great, good love—the Reverend Charles Wadsworth—who had died. And it is only when he did that Dickinson had begun to ask the questions others would have asked in the early days of the relationship. Did he, she asked a mutual contact, have brothers or sisters? How is it possible, biographers have marveled, that she did not know such basic facts about the man she called her "dearest earthly friend?"[51] Is it possible that without reading Emerson's "Friendship," she had perfectly observed its ruling sentiment? Shun "rash personal relations" with your friend. Do not "know his mother and brother and sisters."

She talked with Wadsworth about almost everything of importance to her. She talked with him of religion, of loneliness, of poetry, of gardens, of salvation, and of sadness. But she did not talk with him about real people. She did not talk with him of his family members—or of her own. All too near in spirit, they remained strangers in flesh and facts.

This was her *modus operandi*. This was the way she coped both in verse and in life: "Heaven," she once wrote,

—is what I cannot reach!
The Apple on the Tree—
Provided it do hopeless—hang—
That—"Heaven" is—to Me![52]

Dickinson's style mirrors her substance: She discusses inaccessibility and her lines are littered with em dashes, hesitations, spaces that suggest words omitted, confessions unmade, invitations flouted. If ever there was a literature of things left out—a literature of starvation, a literature of hunger, a literature of lust—Dickinson's is it.

★　★　★

EMILY DICKINSON understood absence—at once literal and figurative, sexual and spatial. This is an understanding we need to regain in our day. We need to rediscover the right to impose distances, the right to remain strangers, the right not to take for granted even those we love, and not to be taken for granted ourselves. Let's admit: There are artificial and adolescent reasons to say "no," as there are artificial and adolescent reasons to say "yes." But there are also excellent reasons to allow—and impose—distances in our closest relations.

It builds character, first of all. It's too easy, simply, to melt into each other—and what is easy soon becomes cheap. Says the twentieth-century German poet Rainer Maria Rilke: In all things except love, "nature herself enjoins men to collect themselves . . . while in the heightening of love, the impulse is to give oneself wholly away." The problem is that "When a person abandons himself, he is no longer anything, and when two people both give themselves up in order to come close to each other, there is no longer any ground beneath them and their being together is a continual falling."[53] To melt into another human being without respite or restraint is to lose your own identity—and therefore your attractiveness to the very person whose affection you so much want to evoke. Seduction entails other-ness.

Second: distances allow clearer sight (a subject investigated in the first chapter). No man is a prophet in his own country. There is little more distorting for the eye or mind than excessive proximity. We must always see our loved ones from the outside as well as from the inside, lest we cease to be able to either critique or admire them.

Third: distances allow rediscovery. It does not matter if it is a city, a culture, or a person at stake; if we stay forever in their proximity, we cease to be surprised by them. To retain our capacity for wonder—and indeed observation—we must periodically step back. In French the expression is *"reculer pour mieux sauter,"* to step back in order to jump forward the better.

Fourth: one of the sublime things about the life of the passions is that we are intuitively attracted to persons at some distance from us. Whereas in casual social life, we incline toward companions who resemble us, who smack of compatibility with us, in love, every man adores a stranger. In love, we take risks. We often respond most strongly to persons most radically distinct from us in experience as well as education, in culture as well as in taste or profession. This is a liminal and generous quality—one we ought to strengthen rather than stifle.

And finally: sometimes one must leave in order to return—at least in order to return with dignity and passion. To stay always in the same place, as does the conscientious brother in the biblical story of the Prodigal Son, is of limited use.[54] It is the brother who leaves home and then comes back who is ecstatic about the lamb on his father's table and who fills his family members with joy— not the one who has always been on location and lost his capacity to appreciate.

Distance and difficulty create intensity. Ease and familiarity enhance equanimity—and ultimately indifference. At the end of the essay that might be called *Love*, Emerson challenges us to choose what it is we most wish to befriend in our companions— for we cannot have everything. "Are you," he demands, "the friend of your friend's *buttons*, or of his *thought*? To a great heart, he will be a stranger in a thousand particulars, that he may come near in the holiest ground."[55] We must choose, sometimes, between the convenient and the sublime, the secular and the sacred.

If we think we know a loved one because we know the rituals of his day, the habits of her hygiene, the externals of his family history, we cease trying to get to know him. Instead of conceiving her as a mystery to be studied, we see her as a caricature to be smiled over—a conglomerate of tics and routines, predictable preferences and repetitive mannerisms.

The same holds true for "biblical" knowledge. Too routine a knowledge of a person's sexuality deadens the senses. "He knows little of the service of women," wrote a thirteenth-century troubador, "who wishes to possess his lady entirely."[56] The strongest erotic rapports are often those that are most circumscribed and most sporadic. Few places are less arousing than nudist beaches, as both defenders and critics will avow.

To savor one another and to savor intimacy, we do well to limit it. Dante was not a naïf. Nor was he a victim of circumstance. He *knew* what he was doing in his courtship of Beatrice. As did Tristan and Iseult, Mary Wollstonecraft and William Godwin, Frida Kahlo and Diego Rivera, Emily Dickinson with her different suitors. We need not imitate their excesses, but we gain everything from seizing their inspiration.

❦

FIVE

"On My Blood I'll Carry You Away": Love as Heroism

Put my eyes out: I can still see;
snap off my arms: I'll hold you hard
in my heart's longing like a fist . . .
and if you set this mind of mine aflame,
then on my blood I'll carry you away.

—Rainer Maria Rilke[1]

WHEN WE FALL IN LOVE, we hand our partner a loaded gun. It is an act of supreme courage, and all the safety measures in the world cannot diminish its terrible implications.

We hand our partner a loaded gun—but in order to kill us he needn't so much as take aim or wish us ill. He need merely doze off over the trigger. In fact, a superior metaphor may be that of the steering wheel: the love affair not as Russian roulette but as a drive through darkened country with an inebriated stranger.

It can be magical; you can end up in places you never expected, embracing in the tall blades beyond the road bend, or you can end up dead in a ditch. Not through anybody's malice, but merely because of a temperament insufficiently alert, a sensibility a little dull, an instance of timing a bit unfortunate.

To love is to risk. We do not always know how much. We imagine we are entering into a "controlled crush," but in fact we are launching into free fall; it can be ecstatic or deadly, depending on factors only partly under our control. We are the more vulnerable for being more feelingful; the more vulnerable for being more courageous; the more vulnerable for having a fine temperament. The emotionally and intellectually dull do not fall in love hard or long.

Almost everything in modern society militates against our falling in love hard or long. It militates against love as risk, love as sacrifice, love as heroism. As presented to us in dating books, matchmaking sites, and advice columns, love is—or ought to be—an organized adult activity with safety rails on the left and right, rubber ceilings, no-skid floors, and a clear, clean destination: marriage. Anyone who embarks on something more ambiguous, more dangerous or difficult to predict is counted all but pathological—especially if she is a woman. For even in today's unprecedentedly safety-proofed social culture, men are still accorded a nominal amount of adventure. They are permitted to recognize "the thrill of the chase"; they are allowed to pursue members of the opposite sex who cause them a bit of trouble and turmoil. It is chalked up in men to high spirits, predatorial adrenaline, to chutzpah, competition, and courage. But when women do the same thing—when women set their sights and stake their bliss on partners who are obviously elusive—it is chalked up to low self-worth.

In fact, the notion that women who go after challenging men have bad self esteem while men who go after difficult women have great testosterone has become endemic. The authors of the fastest-selling dating advice book of the beginning of this century, *He's Just Not That Into You*, blithely assert that men like nothing better than a good fight, a tough race. "We like not knowing if we can catch you," writes co-author Greg Behrendt *in loco* of all men. "We feel rewarded when we do. Especially when the race is a long one."[2] At the same time he counsels his female readers to forgo the very fights that give him such pleasure. "Men don't like it" when women give chase, he says coolly. Men don't like it when women show *any* kind of initiative in romance. They don't like it when women do more, in fact, than sit on their hands and allow passing males to observe their charm and kick the courtship machinery into motion.

No matter that this image is as untrue as it is unfair. Women succeed far more frequently in seducing men—when their desire commands it—than do men in seducing women. Both sexes must be subtle and inventive to realize their ambitions, and both sexes regularly fail. An excess of eagerness turns off amorous prospects of either gender. Thus, women's impatience with the so-called nice man—"the kind of guy who keeps telling you how beautiful you are and immediately wants to spend 24 hours a day with you," as one relationship bestseller disdainfully describes him.[3] A woman who wants to make the first move in a love affair must be as adroit as a man—and sometimes more imaginative. But both sexes can pursue—and the more robust, resourceful, and courageous members of both sexes invariably *do*.

The hottest dating books of the last three decades make it their business to discourage women from this pursuit. In fact, they provide women with long lists of the vilest ilks of men—persons they should not merely refrain from romancing, but actively flee. *He's Just Not That Into You* manages to include on its list most members of the human race. "You, the superfox reading this book are worth" more than any man you might plausibly meet, it says again and again.[4] Under the guise of warning women away from men who are abusive or uninterested, Greg Behrendt and co-writer Liz Tuccillo, manage to warn women away from all men who are in any way at all imperfect, all men who could, in fact, *use* a friend or lover to fortify them.

Among the parties tagged for deportation are men who have poor relationships with their ex-wives as well as men who have *good* relationships with their ex-wives, men who are mourning the demise of their spouses as well as men who would *never* mourn the demise of their spouses, men who worry they have too little money as well as men who worry they have too much money, medical students with an occasional spell of irritation as well as music video directors with a regular case of overwork, men who don't want sex enough as well as men who want sex too much, men who are nice after a break-up but don't really want to get back together again as well as men who are nice after a break-up and *do* really want to get back together again, divorcés who are too comfortable with their erstwhile family, as well as aging singles who are insufficiently comfortable with *your* family

... in short any man who lacks a perfect plastic Fisher-Price shell, any man who does not fall instantaneously, uncomplicatedly, and ecstatically into your arms.

If *He's Just Not That Into You* offers lengthy lists of men to discard, so does its equally successful predecessor, *Smart Women/Foolish Choices*. Published by two Los Angeles psychotherapists thirty-odd years ago and reprinted countless times since, it uses the same arguments to address the same audiences—only more explicitly and, perhaps, more honestly. Where Behrendt and Tuccillo's book tucks its lists of pariahs into chapters entitled "He's Just Not That Into You If . . . He Does Not Want to Marry You" [and other crimes against humanity—fill in the blank], *Smart Women* makes its lists more overt and aggressive. It instructs you to shun, for example, the "Pseudo-Liberated Male," the "Perpetual Adolescent," the "Clam," and the "Walking Wounded." They're losers all. Don't worry about whether or not they are into *you*. You should not be into *them*. At the same time, the book is more candid than its successor. It squarely admits women's attraction to *just those men* and makes some attempt to consider the source of this attraction. Thus, Chapter Five in *Smart Women* is called "How Exciting Men Can Make Women Miserable" and includes sub-sections such as "Bad Boys Can Be Fun" and "The Magnetism of the Rat."

Why is it, ask the authors in these sections, that women are so "prone to rush into dangerous emotional situations," that "the most engaging adolescent characters [to them] are often like Marlon Brando or James Dean—outsiders, loners, the angry ones? . . . Why is it," they demand, "that girls are often drawn to 'rascals' or the bad guys in school?" Is it that they sense these boys are "in touch with the darker side of life?"⁵ Is it that they secretly believe they don't really deserve a "good" boy?

Or could it be—though this is hardly the explanation offered by our two doctors or their colleagues—that girls *like the challenge*? Could it be that they, like their male counterparts, ultimately relish the game of seduction as much as the victory; that they enjoy the wrestling match as well as the prize, the race as much as the medal at the finish line? Could it be that women and girls, like men and boys, are not simply pining for the tranquility of triumph but also for the adrenaline of pursuit? Could it be that the feistier members of both sexes actually *go* for bad boys and bad girls not by accident but on purpose, not because they have been traumatized in their childhoods but because they have been emboldened and have courage and enterprise to spare? Could it be that the choice of a challenging love object signals strength and resourcefulness rather than insecurity and psychological damage, as we so often hear?

For the moment a woman fancies a man who is visibly difficult, the pop psychologist in us begins to inquire about her parenting. What was her relationship with her father? Was she abused between the ages of two and ten? Was she abandoned or intimidated? Harassed or raped? Did she decide, at some pivotal moment, that she *just did not deserve* a happy relationship?

Such questions are fueled more by the sexual double standards of evolutionary pseudo-science (i.e., women are not allowed to enjoy hunting; they are only allowed to enjoy sitting on eggs) than they are by empirical experience. A better question might be: Why should healthy, confident girls who in every other area of their lives are trained to seek out challenges, trained to pursue the most ambitious course and enjoy it; why should these girls be expected in the single realm of romance to spring for the easy option—to choose the sit-home-and-let-destiny-find-me strategy? It seems absurd. A woman who, in all other parts of her life, is a fighter and conqueror stands little chance in her personal life of becoming a wallflower, a pale porcelain doll who waits to be noticed in a coffee shop.

Love, for the strong-hearted and strong-minded woman, is a game like all others—albeit perhaps the most important game. Historically, it has been her particular arena—not because she could not have excelled in others but because she was often excluded from others (politics, the arts, the military). What was hers was heroism in the cause of love, combativeness on the field of emotion. This is hers still. And it remains the noblest field of action for women and men alike—the field with the most affecting victories and, on occasion, the bloodiest fallouts.

*   *   *

IT IS only in recent times that dating books have peddled the extreme prudence we find in them today. The book that qualifies as the first dating book ever written—a 200-page Latin poem published in the year before Christ's birth and entitled *The Art of Love*—urges a different strategy entirely.[6] Addressed to both sexes, brimming with explicit instructions, and penned—to many people's astonishment—by the illustrious Ovid, it likens love not to a safety-padded bumper-car ride but to pitched battle.

"Love is a kind of war," declares Ovid, "and no assignment for cowards. Where those banners fly, heroes are always on guard."[7]

To the first self-help author western civilization has produced, love was not the opposite of war (as it may have been for the children of the 1960s), but one of its essential and sublime forms. The point to Ovid wasn't to "make love *not* war." You made love *as* war. Fighting and loving were both enterprises for the tough not the timid, the intrepid not the effete.

It says a great deal about our age that modern-day editors of Ovid's *The Art of Love* habitually consider it an elaborate joke. A "tongue-in-cheek" parody, they call it, of the serious war literature being written at the time; "polished," to be sure, but finally "rather frivolous stuff" (as one translator puts it in his introduction).[8] Ovid, it's true, was no humorless scholar. Most celebrated for his rambunctious tales of the antics and transformations of Greek gods, *Metamorphoses*, Ovid is forever making fun—both of others and of himself.[9] His temperament is blithe. Like Shakespeare (of whom it has been said that he could never resist a pun, no matter how distracting), Ovid cannot repress a joke. He cannot bypass a rhetorical flourish, a bit of slapstick, a naughty piece of self-deprecation.[10] (Thus he will relate his bedroom disasters with uncommon vividness. Of a night with a beautiful girl on which he failed to rise to the task at hand, for example, he will lament that "she might have done as well using the fringe of her dress"; his "stalk was refusing to burdgeon. . . ." He worries what "my old age [will] be like . . . / If in the days of my youth I am no better than this."[11]

It is an unperceptive audience however—or one incapable of considering love in the heroic vein—who will overlook the sobriety, the gravity, and the astuteness of Ovid's remarks in the midst of all the ribbing. Who can dismiss, for example, his oft-adduced argument that desire runs wild when restrained and ambles to a halt when given free sway? It is a point he elaborates imagistically:

> *Not long ago, I saw a horse that was rebellious and fighting,*
> *Taking a bit in his mouth, flying on wings of the wind,*
> *But as soon as the reins were let loose, and he*
> *knew it, he slowed to a canter . . .*
> *Always our nature insists on things denied . . .*
> *Take my advice,*

he charges, "*don't make temptation more fun by forbidding . . .*"[12] Not the worst advice that one can give possessive spouses—or protective parents either.

Ovid takes his subject seriously. Modesty and jocularity aside (it would not be fitting, after all, for a Roman statesman of his time to discuss his amorous experiences with the tear-stained self-importance of a twenty-first-century talk show guest), he takes Eros dead seriously—never more so than when he discusses its warlike aspects. Indeed, his book begins and ends on a military metaphor: "Arms and violent wars," I will discuss, he announces in the first line. When, by the third line, Cupid "snickers" at the conventional interpretation of this subject matter, swords and armor, Ovid reconceives it as hearts and arrows.[13]

"Lovers are always at war, with Cupid watching the ramparts," he tells us, "take it from me, lovers are always at war."[14] Why? In a word, because they *want* to be. Eros craves competition and exertion; it craves achievement; it wants to move mountains and break ramparts. "What the [military] captains demand, aggressiveness, ardor of spirit" is the same that Eros demands. True lovers have no tolerance for easy targets; they ache to prove themselves against formidable odds. When these odds do not exist, they find them elsewhere. "Let it never be said that love is an indolent calling."

Love is the most demanding calling of them all—and at the same time the most difficult to resist for a person of healthy passions. It can make even a leisured loafer spring willingly into the trenches. Ovid should know: "I was a lazy man," he testifies in the tone of a sinner reformed, "with a bent for bedroom and slippers, doing what work I did half lying down in the shade." Luckily, "love for a beautiful girl took me out of the doldrums; when the order came, I sprang to arms in her camp. / So you see me alert and waging my wars. . . ." The moral? "If you want to forswear idleness, then fall in love."[15] Those whom even love cannot shake from their habitual aversion to risk and inertia are those who are truly unredeemable.

Let's suppose that we are not of their number. Still, it is insufficient to be combative only in the seduction phase of a love affair; it is necessary to be combative continuously. The longer one hopes love will last, the more vigorously one must sustain the battle. Ovid devotes the second section of his first-century self-help book to the maintenance of Love Attained.

To put his point a bit archly: One starts by fighting *for* one's lover and one ends by fighting *with* one's lover. This is not to be construed as unfortunate; certainly Ovid does not construe it thus. Love is not intended to recline. It is not intended to get soft in the belly. It is meant to stand perpetually at attention, to strain and to wrestle, to ring the bells of wedding *and* alarm.

So although you may have won your bride (or groom) and be ferrying happily home on your ship, "your vessel sails in mid-ocean," Ovid warns,

> Far away, still, from the port; harbor and heaven are far.
> It is by no means enough to have won your girl through my singing;
> What you have won by my art, art must instruct you to hold. [16]

Ovid's game plan? Pick a fight. Give her hell. Make him struggle. A high-maintenance relationship is the only kind of relationship worth maintaining. Love ceases when the blood of the participants cools:

> Spirit can grow . . . rank, when matters are going too smoothly,
> Nor is it easy to bear Fortune's continual smile. . . .
> But if you rouse the flame, half-dead, by throwing on sulphur,
> Then it flares up again, brighter in light than before.
> Heat her cooling mind, and let her get anxious about you. . . .
> I would not mind, in that case, if she . . .
> Tore at my cheeks with her nails, frantic and weeping with rage,
> Gave me her angriest looks, and wanted to do what she could not,
> Namely, live without me, what an impossible hope!

One must not draw out the drama interminably, however. It is one thing to have an impassioning fight, another to nurse a long-standing grudge: "How long is the suitable time for resentment?" Ovid wonders. "Not too long," comes the answer:

While she is still in tears, put your arms gently around her,
While she is still in tears hold her close to your breast. . . .
That is the only way; anger succumbs to that peace.

Lest one imagine Ovid's intentions pure, he specifies otherwise:

When she has raged her fill, and seems an enemy, surely,
Take her to bed; you will find she is gentle and mild. . . .
The doves, who were lately at war, join bill to bill in affection. . . .

Not only must one instigate arguments with one's mate, one must also occasionally disappear. "No man of breeding," Ovid warns, "can bear ever becoming a bore. / Never let her say 'I can't get rid of that fellow.'" Be careful to disappear at a time when you are likely to be missed though; there is no point in proving by your absence how easy it is to get on without you:

Don't go away until you know she will be sorry you go.
Then you can give her a rest . . .
Thirsty the dry soil thrives best in response to the rain.
Phyllis's ardor was mild . . . in Denephoon's presence
When his sail was spread, then she broke out into flame . . .

No one wants to become a fixture in the eye of the beloved. One must always be an adornment in the home of one's mate, not a kitchen fixture—or, even, a bedroom fixture:

Rather than offer predictable pleasures, one ought to

Mix in a little rebuff, once in a while, with your fun.
Let [one's partner] lie on the stone, complain the door is too cruel,
Let him be meek as a mouse, then let him threaten and rave.

For "fires that are burning low are fanned into flame by outrage." To be of perpetual interest to one's love, one must be of perpetual worry. So often considered the bane of marriages, even jealousy can be a boon. When we fear someone may lap us in the stadium of our partner's affection, we try harder, we treasure the finish line more: "Your true thoroughbred," says Ovid, "runs his best race when he comes from behind."

Jealousy keeps its victims attuned to the possibilities of their beloved; it allows them to see the persons most familiar to them as intriguing strangers, to see them with eyes unhazed by habit and a heart rendered rawly responsive by uncertainty.

* * *

WHAT IS constant in all of Ovid's advice and insight is this: the harder the fight, the higher the prize. The harder the fight, the stronger the fighter. Or, perhaps, it is the reverse: The stronger the fighter, the harder the fight he tends to choose, the tougher the wars she elects to wage.

Is it any wonder, if this is true, that the most formidable feminists have often been the most formidable lovers? That the women who fought hardest for new social and sexual orders also fought hardest for—get this!—a man? Neither Andrea Dworkin nor Shulamith Firestone, to be sure; not the last century's spate of anti-sex feminists, but their forerunners, the often unheralded Strong Women of history, of mythology, and of poetry.

Take the first powerful female character in English literature. Ask any English major: Who is she? Lady Macbeth? Too little too late. Philip Sidney's Stella, the star of his sonnet book? Hardly. Almost without question the answer is the Wife of Bath from Chaucer's fourteenth-century *Canterbury Tales*.

Who is the Wife of Bath? *The Norton Anthology of English Literature* exclaims upon her "aggressive feminism"[17]—and with good reason: She is the boldest, brashest, loudest, most independent member of the pilgrimage Chaucer describes in his famed verse tales. She is also a career lover.

"Husbands at church door I have had five," she announces to her Christian companions on the pilgrimage they are taking to view the remains of Saint Thomas à Becket of Canterbury. "And all," she swears, "were worthy men in their degree."[18] She's glad to have had all of them—and ready to throttle anyone who suggests that as a God-fearing woman in the Middle Ages she ought not to have allowed more than *one* in her life or bed:

> I was told certain, not long ago it is,
> That since Christ never [went] but once
> to wedding in the [state] of Galilee
> That by the same example taught he me
> That I should wedded be but once.[19]

But this does not convince her. "Man may [argue] up and down," she says wryly, but what they miss is that

> God bade us to wax and multiply:
> That gentle text can I well understand.[20]

And that "gentle text" she applies most urgently—in the thrashing and kicking conquest of spouse after exhausted spouse.

The Wife of Bath, by and large, is too voracious for her husbands. In the lingo of contemporary dating, she is *way too intense* in her relationships. To be married to her is to deliver sexual performances at a clip: "My husband shall have it both eve and morrow," she swaggers:

> I have the power during all my life
> Of his proper boy, and not he . . .[21]

It may be (as she has heard) that "virginity is great perfection" and Christ recommended it to his followers, but "he spoke to them that would live perfectly, / And lordings," she announces triumphantly to her fellow pilgrims, "by your leave, *that am not I*"![22]

Chastity is where her Christianity stops. Docility and forgiveness are also pushing the boundaries. For when the Wife of Bath is not making love with her husbands she is imposing discipline on them: "God it knows I chided them spitefully," she says.[23] When, on an unusual occasion, one of her husbands actually dared to offend her, "By God on earth I was his purgatory."[24] She tortured him until he died—for which reason she now prays that his soul is in heaven.

But if most of her husbands were docile with her—if four of them "loved me so well, by God above, / That I set no value on their love"—the fifth gave her trouble.[25] The fifth gave her a very

great deal of trouble. He fought her tooth and nail. He attacked her
faults, ignored her for long stretches of time, and sometimes hit
her over the head. Not surprisingly, he was her favorite. It is he,
she swears, who will remain the love of her life.

Even before their marriage began it was marked by blood. Still
wed to her fourth husband, the Wife of Bath met her fifth—a scholar
twenty years her junior—in the "fields" near her home.[26] She appears
to have taken some liberties with him; in any case, she let him know
during this meeting that she would marry him in an instant were
she not married already. Soon after, she dreamed that he appeared at
her bedside and laid violent hands on her. The scene was gory:

He would have slain me as I lay [supine],
And all my bed was full of very blood.[27]

And "yet," she told her attacker sprightly,

I hope that you will do me good
For blood betokens gold, as I was taught.[28]

Blood betokens gold to the Wife of Bath. Conflict betokens
passion—and conflict is what defined her relationship with the
scholar. For immediately after she had expressed her wish to be
his wife, her fourth husband obligingly died, and she walked in
his funeral procession with the scholar at her side. A month later,
she and the scholar were married. The war began.

The Wife of Bath had no sooner signed off her worldly possessions to Husband Number Five but she "repented me full sore"
because the cantankerous young man "suffered no thing of my

pleasure" to occur. He did not do a thing she liked.[29] Worse, he lectured her about her shortcomings—a habit she heartily loathed ("I hate him that my vices telleth me"). When she gave him displeasure, he beat her up: "That feel I on my ribs . . . And ever shall," she intones.[30] Not that she did not retaliate.

She fought back like a "lioness"—and never so vigorously as one day when her beloved was poring over his books.[31] She had taken a dislike to these books over time; after all, he delighted to extract from them quotations from famous Roman writers proving the wickedness of women and detailing the manner in which their husbands might justifiably punish them. On this particular day, however, the scholar was reading a book we know well: he was reading Ovid's *The Art of Love*.[32] It is hard to imagine that he was not culling practical wisdom from it, for few men ever applied Ovid's ethic of love-as-war more literally—and, indeed, the scholar perused the book so deeply that the Wife of Bath felt neglected. It is this neglect by her beloved—more than his occasional floggings—that drove her over the edge. One day she simply jump-tackled him:

> When I saw he would never finish
> To read the cursed book all night
> . . . three leaves have I snatched
> Out of his book as he read, and also
> I with my fist so hit him on the cheek
> That in our fire he fell backward down.[33]

Ovid's pages burn in the fireplace. The scholar himself, however, rises from the ashes. Like a "raging lion" he rises,

And with his fist he smote me on the head
That on the floor I lay as if I were dead.
And when he saw how still that I lay,
He was aghast . . .[34]

He had reason to be concerned: The injury he inflicted on his wife left her deaf in one ear. But she too rises from the ashes. She, too, rouses herself from near death to slug her lover back. "Hast thou slain me false thief?" she cries and boxes him in the face.[35] And then, all at once, the tone shifts. To the reader's consternation, the Wife of Bath asks her assailant for a kiss. "Ere I be dead," she says gently, "yet will I kiss thee."[36] Touched to the quick, the scholar kneels over the woman he loves and implores forgiveness: "My own true wife," he vows, ". . . I shall thee never smite [again]."[37] Not only will he never smite her again, but he offers her "sovereignty" in their household.[38] He gives her total "governance of house and land, / And,"—as we are naughtily told—"of his tongue and hand also."[39]

This image of man and woman in primal struggle—the one in the fireplace with his possessions aflame, the other on the floor with a shattered eardrum, blows flying as fast as kisses—could this *possibly* be a vision of love *as an ideal*? Of course it is not to be taken literally: Love can never be a matter of exchanging bruises—but it *is* a matter of exchanging provocations. Like the characters in Grimm's fairy tales, the Wife of Bath is an extreme figure, an impossible figure—but the suggestion her character makes is accurate: Strong, free-thinking women—the kind who defy social convention, challenge religious authorities, go on pilgrimages by themselves, and demand "sovereignty"—are very often the same women who suggest a new romantic order; the same women who wonder if it's possible to have five husbands rather than one; the same women who throw themselves recklessly into their loves and garner wounds as well as wins.

It is telling that the Wife of Bath, accustomed as she obviously was to having the upper hand, feels most in love with the man who offers her the hardest challenge. Given the choice between her intractable scholar husband and his four obedient colleagues (the only wise candidates, according to any modern dating book) she opts loud and clear for the scholar. Her passionate final slugfest with him gives a whole new meaning to "tough love." And it would be hard to argue that she has this slugfest out of weakness. The Wife of Bath is a tower of strength—a self-determining woman at a time that "self-determining" was not a concept and "woman" was hardly a sex, not in any case, a sex to be taken seriously.

Chaucer may have known what Greg Behrendt and the good doctors of California do not: that women can be aggressive as men, that they consciously or otherwise crave excitement as much as they do contentment, and that love is the most obvious and ambitious arena for such cravings—not an escape from real-life competition and conquest, but a culmination of it.

*   *   *

IF THE Wife of Bath provides one literary model for "tough love," the heroine of Shakespeare's most moving play about Eros provides a different one. Let us begin by admitting that Shakespeare was not generally, despite his reputation, a specialist of plays on love. As sublime a job as he does on ambition (*Macbeth*), self-doubt (*Hamlet*), jealousy (*Othello*), pride (*King Lear*), and vanity (*Henry IV*), he is not, first and foremost, a love writer. The plays he penned that have most centrally to do with love are his more frivolous. They are almost all comedies—that is, they are almost all light-hearted: *A Midsummer Night's Dream, All's Well That Ends Well, The Taming of the Shrew, Much Ado About Nothing*—which, while hardly without revelation, are somehow without gravity. The only serious plays that take love as their central subject are *Romeo and Juliet* and *Antony and Cleopatra*. The former is a study of juvenile love. The main characters are barely in their tweens, and their passion has more than a little of the adolescent crush about it. (One example: A few lines before falling in love with Juliet, Romeo is pining loudly for a certain "Rosalind"—subsequently forgotten.)

So it is really *Antony and Cleopatra* that stands as Shakespeare's most important play about adult love. Based on the tempestuous liaison of the first-century BC queen of Egypt with Marc Antony, one of the Roman empire's noblest statesmen, it is a sumptuous play, even by the standards of Shakespeare—replete with resonant lines of passion, high-jinks drama, and stirring sensuality. And, like Shakespeare's comedic plays about love (notably, *The Taming of the Shrew*), it profiles a relationship that is radically and deliberately contentious. It also profiles a relationship in which both protagonists are heroic.

"If you find [Antony] sad, say I am dancing; if in mirth say I am sudden sick," Cleopatra commands her maid in Act One.

Why would you treat Antony thus? asks the lady, abashed. This is hardly the way to keep a man you love!

"What should I do [that] I do not?" Cleopatra demands.

Be *nice* to him, intones the servant: *"In each thing give him way, cross him in nothing!"*

Cleopatra flushes scarlet with rage. "Thou teachest like a fool the way to lose him!" [40]

Convinced that docility in the life of the affections is the road to dreariness, Cleopatra offers Antony a smorgasbord of strategic contradictions. When Antony wishes to ignore a messenger, she orders him to pay attention; when he wishes to lounge in her arms, she reports herself missing; when he desires to go to sea-battle against his enemy Octavius Caesar, she accompanies him, only to flee at the worst moment possible, prompting him to withdraw his ships after her own, and humiliating him before the military world.

As he acknowledges to her afterward,

My heart was to thy rudder tied by th' strings,
And thou should'st tow me after. O'er my spirit
Thy full supremacy thou knew'st, and that
Thy beck might from the bidding of the Gods
Command me. [41]

It is one of the most defiantly beautiful declarations of love in English literature, and Antony makes it deliberately in the language of war. Cleopatra has "supremacy" over him; she knows "how much you were my *conqueror*"; his "sword, made weak by my affection, would obey" her will no matter what it was. [42]

If Cleopatra is the conqueror of Antony, Antony is also the conqueror of Cleopatra. Even as he lies dying at the end of the play—having fumbled his responsibilities in the Roman empire—

he remains for Cleopatra unvanquished. Even as he falls on his own sword, she revels in his mastery, his power, his prowess:

"So it should be," she triumphs: "that none but Antony should conquer Antony." [43] His demise strips the world of all luster, of all manhood, of all virility:

> *Young boys and girls*
> *Are level now with men . . .*
> *And there is nothing left remarkable*
> *Beneath the visiting Moon.* [44]

Cleopatra determines to die with Antony—but not before she flings her

> *sceptre at the injurious Gods*
> *To tell them that this world did equal theirs*
> *till they had stolen our jewel.* [45]

Proud and fiery, they are two warriors in love, Cleopatra and Antony—conquering each other, conquering themselves, and conquering even the "injurious gods."

Cleopatra's methods, to be sure, are the polar opposite of the Wife of Bath's. Where the Wife used crude force to pummel her five husbands into awed submission, Cleopatra uses subtle mental games. Where the Wife imposed her sexuality upon her husbands with great insistence, Cleopatra regularly withheld hers. Indeed, even during Antony's final moments, she makes him fight for it. Sitting high upon her Pharaoh's throne, with Antony drawing his last breaths below her, she refuses to descend to kiss him: "I dare not, dear," she says, feigning fear of Antony's enemies: "Help me, my women, we must draw thee up." [46]

"Oh quick," Antony pleads, "or I am gone." [47]

But no. For all the rapture of her attachment and the valor she shows in joining Antony in the grave, she insists that he be drawn up to her—or rather, that he draw *himself* up to her. It is as though she knows that even in his last minutes under the "visiting Moon," the greatest gift she can give him is a love *for which he must fight*—as she fights for it also.[48]

And this is where Chaucer's Wife and Shakespeare's queen are uncannily similar. Each is a sublimely strong woman who spends her life fighting for "sovereignty" in her society—Cleopatra as the willful pharaoh of ancient Egypt; the Wife of Bath as an outrageous reformer-rebel in medieval Europe—and who pours the same spirit into her love relations. It is the spirit of heroism.

* * *

NOW LET us turn for a moment to a true-minted *military* heroine— a woman for whom heroism was not only political or emotional as for Cleopatra, but martial. Let us look at that group of women whose name has been co-opted remorselessly by workout clubs and herbal supplements, sportswear and online bookstores—the Amazons.

As presented in classical literature, the Amazons were an ancient tribe of women warriors who inhabited Asia Minor and struck both fear and admiration into the hearts of their neighbors. Contemporaneous with the events of *The Iliad* and *The Odyssey*, they stuck to themselves except on the occasions that they resolved to reproduce.[49] At these moments they would invade one of the armed communities in their vicinity, fight with its proudest soldiers, and carry them off into their kingdom. There the soldiers waited until such time as the Amazons announced their famous Festival of Roses, a sexual celebration at which every woman would make love with the man she had conquered in battle. The occasion was an explosion of organized rape, to put it anachronistically, although few of the male victims seem to have resented it. The Amazons were dazzling, desirable, athletic women. And after their sexual harvest of the male soldiers, they liberated them; indeed they threw them out whether they wished to leave or not, and continued their business by themselves. It sounds, in some ways, like a radical feminist's dream: men for reproduction only— then expulsion. A Utopian society of women. One might almost call it the first feminist society.

The queen of this first feminist society—at least at the time of the Trojan War—was a woman called Penthesilea. The accounts that have come down about her differ, but most include her dueling hand to hand—and dueling to the death—with the greatest Greek hero, Achilles. The Amazons had insinuated themselves in the war between the Trojans and the Greeks not out of any political interest in its outcome but purely for the acquisition of sexual hostages. As a result, they freely fought both parties, mixing up enemies and allies, kings and foot soldiers, heroes with mercenaries. And thus it happened that the queen of the Amazons finds herself fighting with the pride of the Greeks. In most stories Achilles conquers Penthesilea, only to fall in love with her as she lies in the throes of death and to press her beauteous corpse to his heart. Later he draws the mockery of his mates by doing what one never does with a sworn enemy, least of all with an enemy who crashed a war that was none of her business: He personally gives her a hero's burial.

But there is a still more interesting version of this story, one that found its way, among other places, into a classic reference book of ancient mythology. It is a reference book picked up by a brilliant German playwright at the beginning of the nineteenth century—a young man who would be known for his extreme life, his extreme death, and his extreme theater.[50] Heinrich von Kleist was only thirty-one years of age at the time he wrote *Penthesilea*, and yet three years later he would be dead—self-slaughtered in a suicide pact with an incurably ill married woman.[51]

The woman and Kleist wandered deep into the forest together one day; shots were heard at a distance; and neither was seen again. Speculation proliferated about what they had meant to each other. Were they strangers linked mainly by their desire to die? Were they friends? Were they lovers? What does it take to kill another human being so ceremoniously, even lovingly, as Kleist did Henriette Vogel, and then to kill oneself? And what was the reason for such an exit by so ingenious and prolific an author as Kleist?

One of the reasons, at least, was the public rejection of *Penthesilea*.[52] It was the play that Kleist called the "closest to his heart." He wept over it as he wrote it, and when it was completed he mailed it to the most famous writer in Germany until this day—the almost sixty-year-old Johann Wolfgang von Goethe. "I write to you on the knees of my heart," Kleist confessed to the literary lion: What do you think of *Penthesilea*? "I cannot make friends with it," answered Goethe. The play was "alien" to him. The exchange about it with Kleist, he said, left him "troubled." It left Kleist devastated. Over the next few years, his productivity flagged. So did his spirits. Impoverished and estranged from the literati of his day, he closed a suicide pact with a woman who was not his wife. It was 1811. He was thirty-four.

But what literature he left behind. He had done a lifetime's work in a decade: eight plays, a collection of stories, essays, poems, and letters. They were rediscovered with a vengeance after his tragic end. And what did one discover? That this end was somehow anticipated in the play he loved so much, the play he mailed to Goethe, the play about the mythical queen of the Amazons.

It is Penthesilea who first falls in love with Achilles in Kleist's play. She spots him on the battlefield as she and her fellow Amazons attempt to identify and conquer their ambulant inseminators. But Penthesilea does not see Achilles as an ambulant inseminator. She sees him as the most captivating human being she has ever witnessed. "Drunk with admiration," she watches his "glittering figure"—all the while realizing that he is her equal; he is a fighter, a sufferer, a symbol, a moody youth, and a myth just as she herself is.[53] This does not diminish her ardor to conquer him by military means. Rather the reverse.

Many weeks after her Amazon sisters have begged her to abandon the war and to pick an easier target than Achilles, she conspires to cross spears with him. Previously she has warned all her comrades away, telling them merely to keep the other Greek warriors at a distance when she will stand before the man of her dreams: "Keep the Greek host engaged," she has commanded,

That nothing thwart my ardor in the fight.
Not one of you, no matter who she be,
May strike Achilles down. A shaft of death
Is sharpened for the one who dares lay hand
Upon his head—what am I saying, upon
A single lock of his![54]

Nobody may harm Achilles. Nobody may touch a lock of his tousled head but Penthesilea.

I, only I
Know how to fell him. Comrades, this metal here
Shall draw him with the tenderest embrace
(Since it's with metal that I must embrace him!)
Closely, and painlessly, unto my heart.[55]

You flowers of spring,

she instructs her warriors,

lift yourselves toward his fall,
That he not injure any of his limbs.
I'd sooner lose my own heart's blood than his.[56]

Though she must "embrace him with metal," yet she would rather die than cause him pain. She must merely lay him gingerly on the ground—so that she may deserve to lie down with him.

The gods have other plans. Achilles, when they fight, lays *her* to the ground. She faints, in fact, at the point of his weapon and wakes only upon her return to Amazon country, where Achilles has accompanied her. Why has he done this unusual deed? Because, in the heat of battle, he has fallen in love himself:

> . . . *Penthesilea*
> *Sinks down, unhorsed, death's shadow close upon her.*
> *And now that she's laid bare to his revenge,*
> *Sprawled in the dust before him*
> *. . . pale he stands, incomprehensible,*
> *Himself a shade of death. Oh gods! He cries,*
> *How she did move me with that dying look.*[57]

Achilles is bewitched. He is enamored. He is certain, suddenly, that the exquisite woman he has just slain is the woman of his life. Not a man to hesitate long over such an insight,

> *He brashly nears where she lies deathly pale,*
> *Bends over her, Penthesilea! He cries,*
> *Lifts her up in his arms, and carries her,*
> *And calling curses down on his own deed,*
> *Moaning with grief, he woos her back to life!*[58]

Not only does he woo her back to life but upon her return to consciousness and the comforts of her Amazon home he proposes to marry her. But it is too late.

If not mortally wounded, Penthesilea is mortally angered. How could the man she loves have inflicted such humiliation on her? He must have seen, he must have known, how great was the affection she bore him.

How could he strike . . .
So shattering a blow? . . .
I'd nestle in between the great bear's paws,
And stroke the panther's fur, that came to me
With such emotion as I brought to him.[59]

She refuses his offer of marriage. Livid at having lost her battle, livid at having had her love unrecognized, her beauty unobserved—or rather observed too late—she resolves to conquer Achilles, or lose him. She will not be his queen on his terms. He will be her king on her terms.

Once again, she sets out on the warpath, but this time she is dangerous. Achilles is gentle as a dove. Acknowledging her pride (since he shares it); understanding her need to win (because he has it too); recognizing her moodiness (because he's famous for the same); and underestimating her hurt, he consents to duel with her a second time. He arrives at the assigned place unarmed, determined to let her win and carry him to the Festival of Roses and make him her lawfully wedded groom. He twirls his lance in his hand like a cheerleading baton, or a chopstick. He has come to play and dine—not to destroy and conquer.

His beloved, however, is in a darker temper. She approaches him with elephants in tow. And wolves. And dogs. Armed to the teeth and enflamed at the core, she aims an arrow at Achilles' approaching figure even before she can see him aright. It pierces his throat. He falls. And then, the tragedy to trump all tragedies. She flings herself upon him as predators upon prey, as lovers made perverse by raw want. She eats him. She consumes him alive.

[She] throws herself on him . . .
With the whole pack [of beasts], and pulling at his crest,
For all the world a dog with other dogs,
One's at his breast, the other takes his neck,
She drags him down so hard it makes the ground quake!
He, crimson with his own blood, writhing, reaches
Out to her soft cheek, touches her, and cries:
Penthesilea! My bride! What are you doing? . . .

His voice is heartrending:

. . . a lioness would have heeded him. . .
[But] Into his ivory breast she sinks her teeth. . . .[60]

Penthesilea is mad with injury. Mad with love. The combination is fatal.

She does not remember her actions afterward. She wakes as after a long sleep to find before her the corpse of Achilles. It has been brought into the court of the Amazons. Her counselors surround her. They are aghast. *Who did this?* Penthesilea asks, a naïf. Silence. Who did this, she asks in agony. You did, comes the halting answer.

Penthesilea cannot outlive such an answer. Having robbed the breath of her beloved, she turns her weapon on herself. It is hard not to think also of Kleist: His gun on the breast of Henriette Vogel, and, moments later, against the roof of his own mouth. But before Penthesilea drowns her blade in her woman's heart, she turns to her counselors once more:

"Did I kiss him to death?" she demands.

"Oh, Heaven!"

"No?" she asks. "Didn't kiss him? Really tore him up? Speak!"

"Woe unto you," wail her attendants. "Go hide yourself away! Let everlasting midnight cover you!"

"So it was a mistake," she says with sudden lightness, as though in a reverie:

> *A kiss, a bite,*
> *The two should rhyme, for one who truly loves*
> *With all her heart can easily mistake them.*

She drops to her knees before the body of Achilles.

"Most pitiful of mortals," she speaks gravely, "forgive me!" It was all a problem of semantics, she explains to him; a misplaced accent:

> *My tongue pronounced one word,*
> *For sheer unbridled haste to say another.*
> *But now I'll tell you clearly what I meant*
> *This, my beloved, just this, and nothing else.*[61]

She leans over his mangled figure and kisses him on the lips.

The taste of his mouth makes her dream. It makes her wonder aloud about the nature of love:

> *How many a maid will say, her arms wrapped round*
> *Her lover's neck: I love you, oh so much*
> *that if I could, I'd eat you up right here.*[62]

And yet this maid does *not* eat up her lover right then and there: a failing, in the trancelike mind of Penthesilea—a sign of insufficient emotion, a passion all too frail. The girl who talks of "eating" her beloved is too soon

Taken by her word, the fool!
She's had enough [of her man] and now she's sick of him.

She no longer wants to consume him. She no longer wants even to touch him, or dig her impassioned nails into his back. This—emphatically—is not Penthesilea's case.

"You see, my love," she says, gazing deep into the eyes of Achilles,

that never was my way
. . . when my arms were wrapped around your neck
I did what I had spoken, word for word.

She *said* she wanted to devour him, and she *did* devour him: "I was not quite so mad as it might seem."[63] She smiles girlishly.

In her own mind, Penthesilea was expressing love for Achilles when she consumed him alive. Her desire knew no bounds, and no manners. Her desire forgot its pronunciation; forgot which word was which—which word hurt and which word healed. And yet how much more forceful, she fancies, was her passion than the well-behaved, temperate, transitory passions of other people.

Penthesilea kills herself. She joins Achilles in the land of shadows. And yet as she sinks down at his side, even those she has most terrified retain an awe for her emotions, an awe for her simple intensity.

The final lines of Kleist's play, spoken by Penthesilea's detractors, are among the most affecting he ever wrote:

"How fragile is this humankind," mavels
the priestess of the Amazons:
How proudly [Penthesilea], who now lies snapped, stood rooted
High . . .
Because she flowered with too much pride and spirit
She fell. The dead oak stands against the storm,
The healthy one topples with a crash
Because his grasp can reach into her crown.[64]

It is not the worst or weakest people who provoke the biggest disasters. Oftentimes it is the strongest, the halest, the healthiest. A dead tree resists the storms perfectly; it is nothing but bare sticks so the wind rushes past them without perturbing them. It is quite otherwise with the young tree, the fresh tree, the tree that teems with leaves and flowers, that teems—in other words—with wind stops. These green and yellow and pink wind stops are the crown of the tree, its strength, its glory; but they are also the handle by which one can seize it and fling it violently to the ground.

Kleist's Penthesilea is no example to follow. But, for all her perversity, for all her madness, she exemplifies an aspect of love we have forgotten. She exemplifies love as voracity, as vigor, as contest. She exemplifies the way in which some women want to make love *and* war, not love *or* war—which historically is the choice they have been given. Either they can devote themselves to the Hallmark universe of romantic sentiments—emotional doilies—or they can turn to the masculine arts: science, politics, social change, philosophy. The notion that love can be a martial art—an active and proactive calling rather than an escape from such callings—is unheard of. The idea that there is a continuum for women between intensity in one realm (social activism, for example) and intensity in another (love) goes unacknowledged. And yet it is a hypothesis with much evidence in its favor.

* * *

CONSIDER THE evidence of Mary Wollstonecraft, author of modern feminism. For much of the period that she has been written about she has been lampooned. Shortchanged. Spoken of cagily, and with a great deal of discretion. Her published texts are irreproachable, indeed, revolutionary. But her life—well, her life, especially for the feminists who should be her champions—is an embarrassment. All the woman did was fall in love. All the woman did was undertake heroic—and on at least two occasions unsuccessful—enterprises to realize her love.

It's painful. She went on months-long business voyages for a man who had already dumped her. She may have gotten a great book out of it all (*Letters Written in Sweden, Norway, and Denmark,* a bestseller at the time) and a lot of adventure; she may even have saved the lives of several dozen sea travelers by persuading her ship captain to take them on board as their own vessel sank, but it was humiliating. She wrote letters to her lover all the time. She threatened to *stop* writing letters—a prospect he probably welcomed—and then she never did stop. Not, in any case, until after two suicide attempts on his behalf. Once she threw herself into the Thames in London; the time before she swallowed laudanum. A feminist, this! She did it for a man!

No wonder that she has been a hard nut for women's rights advocates to crack. And yet, she is a nutritious nut. A more careful meditation about her life will reveal that she—like Penthesilea and Cleopatra—proved a warrior-princess, a uniquely daring lover-revolutionary. Her desire to find new forms of social change and her desire to find new forms of love went hand in hand. Some of her Herculean ventures were singularly successful; others floundered. Nothing ventured, nothing gained. But her sublime courage is evident in her love as in her prose.

Mary Wollstonecraft was born angry. Her parents were alcoholic and abusive; she had a stableful of siblings to care for, and the refuge she found was twofold: friendship and learning. From the time she was a little girl she threw herself into vivid and dangerous affections. "I will have the first place [in your heart] or none," she told a girlfriend in school at the age of fourteen.[65] At the same time, she immersed herself—with equally uncompromising vigor—in study. Hers was the life of an autodidact. Unable to afford more than minimal schooling, she sought her tutors among isolated neighbors and eccentric parish priests, and she found them. With all the advantages of a church mouse living under a floorboard, she became a soaring agent of social reform, a veritable phoenix of erudition and eloquence. The first woman to take on heavyweights like the philosopher Edmund Burke,

whose essay on the French Revolution inspired her hastily written *Vindication of the Rights of Men*, she later penned the even more
audacious *A Vindication of the Rights of Woman*.

It was for the rights of the poor that she first took arms in
Vindication of the Rights of Men—for the rights of the poor against
complacent conservatives like Burke who bewailed the rough
treatment of the French nobility while coolly urging its starving subjects to seek solace in the afterlife: "Surely one can help
them in this life without depriving them of the one to come!"
flashed Wollstonecraft in the first published rebuke to Burke's
much-admired essay. Nor does she stop at polite refutation: "I
have, Sir, been reading . . . several of your insensible and profane
speeches," she informs the sixty-some-year-old sage—and she is
not impressed. "You mourn," she scoffs, "for the empty pageant
of a name"—the name of King—"when slavery flaps her wing.
. . . Such misery demands more than tears—"[66] It demands action.
And action is all that will satisfy her.

But who is this woman demanding action and insulting the
intellectual superstars of her age? At the time Wollstonecraft
attacked Burke, she was a thirty-year-old governess, erstwhile
"lady's companion," and schoolteacher. Struggling for money
and with only minor publications to her name—most of them
for or about children—she was spending her time on the rescue
of (even) less fortunate members of her circle. Just recently she
had acquired notoriety by kidnapping her sister from a miserable
marriage. Divorce was nearly impossible at the time, and Wollstonecraft had helped the suffering girl escape from her husband's
home in the wee hours of the night and then offered her employment in a school of her own founding. She had also rushed to the

deathbed of her best friend in Ireland and henceforth assumed the responsibility for the dead girl's impoverished family.

It was *A Vindication of the Rights of Woman* that catapulted Wollstonecraft definitively from the life of a struggling young female (with many personal rescues to her name) into that of a public intellectual. It was in *A Vindication of the Rights of Woman* that she "threw down her gauntlet" once and for all.[67] Women, she charged, were losing out. They were underperforming in society because they were underpriveleged and miseducated. Men were keeping them down for their own pleasure—and then finding that they were not so pleasured after all. If in the first *Vindication* she assaulted Burke, in the second *Vindication* she assaulted the even more lionized thinker, Jean-Jacques Rousseau. He had just published *Emile*, a book about the education of a man which suggested in a parenthesis that the education of a woman should be the opposite: while males should be enticed to question and explore, females should be nudged to be docile and decorative. *Foul*, cried Wollstonecraft.

Rousseau's opinion is "so puerile as not to merit a serious refutation," she wagers with characteristic audacity—but then proceeds to refute it nonetheless.[68] Women are "naturally" drawn to dressing up, claims Rousseau, rather than to discussing philosophy or politics?[69] That's what happens when you lock people up and radically shrink their sphere of action: "Confined, then, in cages like the feathered race, they have nothing to do but to plume themselves,"[70] Wollstonecraft writes: "Systematically degraded by receiving the trivial attentions which men think it manly to pay to the sex," women soon need rescue from the "frown of an old cow, or the jump of a mouse."[71] At the same time, they are left unshielded against the real threats to their existence: the usurpation of their life choices, the extinction of their genius, the "legalized rape" that was eighteenth-century marriage.

Wollstonecraft was a fearless critic of marriage. She had seen it claim too many victims—her sister, her mother, her best friend, not to mention the many women around her who might have led productive lives but ended up instead as parlor accessories. So it is hardly a surprise that when Wollstonecraft finally fell in love herself—it was after publishing three books, winning international acclaim, and assuming the support of several revolving relatives—she displayed no interest in marriage. Handily, she fell in love with a man already married. Henry Fuseli was a nightly guest at dinner with her publisher in London; he was a famous Swiss painter with whom she got on famously. What did it matter that he had a wife at home who sometimes posed for his paintings? The young model never attended their evenings of conversation; in all evidence, she was exclusively an erotic association. And what Wollstonecraft wanted was an intellectual association.

She had it already, in many ways. At her publisher's home, she and Fuseli vied for the upper hand in argument. Fuseli was witty, contentious, and erudite. He was known for quoting Ovid (and—bizarrely—for having a "Wife of Bath"—a wife, literally, from the town of Bath). He was also known for being difficult, narcissistic, and predatory. One of his students likened him to an emissary of the devil. Fuseli loved to paint devils. He especially loved to paint devils preying upon prone women. His most famous canvas, aptly called "The Nightmare," portrays a transparently clad woman with a leering devil on her breast. Fuseli was no feminist. He thought of women as sensual, subservient creatures—and made no secret of it.

Wollstonecraft fought with him, but she also fell for him. Had she been looking for a Bad Boy, she could not have picked a more obvious candidate. And she *was* looking for a Bad Boy. Like many women of intellectual boldness, she was consciously or unconsciously seeking still another challenge. The world had fallen at her feet. Her publisher adored her without stint. Who could she fall in love with but the edgy, unpredictable, unpolitically correct Fuseli?

He flirted with her relentlessly. He also bragged about her—about the fact that the most famous female intellectual in England wrote him so many letters that he no longer had time to open them. He also bragged that she walked to the front door of his house one day and (ever the champion of unconventional domestic arrangements) proposed to his wife that the three of them live together. The wife, Wollstonecraft said, could have a monopoly on sexual contact with Fuseli; she herself only wanted his mind. It had become necessary to her.

Harebrained? Perhaps. But also intrepid, revolutionary, headstrong, and independent-minded, which was what Wollstonecraft was in all her actions. She never took her social cues from received opinion; she always started from scratch when she tried to formulate her life and the life of others. De facto Fuseli was living with his wife in bed and with Wollstonecraft at the cocktail table; Wollstonecraft wanted to render this official. The fact that she went to his spouse, not to him, to propose as much is further evidence of her mettle. Given her vocal opposition to conventional marriage, it is an initiative altogether in line with the principles and boldness that made her famous. The fact that critics have seen it as a compromise to her feminist integrity rather than as a part of this integrity is their problem.

The same, one might say, holds true for her relation to Gilbert Imlay. Having had her proposal rejected (with some horror) by the understandably less revolutionary wife of her beloved, Wollstonecraft charged on. She apologized to Fuseli and Sophia. She grieved, she knocked herself back into shape, and she charged on to France, accepting a dangerous solo assignment to observe the French Revolution. At a time that, as Wollstonecraft's most sympathetic recent biographer points out, powerful Englishmen like William Wordsworth were abandoning their child and fiancée in France to flee in panic back to England, Wollstonecraft—vulnerable, alone, female, and forever economically challenged—was heading eagerly from London to Paris. It was 1792 when she left.

In the next two years she wrote a book on the French Revolution as well as several essays. She sided, always, with the suffering and dispossessed. She got her hands bloody and dirty. And, at one point, she met an American entrepreneur with idealistic visions for society. On the surface, Gilbert Imlay was a far more appropriate love object than her previous connection. Imlay felt himself a feminist; he hated marriage as an instrument of male tyranny; dreamt of new Utopias; and championed women's social, professional, and personal rights. He was himself a writer who had recently penned a novel about the American frontier.

He also pursued her. Despite their mutual opposition to marriage, he married Wollstonecraft to grant her safety—as an American citizen—from the persecution of English people once the Revolution got hot. When she went into hiding in a small village outside of Paris, he visited her daily, wrote her passionate love letters, planned a future on a farm in America at her side, read her works with gusto, made love with her like no man had ever done before, and ultimately got her pregnant.

Wollstonecraft passed the most ecstatic months of her life with him. And the worst months—as he began to spend more and more time out of town pursuing the money he had lost during the dry spells of the revolution. Being an ardent sort of woman, Wollstonecraft missed him profoundly. Accustomed from childhood to "the first place or none" in the lives of her dear ones, she upbraided him violently. If she could have thrown his copy of Ovid (or of the *Financial Times*) into the fireplace, she would have done so. Instead, she wrote eloquent and aggressive missives, which were fit to persuade an outside audience of the justice of her assertions, but not the addressee.

The addressee started to shrink from the artillery. While reaffirming his loyalty and support for Wollstonecraft and the little girl to whom she soon gave birth, he increasingly stayed at a distance. The more he fled, the more she fought. You are a man "with strong health and gross appetites," she reproved him; if only you would learn "the emotions over which satiety has no power," the emotions that "do not exist without self-denial!"[72] Habituated to achieving her ends by sheer force of argument and volume of industry, she submerged Imlay in correspondence— offering ever more trenchant analyses of his character, pleading her love, and pillorying him with closely reasoned proofs of her own worth. In career-building, such bald intensity often works; in seduction, it regularly estranges. Still, it is not astonishing that robust and courageous temperaments—those in the habit of scoring points through direct intervention and full frontal assault rather than oblique tricks or passive waiting—embrace it instinctively.

After a year, the exchange was interrupted by a suicide attempt. Wollstonecraft swallowed laudanum. Having notified Imlay of her plan to kill herself, she proceeded with this plan. He hurtled to the scene and saved her life.

It was as though the poison were simply another kind of ink for Wollstonecraft—an attempt to underline her emotion, to paint it in primary hues, to color it scarlet for the world to see. *Look*, she seemed to cry, how strong my points are; look how much I will sacrifice for them. The same emphatic rhetoric that distinguishes her political writing defines her erotic behavior; the same relentlessness, the same gift for drama.

Imlay, for all his failings, read her aright. Rather than urge her to convalesce after this attempt on her life, he invited her to embrace even *more* drama, even more risk. Represent me, he suggested, on my most delicate business venture. Here is a document declaring you are my agent, wife, and best friend. Take a multi-month trip to the half-discovered Scandinavian islands—where almost nobody traveled in the eighteenth century—and see if you can't win some compensation for a ship of mine that disappeared, a ship containing silver.

Whatever Imlay's personal motivations for this proposal—some critics suggest he was merely buying himself space—it was the perfect proposal for Wollstonecraft. Strong-willed as she was, nothing was more difficult for her than to stand by passively as Imlay decided what his feelings for her were. To wait is the hardest thing for combative individuals. They cannot bear to leave their weapons idle. Wollstonecraft *had* to write, she had to act, she had to preach—even when she knew that to do so was counterproductive. But here she was—finally—invited to be an action heroine. She had always yearned to travel into dangerous corners of the world. She immediately nabbed a book deal for the story of her trip, and, for all her aching and longing for Imlay, she had a blast.

She set out with an infant daughter and an adolescent nurse-maid. At a time that groups of armed men feared to venture onto the highways because of the number of marauding criminals, Wollstonecraft ventured onto the seaways with two totally un-protected females. Over the next months, she debarked on lonely isles, knocked her skull on rocks, fainted, and revived; inter-viewed cave-dwelling savages, negotiated with the prime minis-ter of Denmark, saved a French crew from drowning, and wrote a stirring book about the whole experience—the most commercial publication of her lifetime. And at the same time that she did all these undaunted deeds she pined for Imlay.

How is this possible? How is it possible that the same woman who threatened her mate with suicide—and reattempted it on her return from the voyage—also delivered so intrepid a feminist perfor-mance on board her ship: driving hard bargains with governments she barely knew existed, clambering onto crags that no foreigner had ever sighted—all the while tending a baby and authoring an explorer's book such as only men wrote in this age? Clearly there is some misunderstanding about what constitutes feminism; what constitutes heroism. Perhaps it is not the proverbial stiff upper lip that does the hero make, but the trembling heart—the trembling and oversensitive heart that feels its fear and advances anyway.

The fact is that Wollstonecraft covered herself with glory on this voyage—in all ways but the two most immediate: She recovered neither the lost money nor the lost Imlay. But she gained worldwide fame as an explorer and memoirist, she gained unparalleled adventures, and, not least, she gained her next love.

Her next love was a far more uncouth character than Imlay. Imlay was smooth. William Godwin—albeit by then a celebrated political philosopher in England—was a rough sort of person. Known for his chilliness and inability to hide contempt for lesser minds, he was "not a man to cultivate disciples," in the words of one biographer.[73] And he had taken a *particular* dislike to Mary Wollstonecraft. He disliked her reputation as a feminist, he disliked the reality of her *Vindication of the Rights of Men* (in which he found grammar errors) and on the occasions they had met in London, he disliked *her*. She talked too much, Godwin observed. He was too much of an atheist, said Wollstonecraft. They quarreled immediately.

Then they met again. Godwin had read *Letters Written in Sweden . . .* in the meantime and adored them. "If ever there was a book calculated to make a man fall in love with the author, this was it," he swore.[74] And yet when they met, they argued again. It is not unfair to say that William Godwin was a far bigger bad boy for Wollstonecraft than Henry Fuseli had been—in any case at first. Fuseli at least had flirted with her. Godwin simply gave her a hard time.

It was no doubt this cross of difficulty and intelligence that compelled her. The attraction was similar to the ones she had felt for her previous boys, but its outcome on this occasion—whether by accident or higher intelligence—was altogether different and superior. The battle-scarred debaters warmed to each other—"it was friendship melting into love," said Godwin.[75] Then, for a while, they cooled. "Full of your own feelings, little as I comprehend them, you forgot mine," Wollstonecraft accused Godwin after one unsuccessful rapprochement.[76] "I know the acuteness of your feelings," Godwin told her earnestly, "and there is perhaps nothing on earth that would give me so pungent a remorse as to add to your unhappiness."[77]

It is remarkable that Godwin, himself notorious for his *deficiency* of affect, admired so deeply Wollstonecraft's *surfeit* of affect. For it was clear that he was impressed as much by the force of her emotions as by the force of her intelligence. It is not Godwin who censured Wollstonecraft for her suicide attempts or impassioned pursuit of impossible men; it was his supposedly more emotive contemporaries who did so. Godwin called Wollstonecraft's letters to Gilbert Imlay "the finest examples of the language of sentiment and passion ever presented to the world" when he published them after her death.[78] And he regarded the attempt she made to kill herself after her return from Scandinavia as evidence of her vehement and noble heart—not for a second as proof of frailty.

You live by the sword. You die by the sword. Wollstonecraft lived at a sharper pitch than most, and she—very nearly—died at a sharper pitch. Upon her return to London after the Scandinavian trip, she learned of Imlay's ultimate insult: He had set up house with a new girlfriend. Wollstonecraft took extreme measures. A grand passion deserved a grand end. Perhaps she had also seen how easy it was to die—so many on her sea voyage had come close to extinction. Perhaps by that time death had something of the familiar about it to her.

In any case, she attired herself in gorgeous clothes. She draped her body in yard after yard of velvet—and to make it yet richer, yet heavier, she placed rocks inside the pockets—and walked onto Putney Bridge. It was night. The sky was black. And when she thought no one was near, she plunged over the railing into the rushing Thames. She waited, and she sank. She swallowed water. She felt her lungs tightening, imploding, collapsing in on themselves. *How long it took, to lose consciousness*, she thought. And then she did.

The Royal Humane Society reported the next morning that they had reclaimed the body of a "Lady elegantly dressed," who had thrown herself into the Thames with the intention of ending her existence.[79] Upon inspection, however, the body was still living. Proudly, they proclaimed that it was delivered to a nearby hospice "perfectly recovered."

Wollstonecraft was not perfectly recovered. Her physical comeback took time—and her emotional comeback took longer. In the midst of her marriage to Godwin—for they did marry, these two hardy matrimonial critics—she still confessed that the injury her heart had suffered with Imlay was unhealed.

But perhaps this is what the game of love is finally about: *playing injured*. Not avoiding injuries, but playing with injuries. It is not the woman who never despairs who is strongest. It is not the man who protects himself most assiduously who is bravest. It is the person who risks everything, loses everything, and risks everything over again who is the true hero.

In war, the willingness to die is counted bravery. It ought to be counted bravery in love. This does not mean we should indulge suicidal moods: "Resolve to be happy," Godwin commands Wollstonecraft during their courtship. "Call up the energies which . . . you so eminently possess." It is sound advice for all of us. And yet, at the same time, Godwin makes his beloved the most compromising confession he has ever made: "Do you not see," he adds, "while I exhort you to be a philosopher, how painfully acute are my own feelings?"[80]

Acute feelings attend acute intellects. They must not be criminalized. They must not be branded unfeminist or unmanly or *weak*. Big emotions belong to big personalities. Godwin *grew* through his communication with Wollstonecraft—which is why he felt with more and more intensity the longer he knew her. Wollstonecraft felt with total intensity from the get-go. She felt with total intensity when she was fourteen years old and smitten with a school friend. For this reason she was extraordinarily vulnerable—but also extraordinarily powerful.

Wollstonecraft lived fearlessly, she loved fearlessly, and—too soon—she died fearlessly. Five months after her nuptials with Godwin, she died giving birth to their daughter, the future novelist, Mary Shelley. She had been viscerally happy in her liaison with the truculent philosopher. It had combined the high-wire conflict of her earlier rapports with the empathy and forgiveness of the gods in which Godwin did not believe.

He believed, however, in his bride. So much so that after her death he entrusted posterity with a full record of her love affairs, a frank and open account of the passions for which he—that once passionless thinker—had so much admiration.

Unfortunately, he overestimated posterity. If Wollstonecraft had enemies in her life, she had exponentially more after her death—many of them because of his *Memoirs of Mary Wollstonecraft Godwin*. A popular poem reflects the way William Godwin's most personal publication was received at the time:

> *William hath penn'd a wagon-load of stuff,*
> *And Mary's life at last he needs to write,*
> *Thinking her whoredoms not enough,*
> *Till fairly printed in black and white—*
>
> *Her brothel feats of wantonness sets down,*
>
> *Being her spouse, he tells, with huge delight,*
> *How often she cuckolded the silly clown*
> *And lent, O lovely piece! Herself to half the town.*[81]

A woman who had probably been intimate with a single man besides the husband in whose arms she died at the age of thirty-eight was stamped a prostitute.

The worst news is that things haven't been easier since. The nineteenth century saw a very partial rehabilitation of Wollstonecraft—but only at the expense of much candor about her love life. Biographers produced whitewashed accounts of her experience that omitted (among other things) all mention of Fuseli—accounts of which one critic wryly commented: "There are some theories which are much weakened by the unfortunate presence of facts."[82]

In twentieth and twenty-first-century biographies some of Wollstonecraft's "irregularities of conduct" (as they are called by Professor Janet Todd) have been reinstated. And yet, as Todd explains, they are usually "found embarrassing rather than enlightening." Even to Todd herself—probably Mary Wollstonecraft's most prolific contemporary defender—they rankle. In her own *Wollstonecraft Anthology*, Todd damns her subject with faint praise. "Wollstonecraft," she closes her introduction, "never *completely abandoned* the ideals of *The Rights of Woman*." As though this failure to "completely abandon" her principles weren't glorious enough, Todd adds—a bit cryptically—that Wollstonecraft also labored "to attain a complete humanity." The triumphant finale? "Her life certainly had much *sorrow and failure*, [but] it also had"—drumroll—"many positive achievements. . . ."[83]

With friends like this, you don't need enemies. Godwin—with all his eighteenth-century prejudices and famed qualities of a cold fish—understood the woman he wed shortly before her death better. He knew that the *"irregularities"* of her temperament were not contradictions to her genius but logical extensions. "We reason deeply when we forcibly feel," Wollstonecraft once declared.[84]

Her life and work are proof. She changed her mind often, but always to embrace a finer, more subtle and magnanimous position. If in *A Vindication of the Rights of Woman*, she had dismissed matrimony as consistently disastrous, she realized later that it could—and *how* it could—be occasionally sublime. If she hailed the French Revolution without stint to begin with, she afterward warned eloquently against the pitfalls of self-righteous rebellion.

Wollstonecraft thought strongly when she felt strongly, and she felt strongly when she risked boldly. At every crossroads in her life she struck the most dangerous path. Even electing to live as a writer was a bodily danger in her age. "My die is cast," she declared fatalistically when she realized "scribbling"—that most un-ladylike and unfinancially sound of activities—was her vocation: "I could not now resign intellectual pursuits for domestic comforts."[85] Attempting to reinvent marriage, whether by attempting to open it to third parties, as with Fuseli, or by installing distances in its midst, as with Godwin, was a terrific risk. Refusing to settle for the social consensus on any subject was daring. Plunging into the roaring midst of the French Revolution was mad. Boating to undiscovered isles with a newborn child on her arm was reckless, as was choosing the lovers she did. Putting her heart into their hands with as little reserve as she had was an act of profound courage.

Even being a feminist was a gamble for Mary Wollstonecraft. Being a *pro-love* feminist was an even bolder gamble—in her time *and* in our time—as her posthumous reputation has proved. For if intellectual females in her own century scoffed that they would not read her *A Vindication of the Rights of Woman* because "the very title is absurd," intellectual women in our own react in much the same way—for the opposite reason. Today we take for granted the argument of *Vindication*, but we take for foolish its author. She dared to love. She dared to love confrontationally and riskily.

Humanity is the beneficiary of this costly emotion. For it *was* costly: Wollstonecraft paid for it, and for the work it produced, in red blood and salt tears. She paid for it in the currency of a hero. Which is one reason she—like Shakespeare's pharaoh and Chaucer's pilgrim—must be counted a hero—not only of literary or social or political history, but of that most exacting and perilous of arts, Eros.

SIX

"Anonymous Except for Injury": Love as Failure[1]

ONLY WHAT WE LOSE BELONGS TO US.

—Jorge Luis Borges[2]

AMONG THE MANY RIGHTS we must reclaim in love is the right to fail. Most great passions, in some sense, are failures—some spectacular failures, some quiet failures, some tragic failures, others comic failures. Dante fell into a faint every time he approached Beatrice; she laughed at him accordingly. Only in the fantasy of his *Divine Comedy* did she treat him with respect, did she walk him sweetly through the corridors of heaven. In reality she probably wished him to hell. By his own admission, she "mocked him" right along with "the other gracious ladies" who witnessed his antics on her behalf.[3] She also, of course, married someone else—as did he. Ditto Petrarch—whose beloved wed another man and gave birth to eleven children as Petrarch wrote ethereal sonnets to her.

And then there are the love affairs that end not merely in hermetically separate lives but in severe humiliation or death. Antony is embarrassed in battle and runs into his sword more effectively than into the arms of Cleopatra. Romeo and Juliet make "love to easeful death" rather than to each other. Tristan and Iseult, Madame Butterfly, Carmen—it seems clear: great love affairs end in tragedy—when they do not end in slapstick. Disguised in green glasses and a sort of trench coat, Stendhal followed the woman who inspired *Love* to her vacation spot; he wanted, he said, merely to "breathe the same air" as she did—to see the same monuments. Instead, she saw *him* as he stepped out of the train, recognized his lovelorn gaze behind the garish eyewear, and chased him right out of town, hurling insults all the while, and swearing she would never speak to him again.

But a love affair cannot be measured by its "success," whatever exactly "success" is. In pragmatic present-day America, success, of course, usually means marriage, and people have a terrible tendency to write off the relationships that did not end with it as more or less regrettable. This is a resounding error. It is also a historical irony given that in the era to which experts still trace "our" notion of romance—the era of the twelfth-century troubadors—marriage was considered the very antithesis of romance. Adultery was romantic, adultery was spiritual, adultery was idealistic; marriage was just an arrangement of physical and financial convenience, a workmanlike solution to pressing quotidian problems.

"It is impossible," declared the Countess of Champagne in the thirteenth century, "for true love to exert its powers between two people married to each other." [4] If this was the opinion of the cosmopolitan countess, it was the opinion, also, of the ethereal nun,

Heloise, a century earlier. Asked if she would marry Abelard, the most dashing bachelor and best-known philosopher of the day, the man who had enamored, seduced, and impregnated her by the time she was eighteen, Heloise recoiled. "I looked for no marriage bond," she flashed. "I never sought anything in you but yourself."[5] And lest there be any doubt about her view of matrimony, she swears to him: "God is my witness that if Augustus, emperor of the world, thought fit to honor me with marriage and conferred all the earth on me . . . it would be dearer and more honorable to me to be called not his Empress, but your *whore*."[6] Whoredom, to Heloise, had more to do with passion than did marriage—and passion is what she had with Abelard; what she wanted to *keep* with Abelard. Conjugal life could only dissipate the ardor between them; it could only damage the philosophical enterprise in which, moreover, they were both so deeply engaged. "What harmony can there be between pupils and nursemaids," she asked, between "desks and cradles . . . pen or stylus and spindles?"[7] She preferred "love to wedlock and freedom to chains."[8]

But it was not only, or chiefly, with respect to wedlock that Heloise and Abelard's famous passion would be considered a failure by twenty-first-century standards. For one thing, they finally did marry (albeit secretly and only in an attempt to temper the fury of Heloise's pious uncle). For another thing, Heloise and Abelard had the hardest run for their money of any pair in medieval or early modern history. At the same time, their tale—known to us primarily through their own letters—is among the most affecting and defiant ever told. If it is a tale of failure, it is also a tale of timeless valor and matchless fealty.

*   *   *

THEY MET at the height of Abelard's fame. He had arrived in Paris from his native Brittany and taken the scholastic world by storm. A rhetorician by training, he came, saw, and conquered in debate all the leading philosophers in the French capital. Possessed at once of astonishing good looks, great charisma in the classroom, and a gift for composing songs, he was the dream—at least according to Heloise—of all the young women of Paris. He also had a reputation for perfect chastity. Until the time he was thirty-eight years old and spotted Heloise, this reputation was earned. He had never had a lover.

Heloise was known throughout the region for her beauty and erudition. Her uncle Fulbert, who raised her, interested himself in the education of his niece with almost incestuous intensity. Abelard knew as much—thus it was a bold move on his part to introduce himself into the house in which Fulbert lived with Heloise. He wished to board there, he said, because his rent in the university was too high. As a successful church canon, Fulbert had extensive quarters. In exchange for low rental payments Abelard would give instruction in philosophy to Fulbert's gifted niece.

The old canon enthusiastically assented—and the affair of the twelfth century began. "With our lessons as a pretext, we abandoned ourselves completely to love," Abelard reports in a letter to a friend known as the *Historia Calamitatum* (*History of My Calamities*). "My hands strayed oftener to her bosom than to the pages; love drew our eyes to look on each other more than reading kept them on our texts. . . . Our desires left no stage of lovemaking untried. . . . We entered upon each joy the more eagerly for our previous inexperience, and were the less easily sated."[9]

Abelard's career took a nose-dive; his work ethic dwindled overnight: ". . . The more time I was taken up with these pleasures, the less time I could give to philosophy. . . . It was utterly boring for me to have to go to the school. . . . My lectures lacked all inspiration and were merely repetitive. . . . When inspiration did come to me, it was for writing love songs, not the secrets of philosophy."[10] Into these love songs Abelard placed the name of Heloise. They were sung about town and before long the entire city knew of the affair. All except Fulbert, whose adoration for his niece and obsequious respect for a thinker of Abelard's stature blinded him to the spectacle under his roof.

It blinded him until the day that he caught his resident philosopher and favored niece in flagrante delicto. Predictably, he went wild. "Almost out of his mind," he went, in the words of Abelard. Especially when Heloise became pregnant and Abelard kidnapped her so that she might give birth in his hometown in Brittany.

It was uncommon—even unheard of—at the time that a philosopher and theologian would marry. And yet Abelard repaired bravely to the house of Fulbert and proposed to marry Heloise. Fulbert was so shocked, he assented. It was Heloise who, when she heard the news, did not assent. She raged against the defilement of their love by law; the profanation of pure emotion by duty and practical interest. "Only love freely given should keep her for me," Abelard reports Heloise telling him. Pushed to marry him if only in order to moderate the murderous rage of her uncle, she relented "among sighs and tears" and she made a fateful announcement: "We shall both be destroyed," she said. Her uncle would not be satisfied with what*ever* they did, and "All that is left for us is suffering as great as our love has been." Abelard's assessment a decade later? "In this, as the whole world knows, she showed herself a true prophet."[11]

Arguments between Fulbert and Heloise resumed immediately after the marriage—and in order to spare her these trials Abelard smuggled her out of Fulbert's vicinity, entrusted her child to his family in Brittany, and hid her in a convent. There she disguised herself as a nun and he visited regularly, seducing her ever more rashly in corners, cafeterias, and sacred spaces. "You know," he reminds Heloise years later, "what my uncontrollable desire did with you there, actually in the corner of the refectory . . . in so hallowed a place, dedicated to the most holy Virgin."[12] Punishment was written on the wall and punishment came. Fulbert, who suspected Abelard had placed his wife in the convent to get rid of her, sent henchmen into Abelard's home at night with orders to commit an act of "such appalling barbarity as to shock the whole world": to seize Abelard in his bed and "cut off the parts of my body whereby I had committed the wrong of which they complained."[13]

The leading philosopher of the age was brutally and bloodily castrated by his uncle-in-law. The scandal spun out of control. "The next morning the whole city gathered before my house, and the scene of horror and amazement, mingled with lamentations, cries, and groans . . . is difficult, no impossible, to describe."[14] The two henchmen were rounded up and castrated in their turn. Pained, diminished, and humiliated, Abelard, on the other hand, fled into a monastery. He would stay in monasteries for the rest of his life.

So would Heloise. For prior to taking vows, Abelard asked Heloise to take them as well. Many tried to dissuade her—young, beautiful, promising, and vivacious as she was. But Heloise—who would happily have followed Abelard into a whorehouse—now followed him into a nunnery. She put on the veil that would part her forever from the world she knew and tearfully recited the lament of Cornelia:

> *O noble husband,*
> *Too great for me to wed, was it my fate*
> *To bend that lofty head?*
>
> *. . .*
>
> *Now claim your due, and see me gladly pay.*[15]

As Heloise later resumed, "I would have had no hesitation . . . going ahead at your bidding to the flames of hell."[16] Hell or heaven were the same to her. Her god was not in the sky but in the heart—it was Abelard.

But gods, like angels, fall. So did Abelard. For if his castration had not yet qualified his and Heloise's love as a flamboyant historical failure, his subsequent fallibility—or rather, his ostensible indifference to her—did.

For twelve years after her entrance into religious life, Heloise heard nothing from the man she loved—in any case nothing personal. He visited her convent on occasion—but only to deliver public instructions. For he soon became an abbot—as she soon became an abbess. Separately but symmetrically, they rose to power and glory in their respective theological places. Heloise became the admired leader of an important community of nuns.

Abelard turned his prowess in philosophical debate into prowess in biblical controversy—indeed he was soon making radical arguments about the Trinity that won him the ire of religious authorities across the land. He also provoked the envy of his fellow monks who began, in due course, to attempt to stab as well as poison him. The revenge of Fulbert, Abelard learned, was nothing compared to the revenge of the servants of God.

It was his trouble with the monks, in fact, that drew Abelard back into Heloise's sphere, for it was these troubles that prompted him to write the now famous *History of My Calamities*—which ended up somehow in the hands of Heloise.

History of My Calamities is a compelling example of a phenomenon one might call Competitive Suffering. Abelard opens by informing his friend that "In comparison with my trials you will see that your own are nothing . . ."[17] The excuse for such braggadocio? The hearer will presumably feel better knowing Abelard's lot is harder than his own lot; that he does not have to "keep up with the Joneses," because the Joneses, in fact, have it much worse than he. Such, at least, is the official excuse for medieval epistles that follow the model of Abelard's. They have become known to scholars as "letters of consolation."

But Abelard's *Calamities* did anything *but* console Heloise. It was with mortal terror that she read that the lover to whom she had dedicated her life "guarded as well as I could against the daily assaults" of his brothers in Christ; that these brothers "tried to destroy me during the very sacrifice of the altar by putting poison in the chalice" and later served him food that was passed to a companion "who knew nothing of their intentions, ate it and dropped dead."[18] Horrified by such reports, Heloise ventures—for the first time in a dozen years—to write to the man she has never forgotten. Not, as we shall see in the letters that follow, for one hour of one day since their separation.

"To her lord, or rather father; to her husband, or rather brother . . . from his wife, or rather sister, to Abelard, from Heloise," rings the salutation.[19] It reflects all the confusion of their bond: Abelard is at once to her a "holy father" (a priest); a "brother" (since he is an abbot and she an abbess); a "lord" (i.e., a husband). She is at once his secular wife and his sacred sister.

She begins by exclaiming upon his misfortunes and enjoining him to explain them in more detail. She goes on to express disappointment that he has not—for twelve years—written her. He has wasted his words on ungrateful monks who try to kill him; even while neglecting the woman (and her community of nuns) who is hungry for his instruction, starving for his thoughts. "The love I have always borne you," is "a love which is beyond all bounds," she writes. "You know . . . as everyone knows, how much I lost in you, how . . . that supreme act of flagrant treachery robbed me of my very self in robbing me of you. . . ."[20]

Lest we reassure ourselves with the gentle fiction that Heloise joined the nunnery for good reason; that she was somehow destined for a religious life, or at least had come to appreciate it over time, Heloise thrusts a stake into our illusions: "It was not any sense of vocation which brought me as a young girl to accept the austerities of the cloister, but your bidding alone," she tells Abelard. Her fate is black—and she looks it straight in the eye: ". . . If I deserve no gratitude from you . . . I can expect no reward for this from God, *for it is certain*," she says, *"that I have done nothing yet for love of him."*[21]

It is impossible to overestimate the blasphemous boldness, the suicidal courage of such a statement in the Middle Ages; of such a statement made (of all people) by the head of a great Christian abbey. It is as though the Pope stood up today and announced that he had never believed in Jesus. Heloise is risking everything—her soul, her career, her reputation, her equilibrium, in order to get through to Abelard; to make her predicament real to him.

She wants Abelard to feel how authentically she still loves him. If the trials they have passed accomplish nothing else they must accomplish this: They must show Abelard that Heloise's love for him is holy. It is, in fact, the *only* thing holy in her life. "While I enjoyed with you the pleasures of the flesh, many were uncertain whether I was prompted by love or lust," she notes, "but now the end is proof of the beginning." Abelard can give her nothing now. He can give her nothing sensual, nothing worldly. And yet *"now, even more, I am yours."*[22]

She ends her letter by requesting a sign of life—a sign, really, of love. People think you only pursued me because you desired me, she says. Lust gone, love gone. Tell them they are wrong, she asks. Tell *me* they are wrong.

Abelard's response is an exercise in obtuseness. To Heloise's red-hot soul it must have been a snowdrift. It is not indifference, he tells her evenly, that kept him silent for twelve years, but *trust in her intelligence*. She did not need his moral instruction. "God's grace has bestowed on you all essentials . . . to comfort the weak, and encourage the fainthearted"; so what's the point communicating? "Any teaching or exhortation from me would be wholly superfluous." So it appears to Abelard. Should it appear otherwise to Heloise—should she imagine she has "need of my instruction and writings in matters pertaining to God," why then she should "write to me what you want, so that I may answer as God permits me."[23]

Having dispensed so efficiently with Heloise's problems, he moves to his own. "Thanks be to God who has filled all your [and your nuns'] hearts with anxiety for my desperate, unceasing perils, and made you share in my affliction." On this subject Abelard is expansive. He sends Heloise a psalm book so she may "offer a perpetual sacrifice of prayers" for the "dangers which daily threaten me."[24] He writes her some custom-made prayers that he charges her to recite on his behalf together with her sisters. Paragraph after paragraph sees Abelard relentlessly rehearsing how important it is that she pray—*for him*. At the end of the letter he urges her to prepare, also, for his death. "At present you are over-anxious about the danger of my body, but then your chief concern must be for the salvation of my soul, and you must show the dead man how much you loved the living by the special support of prayers."[25]

Not a word about her despair. Not a word about her love. Not a word about her lack of *faith* in the prayers he is foisting upon her. Not a word either about her lack of faith in the entire monastic life that she is leading on his account.

Heloise's second and most famous letter to Abelard is an exercise in *explicitness*. For one more time in her life—and *only* one more time—Heloise gives Abelard the benefit of the doubt and assumes he simply did not understand the love she expressed to him so lavishly. Or did not believe it. Or dared not rely on it. "My only love," she charges, listen to me. Why do you address me as a stranger? How can you write as though I could with equanimity contemplate your *death*—when you are all I live for? "Never," she exclaims, "let God be so forgetful of his humble handmaids as to let them outlive you." *Should* he do so, she would pelt "him with complaints instead of placating him with prayers."[26] In the event that Abelard missed the blasphemy of her previous letter, there is no chance of his missing it this time.

For if Heloise loses Abelard, what is left to her? "What reason for continuing life's pilgrimage, for which I have no support but you, and none in you save the knowledge that you are alive, now that I am . . . denied even the joy of your presence . . . ? O fortune, that is only ill fortune. . . . She has emptied a full quiver on me, so that henceforth no one else need fear her onslaughts, and if she still has a single arrow she could find no place in me to take a wound."[27] Heloise has joined, in some sense, the campaign of Competitive Suffering—but unlike Abelard, she is suffering only for love.

She is also *savoring* love—at least in her imagination: "Everything we did and also the times and places where we did it are stamped on my heart," she tells her lover. ". . . I live through them all again with you. Even in sleep I know no respite. Sometimes my thoughts are betrayed in a movement of my body"—other times they are betrayed by a cry or an "unguarded word." Heloise's confessions border—by the standards of their day—on the pornographic. Even during Mass, she attests, "when our prayers should be purer, lewd visions of those pleasures take such a hold on my unhappy soul that my thoughts are on their wantonness instead of on prayers. I should be groaning over the sins I have committed, but I can only sigh for what I have lost."[28]

Heloise's honesty and bravery are heroic, even if her Christianity—by conventional measures—is not. "At every stage of my life . . . I have feared to offend you rather than God," she confesses to Abelard; I have "tried to please you more than him."[29] This does not disturb her, one senses—she takes a kamikaze pride in it. What does disturb her is the deceitful life she is obliged to lead. "Men call me chaste," she observes dryly, "they do not know the hypocrite I am. . . . They consider purity of the flesh a virtue, though virtue belongs not to the body but to the soul. I can win praise in the eyes of men but deserve none before God, who searches our hearts and loins. . . ."[30]

Ever a searing self-critic, Heloise is also a searing critic of social authority. "I am judged religious at a time when there is little religion which is not hypocrisy," she proffers, "when whoever does not offend the opinions of men receives the highest praise."[31]

"*Do not think me strong*," she concludes with sudden urgency, "lest I fall before you can sustain me. Do not feel so sure of me that you cease to help me. . . . Do not suppose me healthy lest you withdraw . . . your healing." I am *not waving but drowning*, she seems to say, as has a modern poet.[32] Do not use my rosy cheeks and smooth brow as reason to neglect me: "No one with medical knowledge diagnoses an internal illness by examining only outward appearance," she says.[33]

Heloise's strength lies, ironically, in her intrepid proclamation of weakness. It lies precisely in the way she refuses to let Abelard nurture the comforting piety that she is a tower of virtue and strength. He does not become a doting lover as a result, but at least he doffs his disguises. He gets angry. He bristles at her "recital of . . . the wrongs you suffer" and especially at her "old perpetual complaint" about the way he was castrated and they were forever separated.[34] It is clear: Abelard—whether for reasons of intellectual conviction or emotional survival—has become a true convert to his faith. He will no longer allow himself to imagine that his castration was not for the best. "You know the depths of shame to which my unbridled lust had consigned our bodies, until no reverence for decency or for God even in the days of the Lord's Passion . . . kept me from wallowing in this mire," he says. Well, guess what? By one "wholly justified wound in a single part of my body," God saw that "he might heal two souls."[35] And so he did. "Consider the magnanimous design" of it all! He saved Abelard from the flames of damnation and Heloise at the same time! "You should not grieve because you are the cause of so great a good, for which you were no doubt specially created . . ."[36]

If there is something insufferable and narcissistic about such pronouncements, there is also something tender. "Come . . . my inseparable companion," he addresses Heloise, "and join me in thanksgiving. . . . See then, my beloved, see how with the drag-nets of mercy the Lord has fished us up from the depth of a dangerous sea." People took the rhetoric of heaven and hell literally in the Middle Ages. Hell was flames and horns and three-pronged spears—and escaping from it was splendid good fortune. But Abelard not only salutes Heloise on having escaped hellfire; he salutes her also—and most interestingly—at having escaped the curse of childrearing and of marital life. "How unseemly," he exclaims, "for those holy hands which now turn the pages of sacred books to have to do the obscene degradations of women's work!" Imagine, says Abelard (the most unlikely feminist the world has ever wrought), if you had been forced to "bear in suffering a few

children . . . when now you are delivered . . . of numerous prog-
eny in heaven!"[37]

Heloise's biological child was raised by Abelard's family; her
real children were the women whose spiritual life she inspired.
Unlikely as it sounds to the modern ear, Heloise did achieve far
more and become far more celebrated for her consignment to
a nunnery than ever she would have if she had married Abelard, moved in with him, and lived happily ever after. Both
Heloise and Abelard rose in the world's esteem by their spectacular *failure*. Through this failure, as Abelard says, God did
"draw us to him by force."[38] Abelard is not today remembered
for his philosophy—even if there are textbooks and scholarly
articles that speak of it—he is remembered because of his tragic
love. For Abelard as well as for Heloise the famous line of poet
Philip Larkin holds absolutely true: "What will survive of us is
love."[39]

What survives of them is *indeed* love—and not only that: *failed
love*. On the surface, Heloise's failure is still greater than Abelard's.
Where Abelard gets physically brutalized, Heloise gets mentally
and emotionally brutalized. She is the one of the two who feels
and desires and dreams more, and therefore she is the one who
suffers more. Not only is she imprisoned in a monastery by the
impersonal forces of fate but she is rejected in a most personal
way—at least romantically—by the man of her life. She pines for
Abelard; he reprimands her. She is alone in some way with her
very powerful emotion. She is alone, also, with her capacity to
put herself into another's shoes. Abelard is comfortably trapped
in his own consciousness. He cannot imagine Heloise's feelings
any more than he can imagine or relate to the feelings of the

monks around him; perhaps that is the reason he gets on so badly with them. Heloise got on well with everybody—even with the enemies of Abelard. She had the power to feel her way into the frames of other people; she first learned to do so with Abelard.

Her third letter to him is living proof. With a kind of grace, dignity, empathy, and self-collection rarely seen in the correspondence of disputing lovers, Heloise abandons her attempt to converse with Abelard on the level of Eros. One phrase or two, and it is over: "I have set the bridle . . . on the words which issue from my" pen, she declares. ". . . In writing at least one can moderate what is difficult or rather impossible to forestall in speech. . . . Would," she adds affectingly, "that a grieving heart would be as ready to obey as a writer's hand."[40] With that she changes subjects—forever.

"As one nail drives out another hammered in, a new thought expels an old," begins her next paragraph. Give me a new thought, she says to Abelard, almost coyly. Whatever your changed convictions, "you have it in your power to remedy my grief." Talk to me about theology, for instance—and with that she plunges into a vortex of very precise and learned questions about the history, purpose, and everyday management of female convents. ". . . The Rule of St. Benedict is professed . . . by women as by men," she will say, for example—but in reality "it can only be obeyed by men. . . ."[41] What, then, is a girl to do? What is a nun to do who wishes to abide by a church law that she is physically incapable of observing?

By asking questions such as these—and many others—Heloise spawns what has been called "the most important body of work on women's place in religious life written in the Middle Ages."[42]

Her diplomacy and self-control work wonders: Abelard responds to her in a way he has never responded to another human being in his life. He responds to her with intimate reflections and ambitious theories, hymns and precepts, prayers and sermons—all of them written expressly and only for her—and for the troop of nuns under her direction. Two hundred odd hymns he is reputed to have written for Heloise. His religious production on her behalf equals and exceeds the very considerable romantic production he had put on for her in earlier days.

It was not the success Heloise wished, but it was success of a sort. Abelard's dying wish was to be buried near Heloise—in her convent rather than in his own much grander monastery. He left to Heloise alone his last will and testament. Within the limits of his changed personality, he gave her the best he had. She had better. Which is why she looks like she comes out of the relation a loser. But this is an error. She comes out of the relation a winner because she is more richly endowed than her lover. She gets the best Abelard has to give—and she understands and embraces it. He, in his turn, never understands the totality of her passion and intelligence. As a contemporary scholar has noted, Abelard is forever "tagging along behind" Heloise in matters of the heart.[43] So he is. But it is not for this reason that Heloise is the one we should pity. It is not because she is *leading the way* that she comes out last; it is rather the opposite. She may indeed suffer more than Abelard, but hers, for all that, is the greater achievement, the greater wealth, the greater self-conquest, the greater victory.

In failure, Heloise triumphs; in subservience, she soars. It is her voice, far more than Abelard's, that echoes through the literary psyche of all time. ". . . [I]f Augustus, emperor of the world,

thought fit to honor me with marriage . . . it would be dearer
. . . to me to be called not his Empress, but your *whore*.”[44] The
dust will not settle on such words. They vibrate with the reckless,
beautiful boldness of the pure lover; the union of gritty abandon
and lofty devotion, sensuality and religion. How can one call Heloise a failure? Unless failure is—or can be—the highest form of
success.

★   ★   ★

THIS WOULD almost certainly be the opinion of “Young Werther,”
the hero of the biggest cult-novel of the eighteenth century—and
perhaps of all centuries. Failure is the highest glory. Pain is the
sweetest triumph. Suicide is the surest immortality. And it would
be true in his case.

When Johann Wolfgang von Goethe published *The Sorrows of
Young Werther* in 1774, he was twenty-four years old. He was not
yet the most famous writer Germany has ever produced. He was
young and heartbroken—and floored, soon, by the success of the
novel he had penned in only four weeks. Its success pursued him
for the rest of his life. The novel eclipsed in the mind of many
critics and readers his “greatest” achievement, the long dramatic
poem, *Faust*.[45] It unleashed a frenzy of both consumption and extinction. “There were Werther memorial processions, Werther
clubs, Werther china figurines . . . , Werther waxworks, eau de
Werther.”[46] It also unleashed suicides across the European conti-
nent. Young men in yellow vests and blue jackets packed a copy
of Goethe’s paperback (in which the hero also wears a yellow vest
and blue jacket) and tossed themselves into rivers and chasms,

highways and ditches. They shot themselves through the head with Goethe's novel open on their laps. *Werther fever* it was soon called.

Where did it come from? Who was this Werther who inspired the masses to alternately extinguish and adorn themselves? He was—to put it bluntly—a resounding failure, a man who specialized in *tristesse* and tears, inefficacy, unmanliness, surrender, and collapse. Let us consider his tale.

It is an epistolary tale—one told almost exclusively in fictionalized letters to his school friend. "Dear William," Werther may begin, ". . . You have never known anything so wildly fluctuating as this heart of mine . . ."[47] His narration is full of pose-striking. The writer portrays himself as a man of extraordinary emotion—and therefore of extraordinary suffering. "Oh you sensible people," he will rail as he watches his peers, ". . . you respectable ones stand there so calmly. . . . Upbraid the drunkard, abhor the madman. . . . I have been drunk more than once and my passion often borders on madness and I regret neither. . . . I have learned that all exceptional people who created something great, something that seemed impossible, have to be decried as drunkards or madmen."[48]

Early in *The Sorrows of Young Werther* we encounter a defense of suicide. To take one's life is a sign of lavish passion, not deficient willpower. "I have heard tell of a noble breed of stallions who, when they are overheated and run wild, instinctively bite open one of their veins to relieve themselves. I feel like that often," he meditates: "I would like to open the vein that would give me eternal freedom."[49]

What gives him occasion to feel thus? A love affair with

a taken woman. Werther knows Lotte is taken even before he meets her: He is forewarned. "You are going to meet a very pretty girl," someone informs him: "Watch out that you don't fall in love with her." Why not, says mischievous Werther. "Because she is engaged," he is told.[50] The next day Werther is in love with her. He sees her among her little brothers and sisters; she is a picture of grace and kindness. He talks to her; she is an exemplar of poise and sensitivity. From that moment on, he abandons all hope of gainful employment, all social aspirations, all semblance of normal activity.

"My mother, you say, would like to see me actively employed," he asks his friend William. "I have to laugh. Am I not actively employed now?"[51] He may have given up his one-time work as a lawyer, but he is *hyper*-actively employed chasing Lotte. And yet he does not seem to chase her with any real eye to success. Indeed he declines William's advice to "either have hopes of winning Lotte or . . . none," to either pry her away from her fiancé, Albert, or to forget about her.[52]

Almost perversely, he takes a liking to Albert. He decides that Albert is "the best, the most noble man in the world," that he is a person, moreover, "of strong feelings and knows what a treasure he has in Lotte."[53] How could he steal her away from such a paragon? Instead, he befriends him—and clears the path to Lotte's marriage.

At the same time, his feelings for her assume an increasingly religious cast. "Is not my love for her the most sacred . . . ?" he asks William. "I am experiencing the kind of happiness that God dispenses only to his saints."[54] Even witnessing the small rituals of Lotte and her family—a little sister's washing herself in a stream at Lotte's command—takes on the hues of holiness: "I never attended a baptism with more reverence," he asserts, "and when Lotte came up the steps again I longed to throw myself at her feet, as one throws oneself down before a prophet who has just washed the people clean of sin. . . ."[55]

To anyone who might object that Werther is delivering himself to a sort of *excess*, he would say *yes*. I am excessive, and that is the *only* way to love. Passion and moderation keep no company. The heart that loves reasonably does not love at all. Werther invents his own parable: "A young man's heart belongs to a certain girl. . . . Along comes a Philistine . . . and says to him, 'My dear young man, to love is human, but you must love properly. Arrange your time more circumspectly into time for work, and spend only your hours of recreation with your sweetheart. Count your money and give her a present out of whatever remains after paying for the necessities of life . . . only don't do it too often . . . for her birthday, let us say. . . .' If the fellow obeys, you have a worthy young man. . . . But as far as love is concerned, that's finished."[56] To regulate love is to betray it.

Unregulated love, however, is a high-risk activity—in particular when shot through with religious significance. Before long, Werther arrives at what one senses is the inevitable end of his excess. Asked by Lotte to "limit" his visits to her home so as not to arouse the ire of her now-husband, Werther refuses to cooperate. Instead of staying away, he comes to Lotte's house and reads her ancient old songs of love. And suddenly both Lotte and Werther are in tears. Both Lotte and Werther see their own fate mirrored in the fate of the songs' doomed pair. Werther falls to her feet. Lotte "became confused and pressed his hand tightly against her breast. . . . Their burning cheeks touched, and the world ended for them."[57]

The world ended for them, and there was no real way for it to resume. That is the crux with ecstatic love, excessive love. It abides no tomorrow. What do you do after you unite—in flame and fire—with the object of your devotion, the god of your soul? Check the mail? Stoke the fire? Make biscuits? There is no satisfactory continuance. Perhaps this goes some way toward explaining post-coital depression. Having come so far beyond practical, proper life, it is difficult to return to it. Werther and Lotte do not.

They break apart, each dizzy with the touch of the other, each persuaded of the love of the other. "You shall not see me again," says Lotte. Werther leaves her house and prepares his death. He plans it in such a way that Lotte is complicitous. He sends a servant to borrow guns from—of all people—her husband. The servant makes an excuse about Werther's going on a wilderness trip. Albert nods at Lotte. "Give him the pistols," he tells her. "The words fell like a thunderclap on Lotte's ears."[58] And yet she retrieves the guns from their hanging place on the wall, cleans them tenderly, and hands them to Werther's servant. She knows Werther's intention and she collaborates with it.

What most of the world would regard as an irrational and unnecessary failure, becomes, to Werther, a religio-romantic climax. Werther's death—his penetration by the bullets from Lotte's pistol—replaces and transcends all other penetration. He kisses the guns as he takes them from his servant. "They have passed through your hands," he writes in his final note to Lotte. "You brushed the dust from them. . . . The spirit of heaven favors my decision, and you, Lotte, hand me the weapon—you from whom I wished to receive death and now receive it."⁵⁹ The gravity and the intimacy of the exchange is like lovemaking to Werther. In some way, he prefers it to the compromises and enforced moderation of a more quotidian union. He feels triumphant as he moves toward his death. He knows Lotte loves him, he knows this love was sealed by their burning touch, and he knows it will be immortalized by his suicide.

While Lotte's affection for Albert will become tarnished over time, her passion for Werther will only become purer. Werther will become to her an eternal myth even while Albert dwindles into a tobacco-stained reality. "What difference does it make that Albert is your husband?" Werther writes disdainfully. "Husband—that's a word for this world, and for this world it's a sin that I love you. . . . Very well then, and I punish myself for it. [But] I have tasted this sin in all its divine rapture, I have sucked its balm and strength into my heart. From now on you are mine—mine Lotte!"⁶⁰

He speaks with a confidence he has never possessed before. ". . . No eternity shall erase the glowing life I experienced on your lips yesterday and that I feel within me now. She loves me. These arms have held her; these lips have trembled against hers . . . she is mine. You are mine, Lotte, forever."⁶¹

In death—in failure—he embraces his beloved more perfectly than ever he might have done in life or victory. A shot is heard in the night; a flash of gunpowder is spotted by a neighbor. In the morning Werther is found at his desk with a bullet hole over his eye. The moment is frozen in time; Werther's passion is writ in blood. His admirers are multiplied. "With hot tears streaming down his cheeks," Lotte's father "kissed the dying man. His oldest sons . . . fell on their knees beside the bed in attitudes of the wildest grief, kissing the dying man's hand, his mouth. . . . At twelve noon, Werther died." Albert could not bring himself to follow the bier. Lotte had fainted and not yet revived. "They feared for Lotte's life."[62]

The point here is not to idealize suicide—though that, certainly, is the effect *Werther* had in its immediate aftermath. Unaccustomed to novels that rendered human sentiment with any explicitness, eighteenth-century readers responded to *Werther* with shock, wonder, and not a little infatuation. This, many decided, was true love. This was what one did when one was young and daring and impassioned. Love was unfulfillable in real life; it yellowed at the edges and turned up at the corners and became brittle. Here was a way to immortalize it—a way to keep it divine.

Such reasoning may be sentimental and self-indulgent—as the character of Werther himself can easily be viewed. And yet it is not completely wrong. It contains a nugget of truth—if only a nugget—that has been forgotten in our own day: the stronger your sentiments, the greater your chance of failure. Failure happens more often to the brave than to the docile. This is not emotional snobbery, it is reality. The higher you aim, the greater the chance of missing your target. The more you have to invest, the more you also have to lose. Failure is no shame, by this token, but a badge of courage, the insignia of wealth.

A Parisian scholar meditating on the letters of Abelard and Heloise in the middle of the last century marvels at the "beauty of souls large enough to have been promoted to such sufferings."[63] It is a phrase that jars us today: "promoted"?—"to suffering"? Aren't we promoted to *comfort*, promoted to riches, promoted to happiness? Indeed we are—sometimes. But not Abelard or Heloise, and not Werther. The whole genre of which Abelard's *History of My Calamities* is an example illustrates the popularity, as far back as the thirteenth century, of self-regarding pain.

Such pain is as uncommon in our own day—where the fashion is rather toward strenuously exhibitionistic happiness—as it was common in earlier days. Asked, in our time, how our relationships are going, we often answer with a volley of praise for our significant other and an oath of how happy we are. Dysfunction is allowed in our family trees but only pure harmony in our couples. Mothers and fathers are permitted to have been abusers and addicts, but spouses are obliged to be saints. Every candidate for public office declares his wife his "best friend." Every book author swears in her acknowledgments how "supportive" was her mate during her literary travails. To recognize just how unusual this is historically, it helps to recall the words of statesmen and public figures in previous eras.

Far from singing the praise of their relationships, public figures of old demonstrated their courage and sensitivity by boasting of the misery in their love lives. Born only three decades after Dante and exiled (with his father) from Florence in the same year, Petrarch was known as the "poet-diplomat." And yet the sonnets he wrote to Laura were chronicles of romantic failure. "Love has set me up as a target for arrows," he would write, "like snow in the sun, / like wax in the fire . . . I am already / hoarse, Lady, with calling for mercy. . . ."[64] If Petrarch's contemporaries thought him the lesser man for such public self-immolations they did not show it. Indeed Petrarch's sonnets spawned imitations for several centuries—imitations in Italy and imitations in England, imitations by perfect Renaissance knights and politicians such as Sir Philip Sidney and imitations by William Shakespeare himself.

In some way, Werther is an heir to these powerful lamenters. In other ways, he completely outdoes them. And yet, for all his self-regard, he is not wrong when he writes that a powerful heart is "the source of all things—all strength, all bliss, [and] all *misery*."[65] He is not wrong when he contends that every fine emotion is "as fragile as it is . . . beautiful."[66] Fragility and beauty go hand in hand. If our souls are "large enough" to accommodate great joy, they are large enough also to hold great agony. For precisely the same merits we can be "promoted" to profound suffering or true joy.

If Werther overromanticizes the dark side of love, we underromanticize it. With our cult of success we have all but obliterated the memory that in pain lies grandeur. If the soul is a garden, as Voltaire once suggested, a *complete* soul will never be spared bitter fruit. It will never be spared poisonous fruit. For every sweet plum there will be a toxic berry. For every cluster of roses there will be a tangle of thorns. "All things the gods give to their favorites abundantly," Goethe wrote later in life, "all joys abundantly, and all pangs abundantly."[67]

Loving is like gambling; the only way not to lose is not to stake too much. Mary Wollstonecraft staked everything. Her widower, William Godwin, compared her to Werther.[68] He was proud to have a wife, albeit a prematurely deceased wife, whose amorous abandon and tragic intensity brought to mind the great lover of German Romanticism.

Mary Wollstonecraft has a soul-sister across the Atlantic. She has a soul-sister in America—a soul-sister with the same terrifying capacity for emotion, the same boldness, revolutionary feminism, writerly prowess, child out of wedlock, sunk reputation, philosopher-lover; the same untimely death. Her name was Margaret Fuller. Her story bears the telling.

*   *   *

SHE WAS born fifty-odd years after Wollstonecraft in Cambridgeport, Massachusetts. Not that she appears ever to have been at home there. To all who met her she seemed "a foreigner from some more sultry and expansive climate," in the words of Ralph Waldo Emerson, the philosopher who wrote her memoirs after she died, as Godwin had written the memoirs of Wollstonecraft.[69] Both accounts plunged their heroines into deep scandal, though both were well intended. Emerson's remembrance of Fuller was certainly colored by guilt at having done so little, whilst there was still time, for the woman he esteemed and—yes—loved—so much.

Why did Emerson love her so much? She was an "imperial creature," as the luminaries of her day attested, "alike in ideal excellencies and in bearing, mythological!"[70] Wherever she appeared—Boston or New York, England or France, Italy or Germany—Fuller commanded the conversation. Her erudition and imagination, combativeness and wit glinted like precious metal in a field of asphalt. When she spoke, Thomas Carlyle shut up—and that, as the English essayist's biographers and acquaintances can vouchsafe, was a legendary occurrence.

Margaret Fuller knew her worth. She was only thirty-one

years of age when she declared to Emerson that "I now know all the people worth knowing in America, and I find no intellect comparable to my own."[71] If the remark was greeted with eye rolling when Emerson first recorded it in his memoirs, it has been approved since. "From the perspective of American intellectual history," writes Pulitzer Prize–winning historian Perry Miller, "her observation may, in fact, be the simple truth."[72]

Fuller was unflinchingly brilliant. Coming of age under difficult circumstances—by age twenty-five her father had died and she found herself financially and pedagogically in charge of seven younger siblings—she nonetheless found time not only to master the learning of her own tradition but also to become expert in several foreign literatures and cultures. Emerson could never fathom where and "when she had learned all the languages she suddenly knew." It is the young Fuller who introduced the American public to German literature, Fuller who first translated its superstar, Goethe, into English. Subsequently called "the best literary critic whom America has yet seen," she wrote path-breaking essays on *Werther*, defending Goethe's alter ego at a time when his American commentators viewed him only as evidence of European weakness and depravity.[73] Werther "must die because life was not wide enough and rich enough" for him, she proclaimed.[74] It is not his frailty that damns him, she wagered, but his strength, his breadth. Werther perishes because he is *too good for the world*— not, as Fuller's countrymen thought—because he is too weak.

Her championship of *Werther* is not, of course, accidental. For in addition to writing the most important works of literary criticism of her day, in addition to becoming the first female member of the New York working press, the first editor of the elite journal,

The Dial, the first woman in America to report on a foreign war, and the first author of a tract advocating gender equality, *Woman in the Nineteenth Century* (1845); in addition to all this, Margaret Fuller also threw herself with abnormal aplomb and intensity into her personal relationships.[75] There was an air of "romantic exaggeration" about Fuller's friendships, said critics.[76] Whether they involved men or women, whether they were conducted when Fuller was a child or an adult, they inevitably smacked of Olympian passion.

Like Fuller herself, they were larger than life. Take her friendship with Anna Barker, a beautiful and accomplished heiress from New Orleans whom Fuller met while still in her teens. Almost immediately the two began exchanging heated letters, letters in which they shared secrets and declarations, letters in which Fuller called Anna Barker her "queen" and her love, in which (for all the evidence that Fuller went bodily untouched until her late thirties) she discussed sleeping with Barker in terms that would be taken for frankly homoerotic today. And yet, Margaret Fuller was acutely aware that the woman she so esteemed could not keep emotional pace with her. Anna Barker, she wrote in her journal, "loved me, too, though not so much, because her nature was 'less high, less grave, less large, less deep.'"[77]

It was precisely because of Fuller's "graver, deeper" nature that she ran into resistance from the objects of her affection. She felt more than they, and so she often asked more than they—and got less. It was much the same with another gifted young woman, Caroline Sturgis, who admired Fuller for much of her life as Fuller admired her. And yet, when Fuller got tempestuous on a beach holiday one day, and demanded of Sturgis whether she "loved her," Sturgis (as one biographer puts it cagily) "was not immediately able to answer."[78]

If women let Fuller down, so did men. "Men disappoint me so," she once exclaimed. "I wish that I were a man, and then at least there would be *one*. I weary in this playground of boys, proud and happy in their balls and marbles. Give me heroes, poets, lawgivers. . . ."[79] Give me lovers! she might have added—men who have the courage of their convictions and the emotion to go along with their reason! Give me a man "with the intellect and passions in due proportion for a full and healthy human being. . . . How much time have I wasted on others!" Most men she met were as effete in their emotions as they were astute in their calculations. The first such man was Samuel Ward.

A sensitive young New Englander who hesitated between becoming a painter and a banker, Ward was Fuller's soul mate for many years. They talked of art and German literature, nature and intimacy. Their friendship melted into love. They became inseparable. Until the time that Fuller became, as usual, too intense for him. She diagnosed his retreat quickly and with characteristic sobriety: ". . . Never, since we were first acquainted, have we been so far removed from one another as at present," she wrote him. "The kernel of affection remains . . . the same . . . but [in you] it lies dormant in the husk. Will ever a second Spring bid it put forth leaf and flower?"[80] She thought not.

She was right. Her next letter begins "You love me no more."[81] And indeed he didn't. To add insult to injury, he was in the process of getting engaged to Margaret Fuller's other great love, Anna Barker. It was a bitter irony for the passionate Fuller. But to her great credit, she bore it with uncanny grace. If she could not be

Ward's wife, she would try to act like his "Mother, and I will be
. . . as tender, as delicate . . . as if I had borne you beneath my heart
instead of in it."[82] She understood what he was doing. And it was
all right. If once she had believed that the end of their romantic
intimacy would spell the end of their whole communication—for
"I knew myself incapable of feeling or being content with an ordinary attachment"—she believed so no longer. She would let him
go; she would let him be himself.

Fuller's grace in leaving a relationship surpasses most people's
in entering one. Always queenly, ever magnanimous, she was as
intense in her own feelings as she was tolerant of the feelings of
her partner, even when they led him away from her. It is simple to
be easygoing, as Fuller was, when you don't care that much. But
Fuller cared *too* much. She cared as much as it is possible to care,
and still she loved with an open hand—giving and releasing, as
the object of her affections needed.

"The art of losing is not hard to master," writes poet Elizabeth
Bishop—and yet it is the hardest to master.[83] Fuller was a sublime
loser. She lost as if to lose was to win. She never parted from her
self-respect in parting from her beloved—nor did she ever part
with his esteem.

At once Fuller's most brilliant and most difficult sparring partner was Ralph Waldo Emerson. They were opposites, in many
ways. "You are intellect," she once told him, "I am life."[84] By the
time she was a young schoolteacher, he was already internation-
ally famous. His philosophy, his lectures, his ideas on self-reliance
and Transcendentalism were being discussed all over the United
States and England. Fuller revered these ideas. But when she approached their author she did it on unbended knee. She had not

known Emerson long before she attacked him for canceling a speech he was to give on "Genius": "How could you omit your lecture?" the young woman flared at the sage. "Could you not have taken some other time for your 'slight indisposition'?"[85] she demanded. She had imagined Emerson's wife must be on her deathbed for him to miss so important a lecture, but when she sent a messenger to inquire, the messenger returned "all smiles to tell me that Mrs. E. was quite well, that Mr. E. had lost a night's rest!! . . . Imagine my indignation," Fuller railed: "lost a night's rest! As if an intellectual person ever had a night's rest!"[86]

Fuller had not had a night's rest since she was a child. Emerson's self-protective and self-isolating temperament was utterly foreign to her. Where he sat in his lakeside mansion surrounded by books and silence, avoiding any distraction lest it "put him out of tune for writing" her life was nothing *but* distraction.[87] She led her contagiously popular "Conversations"—in which she introduced Boston's women to Shakespeare and Goethe, Platonism and feminism—she freelanced for countless papers, taught countless pupils, wrestled with countless intimates, tended seven siblings, before burning the midnight oil to do her "real" working, translating, and thinking.[88]

If Emerson suffered, over the next few years, from writer's block, Fuller blamed his too tranquil lifestyle. The Muse, she teased him, was darting about right in front of him: "I have seen her peeping through your shudders which are always closed"—but since he was forever staring only at his pencil, the Muse flew away again in irritation.[89] As deeply as Fuller admired Emerson, she was never once obsequious with him, never once awed into politeness by his renown, by his eloquence, or by his notoriously chilly manner.

Perhaps she feared coming to resemble Bettina Brentano—a young woman with whom Goethe had exchanged flirtatious letters at the height of his fame. Bettina Brentano later published their notes under the title "Goethe's Correspondence with a Child."[90] Examining the volume for her Goethe studies, Fuller was shocked. She was appalled by Bettina's bald flattery, appalled by her casting of herself as a minor and an inferior, appalled, also, by Goethe's highhandedness. "Observe this, young idolaters," she charges her audience in an essay for *The Dial*: "Have you chosen a bright particular star for the object of your vespers? You will not see it best or revere it best by falling prostrate in the dust. . . . Stand erect," she cries, "though with upturned brow. . . ."[91]

This is what she did herself. For all her waxing passion for the man who was her ideal opponent, her provoker, her kindred spirit and her muse, she never stooped to him. Even when— roughly in the time she penned her essay on Bettina—she was drifting into an erotically charged intellectual tango with him, her chin remained well above his forehead. "You are mine and mine shall be," she told him one day, "may you dally how long soever in this or that temporary relation."[92] By "temporary relation" Fuller meant everything from his half-century-long marriage to his rapports with the men and women to whom she, Fuller, had introduced him. She knew these persons enriched his life; she also knew she was the pivot of this life. In two short years she had become Emerson's most necessary debate partner, his nearest confidant. When she died, half a decade later, Emerson said that he had "lost in her my audience."[93] His essays had begun to be written to her and in dialogue with her; when she sent him a letter on friendship he paraphrased or rebutted her in his next essay on friendship; when she later published an article on Goethe, she rebutted his rebuttal.

And yet Emerson could not recognize their interdependence. He could not recognize their love. Whenever Fuller—intrepid interlocutor that she always was—pushed him to acknowledge, to express, to expound upon it, he ran for cover. "I have your frank and noble and affecting letter," he writes after receiving an especially tender missive, "and yet I think I could wish it unwritten. I ought never to have suffered you to lead me into any conversation or writing on our relation. . . ." The topic "will not prosper with me," he says. He *assumes* their "relation"; he appreciates it; but he cannot discuss it.[94]

Perhaps all too tellingly, he compares himself to his three-year-old son: "I see precisely the double of my state in my little Waldo when in the midst of his dialogue with his hobby horse in the full tide of his eloquence I should ask him if he loves me?—he is mute and stupid." I, too, am an emotional toddler, he seems to confess. I, too, am "mute and stupid" when you speak to me of adult passion. The only way I can afford to live this passion—however imperfectly—is not to talk about it.[95]

And "imperfectly" is the word. For Emerson knew how far he lagged behind Margaret Fuller in matters emotional. Even while he calls her "Oh divine mermaid and fisher of men," even while he attests he "cannot spare" her, he tells her also that he can neither understand nor deserve her. "You appeal to sympathies I have not," he declares.[96] "Can one be glad of an affection which he knows not how to return?" he asks. "I am. Humbly grateful for every expression of tenderness—which makes the day sweet and inspires unlimited hopes." He cherishes her love even though he cannot reciprocate it.[97] A tragic situation, in some ways—leavened for Fuller only because she knows that at the core of Emerson's strangely hampered heart, he values her above all others. And will continue to talk, write, and keep company with her as long as she allows.

Compared to Fuller, nobody in Emerson's mature life aroused much attention. His relationship with his wife was anodyne. She supported him blindly, tended his house, received his guests; he treated her with kindness and a sort of underheated gallantry. When she asked if he loved her, his answers were not more satisfactory—and probably less sincere—than his answers to Margaret Fuller. The sparks never flew between the two as between Emerson and Fuller; nor did the compliments, ideas, or arguments. Emerson had had one earlier love, as an adolescent—his first wife, Ellen Louisa Tucker, who had tragically died at age nineteen. After this blow, Emerson never exposed himself in the same way again—in sharp contrast to Margaret Fuller, who opened and reopened her resilient heart, though it got battered to a pulp a thousand times.

Fuller was brave and generous in her passions; Emerson timid. It is for this reason that he felt perpetually in her debt. "You have a right to expect great activity, great demonstration from your friends," he once wrote her, "and though you do not say it you receive nothing. You may as well be related to mutes and to uncommunicating egoists. . . ." (The metaphor of the mute runs through his entire correspondence with Fuller.) "It is imbecility, not contumacy" that causes him to give Fuller so little, he tells her.[98] It is inadequacy, not contempt.

What Emerson lacks in ardor he compensates for in self-awareness. Where a lesser man might have supposed himself superior to a woman he was rejecting, Emerson knew his rejection of Fuller stemmed rather from his own inferiority. "All natures seem poor beside one so rich," he writes of Fuller in his journal, even as he backs away from her.[99]

Fuller's next beloved, James Nathan, was not so perspicacious; he was neither so honest nor so good for Fuller. For though Fuller's heart was periodically broken by Emerson, her friendship with him lasted for the rest of her life. Even as she tossed in the tempest of European revolutions years later she still reached out, over the oceans, for "his healthful, even pulse." It was there for her as it had always been; she rested her trembling fingers on it, and both profited. "Intellect" gained "life," and "life" gained calm.

No such profitable conclusion can be said to have been needed between Fuller and Nathan, a German businessman she encountered when she left Boston for Manhattan to become America's first full-time female journalist. She fell in love with him as she was writing columns about insane asylums she explored, poverty she investigated, music, theater, and literature on which she had grown nationally expert. Her imagination aflame as never before, she saw many a marvel in Nathan's quiet traits. When he confided in her his failures and sufferings in love, she was touched to the quick. One of her first letters to him is a stirring defense of pain: "My dear friend," she addresses the young German man, ". . . It is great sin even to dream of wishing for less thought, less feeling than one has. . . . The violet cannot wish to be again imprisoned in the sod, because she may be trampled on by some rude foot."[100] Who knew better than Margaret Fuller how easy it was to be trampled? And yet, who pushed her delicate self more insistently forward into the line of fire and footprints?

If Fuller initially charmed Nathan with her empathy and lyricism, she also soon became too much for him. He was a sweet-talking opportunist at bottom, a simple man looking for adventure. He could talk a good game and clearly did—he spent days and hours doing nothing but taking long walks and conversing with Fuller—but before long he made a sexual overture and realized that he was in over his head. Fuller responded to his overture with mortal shock. She was a virgin. She attached mystical importance to any sexual act. The absence of such importance was, to her, a cardinal crime. Nathan made clear that he did not share her feelings. Indeed, he must have told her that he was not a free man, that the best he could offer her was some sort of part-time erotic "arrangement." She recoiled in horror.

". . . The sweet little garden with which my mind had surrounded your image lies all desecrated," she exclaimed.[101] Even after she began, step by step, and month by month, to reopen her heart to Nathan, to overlook or to excuse or to explain away his incomprehensible sexual misstep, Nathan hung back. He had been burnt. He knew Fuller's erotic philosophy now, and he knew he could not be with a woman so serious. So even when Fuller began to hint at a new receptivity to his physical love—when she began to wax poetic about the role he might play in initiating her into the secrets of the universe—he remained skeptical. On one hand, he told her avuncularly that she needed to "become human," she needed—at age 35!—to get out of her damn head and into her body; on the other hand, he no longer promised himself any wild nights with her. His fantasy of the liberated American sex-bomb was finished.

So when Fuller told him that she "longed to be human, but divinely human," he ignored her.[102] When she told him that she wished to be attached "more firmly to the earth"; and asked him to "choose for me a good soil and a sunny place, that I may be a green shelter to the weary and bear fruit enough to pay for staying," he thought that sounded like a lot more trouble than it was worth.[103] He began to move away, to allude to an "English maiden" whom he needed to escort back to the British Isles. Ironically, such confessions only made Fuller trust him more. She waited for Nathan, and she pined for Nathan: "You come not," she wrote one night when he did not appear at her door, "and now I realize that soon will be the time, when evening will come always, but you will come no more."[104]

Soon he really came no more. He departed for Europe in the summer of 1845 and told Fuller he would return by year's end. She followed him on his travels with thoughts and letters—she wrote him more letters more often than she wrote any other man in her life. For all epistolary purposes, she was happy that "thou art living and growing," she begrudged him nothing, and rejoiced rather that "in all that enriches and dignifies thy life I have my part."[105] To the degree that one can be an exemplary partner—generous, trusting, and at the same time thought-provoking—Fuller was an exemplary partner. And yet the fates did not reward her. Months later Nathan wrote to inform her he was not coming back. He had agreed to marry a German girl.

Fuller ripped the letter, rushed out into a rainstorm, and spent the night battling bareheaded, like Lear, with the raging winds. Was it a suicide attempt? All that is clear is how much Fuller suffered. She had an unbroken record of romantic rejection at this point. This accomplished woman, this "fisher of men" had become a specialist in catch-and-release.

Fuller dramatized her predicament rather perfectly in an idiosyncratic travel narrative called *Summer on the Lakes*. In this novella, Fuller introduces a heroine, Mariana, whose emotional intensity at once tantalizes her men and terrorizes them. Never "content to receive her companions quietly," she "threw herself too much into the tie. Like Fortunio, who sought to do homage to his friends by building a fire of cinnamon, not knowing that its perfume would be too strong for their endurance, so did Mariana. What she wanted to tell, they did not want to hear; a little had pleased, so much overpowered, and they preferred the free air of the street, even, to the cinnamon perfume of her palace."[106] Mariana fails because she is too potent. Her suitors can take her in small doses but not in the doses natural to her, not in the doses she wants to give. A little of Fuller's energy always pleased her interlocutors; the whole of it put them to flight. It was too much for them, too sweet, too pungent, too intoxicating. They had to hurry outside to clear their heads. Their natures were not strong enough to inhale Fuller's undistilled emotion.

Was it Fuller's problem? Or the world's? All that can be said is that Fuller was a lover *par excellence* and nobody in her environment was her equal. The "heroes, poets, lawgivers" whom she sought eluded her.[107] Their absence, on the other hand, inspired *her* to heroism, poetry, and lawmaking. Never did Fuller act as boldly, write as gorgeously, or argue as acutely as when she loved. Her public treatises often pale next to her letters. She knew as much. "What a vulgarity there seems in writing for the multitude!"[108] she once erupted. She preferred to write to a single human being for whom she ached. Perhaps it was the personal chord that inspired her; perhaps it was the pain. As Emerson noted in a letter to her, "Nature does rarely say her best words to us out of serene and splendid weather."[109] Fuller's best words came—like Lear's—out of the eye of the storm.

Fuller believed in suffering. She believed in its purifying force and in her own capacity to bear it. Sometimes she wondered whether or not her sex was especially suited to face suffering. She pointed out that where the men in the life of Christ regularly fled in his hours of need, the "women could no more stay from the foot of the cross than from the Transfiguration." The women who loved Christ would not be "exiled from the dark hour."[110] They demanded to learn from it. They demanded to be deepened by it—as Fuller was deepened by her tragedies.

It is an irony that the one apparently unambiguous *success* in Fuller's romantic life—the final liaison she had with a young Italian soldier she met as she was covering the Italian revolution for the *New York Tribune*—was also considered a failure—if not by Fuller herself then by her censorious New England contemporaries. Count Giovanni Ossoli was eleven years Fuller's junior, and he was not an intellectual. Never mind that he possessed several times the courage, the virility, and the large-heartedness of her Cambridge boys; never mind that he embraced Fuller's multifarious passion unambiguously, that he doted on her, and fathered a child with her in whom they both appeared to delight. America's East Coast could not comprehend the tie, and therefore damned it. Sitting among the cannonades and hospital injuries that had become her new life, Fuller wrote to her erstwhile intimates, Samuel and Anna Ward in Boston. "My friends remain in their place," she said sadly. "I seem to have more clue to their state than they do to mine. Across the stream I see them; they look fair and tall, but I must go to them; they cannot come to me."[111] She knew they no longer understood her. Their circumscribed experience defined their circumscribed judgments. They grasped neither the horror of war that she grasped nor the glory of love. Gingerly, she offered to "cross the stream" and explain herself.

She never made it. Her ship capsized several dozen yards from the coast of New York, taking with it to the ocean floor her new partner, her new child, her new book, and herself. Some historians have speculated about a suicidal action on her part. There is evidence she might have saved herself had she been willing to proceed without son and lover. She was not. She ended her life as she lived it—with violence and grace.[112]

Fuller's failures are several times more sumptuous than other folks' successes. And perhaps that is something we need to admit about failure: It can well be more sumptuous than success. In fact, people are more often tempted to imitate beautiful failures than blithe successes. Consider the copycat suicides spawned by the Hungarian World War II song, "Gloomy Sunday," which tells of a love death—to say nothing of Goethe's *Werther*.[113] Somewhere in our collective unconscious we know—even now—that to have failed is to have *lived*.

It will not do to romanticize failure. But neither must we criminalize, demonize, or disdain it. To be heroic is to be endangered. As bruises are part of battle, failure is part of love. If we have no wounds, chances are we haven't put up a fight. Chances are we have loitered timidly on the sidelines of the great skirmish.

Jean-Paul Sartre envied those who felt great emotional pain.

A rationalist by temperament, he writes, in his autobiography, *The Words*, of the jealousy he felt as a child when contemplating the troubled lives of artists. They "suffered manfully," he says. "I conjured up their torments with a somewhat cheerful pity: how pleased those fellows must have been when they felt most unhappy; they would say to themselves: 'What luck! Here comes a beautiful verse!' "[114] He himself could not feel as much. It was Simone de Beauvoir who too often spent the night in tears— but who also, as one of her most important partners averred, had a veritable "gift for happiness."[115] Tears and joy, sorrow and creativity—the two, in an uncanny way, go together.

Margaret Fuller, Heloise, and Werther brought more nobility to their failures than most bring to their successes. There is a certain truth to Tolstoy's old argument that "Happy families are all alike." It is the unhappy ones that are unique, the unhappy ones that arrest us. What is important in absorbing or living these tales is only this: to retain faith in love. "Happy the survivor if in losing his friend, he loses not the idea of friendship," writes Margaret Fuller. "Be not faithless thou whom I see wandering alone amid the tombs of thy buried loves. The relation thou hast thus far sought is possible. . . ."[116] It is possible—and it is closer to *your* grasp, you who have suffered, than it is to the grasp of those whose thick fingers never burned.

⌒

SEVEN

Carving in the Flesh:
Love as Art

FOR ONE HUMAN BEING TO LOVE ANOTHER:
THAT IS PERHAPS THE MOST DIFFICULT OF OUR TASKS,
THE ULTIMATE, THE WORK FOR WHICH ALL OTHER
WORK IS BUT PREPARATION.

—Rainer Maria Rilke[1]

ANYONE WHO HAS EVER FALLEN IN LOVE knows it's a full-time job. This is why we only rarely obtain theories of love from the pen of lovers: If they were ardently enamored, they'd only find time to write the beloved. On some occasions, poets in love can compose poems; those, after all, are approved instruments of seduction. But philosophers in love cannot produce systematic treatments. Book authors in love are in over their head when they try to complete books. Love is a jealous god, and does not leave its new recruits much more time than for the composition of let-ters, e-mails, text messages. Abstract disquisitions about Eros are far too remote.

Much of the strongest writing about love comes, therefore, in the form of correspondence. This is not a sign of moral turpitude. It is certainly not a sign of flagging industry. Almost no one is more industrious than the woman—or man—in love. Activity is all the lover craves. On the edge of her chair from nervous and erotic energy, she clamors for action—but can focus only on entertaining the object of her affection.

"Both Stendhal and Chateaubriand took their love affairs much more seriously than their work," observes the Spanish philosopher, Ortega y Gasset: "It is curious that only those incapable of producing great work believe that the contrary is the proper conduct: to take science, art, or politics seriously and disdain love affairs as mere frivolities."[2]

There are few enterprises that demand the same amount of subtlety, commitment, imagination, and resolve, as that of a courageous love relationship. Many have tested their mettle on it; most have fallen short. One need think only of the consuming intensity that goes into a courting couple's exchange of messages, be they epistolary or electronic. A fraction of such intensity probably goes into the building of portfolios, the running of offices, the building of careers. Even the silences in a lovers' correspondence cost their authors dear—dearer, often, than the mad flow of words. Pauses are part of a symphony and they are part of an amorous dialogue—frequently the most difficult part. "There is nothing harder for a passionate woman than to wait" patiently for a response, says Simone de Beauvoir.[3] There is little harder for a passionate man than to impose limits on ardor, to bound what would be boundless.

"I am trying very hard to be *dry*," says Stendhal in *Love*: "I am continually beset by the fear that I may have expressed only a sigh when I thought I was stating a truth."[4] It is the horror of every lover: that instead of disarming his idol with the singularity of his sentiment, he merely anesthetizes her with exclamations and repels her with the relentlessness of his devotion.

For love objects are also love subjects—and subjects like to choose. Subjects like to initiate. Male or female, we are all hunters as gladly as we are hunted—some of us *more* gladly. So even while lovers are striving to be truthful about their feelings to their quarry, they must hold something back for the quarry to hunt in *them*. Even while we are conquerors, we must leave something for the Other to conquer in us.

This is so delicate a proposition that it's no surprise people break their heads and hearts over it regularly. No wonder we often find it easier to charm a person we don't care about all that much. The simplest way to be successful in matters of the heart is to be heartless. To adapt the words of Horace Walpole, love is "a comedy to those who think, and a tragedy to those who feel."[5]

The correspondence between artful lovers is sometimes the most important artwork they produce. It is no accident that so many novels of love revolve around letters—from eighteenth-century classics like *Pamela* and *Clarissa* (which consist entirely of epistles between beautiful young heroines and dodgy older heroes) to *Love in the Time of Cholera* (starring a compulsive scribbler who works in a telegraph office and pens love letters not only for himself but for paying customers).[6] Nicole Krauss's contemporary bestseller, *The History of Love*, hinges on illicit letters.[7] In all these works of fiction the lovers are revealed through their correspondence, compromised through their correspondence, aroused, arraigned, and, in some cases, immortalized by their correspondence. There may be more sexual tension between the sheets of their mail than between the sheets of a honeymoon bed.

Nor are fictionalized correspondences the most potent; real life correspondences frequently eclipse them. Take the missives of Heloise and Abelard; or the lyrical love post of Mary Wollstonecraft and Margaret Fuller. For all their industry and their genius, they wrote little that was greater. The same might be said for such motley figures as Benjamin Constant, Ralph Waldo Emerson, John Keats, and Voltaire—or, indeed, Horace Walpole, who invented the Gothic novel. For if a man like "Voltaire threw off his letters in the intervals of multifarious literary activity," as one critic has observed, Horace Walpole "did not snatch moments from life to write letters in: he snatched moments from letter writing in which to live."[8] Walpole's letters today are far more compelling than his fictions. The letters of the eccentric Frenchwoman who was, for a decade-and-a-half, his favored interlocutor are more compelling still.

Like many literary ladies of her age, the Marquise Marie du Deffand did not take her writing career seriously. What she did take seriously was her correspondence. Born in 1697, she married in 1718, only to separate from her husband, become mistress to the Regent of France, entertain a series of prestigious lovers, and cultivate a social life second to none. Renowned as a brilliant conversationalist and formidable debating adversary, she soon found herself in command of her own literary salon in Paris. It was here that she met the majority of her illustrious correspondents, here that the great and would-be great convened over intoxicating libations and traded ideas as though they were stamps. Between the ages of twenty-five and sixty-five, Madame du Deffand carried on correspondences with Voltaire, with Madame de Stael, and with Montesquieu. Each of these correspondences is riveting in its own right.

By 1754, however, the Marquise du Deffand had begun to go blind. It was only after she had lived in darkness for a full decade that the feisty Parisienne met the effete Englishman, Horace Walpole. When he came to visit Paris in 1765, she was sixty-eight and Walpole forty-six. He was a large-scale wit, a small-scale novelist, and—to much of the French society members he encountered—an extraordinarily winning personage. "It would sound vain to tell you the honours and distinctions I receive, and how much I am in fashion," he reported to a friend in England.[9] He was particularly in fashion with Madame du Deffand.

She took an instant liking to him. Tired, perhaps, of the relentlessly French constituency of her salon, she warmed to Walpole's Otherness, to his exoticism, to his Englishness. His voice was "supremely gentlemanly"; his rhetoric inimitable.[10] He had taste, snobbery, and a sense of election—much like the Marquise herself. Yet where she was full of bravado and recklessness, he was a creature of high prudence and easy embarrassment. Where she was nearly seventy—and visibly ailing—he was in his forties and in the prime of life.

He adored her, however. "Madame du Deffand . . . is now very old and stone blind," he wrote home, "but retains all vivacity, wit, memory, judgment, passions, and agreeableness. . . . She corresponds with Voltaire . . . contradicts him, is no bigot to him or anybody, laughs both at the clergy and at the philosophers.

In a dispute, into which she easily falls, she is very warm, and yet scarce ever in the wrong. . . . Nor am I ashamed at interesting myself exceedingly about her."[11] In the last months of his half-year residence in the French capital, he saw her either every day or every other day. He confided in her, doted on her, and—as he traveled back to England—wrote her an exceptionally emotional letter. The letter is no longer extant, but her response suggests how uncharacteristically Walpole must have revealed himself in it:

"I was very surprised on receiving your letter," she wrote, "I did not expect it, but I see that anything can be expected of you." She goes on to assure him of her discretion: "No one will know of our correspondence and I will do exactly as you stipulate." She marvels at his confession of sentiment for her: "Had you admitted earlier what you thought of me, I would have been calmer. . . . The desire to conquer, and having conquered, to advance, makes for imprudence." Had she known what he hid in his heart she would not have needed to pursue him as flamboyantly as she did during his Parisian sojourn.

Now that "no one can hear us," however, she aches to tell him "that it is impossible to love more tenderly than I love you. . . . Be persuaded that I am more yours than mine." Walpole gives her joy unlike anyone has done in all her years. She wishes him to speak to her as though they "were alone by the fireside." At the same time, she does not saddle him with the obligation to speak incessantly: "I do not beg you to write often," she notes. "Saint Augustin said: 'Love and do as you please.' It is certainly the best thing he said."[12]

The letter is a model of magnanimity and tenderness, passion and poise. And yet, Walpole responded to it with anger. The memory of his own indiscretion evidently tortured him—and he spent the next fifteen years punishing himself for it—and punishing Madame du Deffand.

Once again, we do not have the letter he sent her in reply—the majority of his correspondence having been mailed back to him at his request and destroyed by his literary executor. But we can deduce its content from the Marquise's response:

"If you were French I would not hesitate in thinking you a great fool," she begins, but "you are English, so you are only a great madman. From what do you deduce, pray, that *I am given to indiscretions and romantic transports?*"[13] All her life Madame du Deffand has told her suitors that she has "neither temperament nor romance."[14] And now here is Horace Walpole, avowed bachelor (and possible homosexual, as editors have suggested), accusing her of romantic excess. The insult! "Let the *indiscretions* pass," she continues, ". . . but as for romantic *transports*, they make me furious, and I would willingly tear your eyes out which are said to be so beautiful but which you can certainly not suspect of having turned my head." Even in injury, the Marquise du Deffand is high-spirited and holds her own. Indeed, injury sometimes seems to bring out the most colorful side of her. The more she is needled by Walpole, the more wicked becomes her own pen; the sharper becomes her own irony. Having gregariously defended herself, she turns to measured mockery. She has met another interesting foreigner in her salon, she informs Walpole, a certain "Monsieur Shuvalov," and "I want it to be said of the latter that he has turned my head and that I have quite forgotten the English for the Russians."

Coy but combative, sweet-natured but self-assured, the seventyish-year-old Marquise is a study in contrasts, her correspondence with Walpole an artful game of push-and-pull. Were their letters to each other merely saccharine we would tire of them. There are few things as cloying as the dialogue of two lovers who are forever of one mind. But Walpole and Deffand are united by a thousand differences. They seem elected to fight each other, as well as themselves.

Their passion is "the love that dares not speak its name," as much as any Oscar Wilde may have had in mind when he coined his signature phrase. After their initial *rapprochement*, they never again used the word "love" to describe their tie. Indeed, Walpole bristled when Deffand so much as overdid her signs of *affection*. After he visited her in Paris a second time and departed again for England, the Marquise mailed him a melancholy reflection about their friendship: "I will not see you again," she opines, " it was not worth your coming to resuscitate me. . . . When you will have been absent several months I greatly fear that you will discover that your friendship for me was no more than a preference you gave me over those you found unbearable. . . ."[15]

Rather than reassuring her, Walpole boxes her on the head. Your letter, he says sharply, "could not cause me greater chagrin. . . . Must your complaints, Madame, be unending? You make me greatly regret my candour . . . I should have restricted myself to simple acquaintanceship: why did I avow you my friendship? . . . Really, if friendship is to have all the inconveniences of love and none of the pleasures, I can see no temptation to try it. . . . If you want our correspondence to last, put it on a less tragic note. . . ."[16]

Thus resumes an exchange that will number 1500 letters—half by Walpole and half by Deffand. And yet the barbs between the two were real—and strategically placed to inflict pain. The Marquise's devotion, Walpole notes, can give him "none of the pleasures" of love; she is old and ugly. That must have hurt. But she fires back with well-turned sarcasm about Walpole's cherished Englishness: "I do not know if the English are hard and cruel," she proffers, "but I know they are presumptuous and insolent. They see expressions of friendship and warmth, ennui and sorrow, regret at separation and desire to meet again as unbridled passion . . . and they announce it with so little tact that one has the impression of being caught in flagrante delicto."[17]

Over the next decade, she teased him mercilessly and criticized him artfully. "You have one unpardonable weakness to which you sacrifice your feelings and to which your behavior is subject, this is the fear of ridicule," she tells him variously. "[I]t makes you dependent on the opinions of fools, and your friends are not protected from the impressions that fools wish to give you of them."[18] Walpole, she knew, lived in mortal fear of being identified as the comical young beau of an old blind lady. It is this fear that fueled his prickliness; it is this—very English—sense of violated propriety that caused him to urge all the exaggerated discretion he did. His weakness saddened her, but it did not make her despise him. She was, in a real sense, above it all.

"We have been mocked, you say, but here [in France] everything is mocked," she says coolly, "and instantly forgotten." She did her best to raise his insecure spirit to the height of her own, but when he fell short, she accepted as much. One failing, after all, did not a relationship unmake—nor a man. For all Walpole's huffing and puffing, she knew he would not blow her house down; she knew he would never cease to write, love, or secretly worship her. "Neither all your lectures nor all your arguments against friendship will," she tells him blithely, "persuade people that you are not the man most capable of it in the world."[19] And so he was. He never left the Marquise and he never flagged in his devotion to her. She, in turn, retained her soaring style, brushed aside his occasional tantrum with her great feathered wing, and continued on her sun-filled flight.

Time and again, he rewarded her sangfroid by sending letters that made her "drunk" with joy; letters so "enchanting" she felt "disturbed" by them. (Once again, they were destroyed by his literary executor.) He sent her poems in praise of her wisdom, compliments on her radiance, comparisons to the other great letter writer of the period, Madame de Sévigné. Clearly, he esteemed Deffand. He also visited her regularly—and spent what must have been delightful times. On one occasion the Marquise was so excited by his arrival in the late evening hours that rather than wait until the next morning, rather than wait until her traveler was rested, she installed herself in his bed chamber and chattered the night away, not even leaving when he washed, undressed, or reclined. "There is no indiscretion," she exclaimed triumphantly, "I am stone blind!" He seemed to accept this argument—and spent hours and nights with her more intimate than any he would spend, in his chaste lifetime, with another human being.

There was, to be sure, something bittersweet about their relationship: Deffand was never given "full satisfaction"; the intimacy they incontrovertibly felt with each other was never consummated, and yet it radically enriched both their lives. It enriches *our* lives as readers. There is more drama and insight and humor in the joint epistolary masterpiece of the Marquise du Deffand and Horace Walpole than in many a romantic comedy or tragedy, in many an ambitious disquisition on love. The bittersweetness of the tale increases its power. There is no joy as intense as the joy that verges on tears. No one knew this better than Madame du Deffand. "It is destiny," she writes Walpole, "I can never have any pleasure unless it be counterbalanced by great pain."[20]

Their liaison was exemplary in this sense: Its rhythms of pain and pleasure, its systole of severity and its diastole of tenderness mirrored life itself. To Walpole and to Deffand it *was* life—and could only end with death. "I would like to be able to send you my soul instead of a letter," she once wrote him.[21] Perhaps she left her soul in his possession when she died at age eighty-three. Perhaps she left her soul in his guarded bosom. What is certain is that he never opened it to someone else as he had to her. Their correspondence remained the emotional pinnacle—as well as the artistic pinnacle—of both their lives. Most people today who read Walpole's once famous novel, *The Castle of Otranto*, do so only for historical reasons. His correspondence with Deffand, on the other hand—once considered a mere historical footnote—we may read right now the way we read an arresting novel, the way we contemplate literature that is marked for eternity.

★   ★   ★

THE EPISTOLARY love affair of novelist George Sand and poet Alfred de Musset was quite another thing. First of all, it was interrupted—if never eclipsed—by a sexual relationship of crystalline intensity. Both Musset and Sand were reputed in early nineteenth-century Paris for their erotic voracity. Sand was understood to be a nymphomaniac and Musset identified himself as a man incapable of physical fidelity. When they met in 1833 Sand was twenty-nine; Musset was twenty-three. She was better known than he, having already published several novels, among them the quasi-pornographic *Lélia*. She would publish at least thirty-five other novels in her productive lifetime. He, on the other hand, was a handsome dilettante who had dabbled in a number of arts but begun to distinguish himself in only one: poetry. His golden locks and silver tongue did more to recommend him to Left Bank literary society than his oft-quoted comparison between the moon over a belltower and the dot on an "i". He consumed women like a tiger consumes zebras—casually, brutally, and habitually.

Sand had had several lovers too by the time they met—and one husband. When she was seated next to Musset at a literary dinner, however, the two swiftly resolved—like Deffand and Walpole—to be platonic friends. But unlike Deffand and Walpole, they did not stick to the rules of their agreement. They had known each other for little over a month when Sand received this deadpan letter from her chaste young companion:

> *My dear George,*
> *I've something simply ridiculous to tell you . . . I am in love with you. I've been in love with you since the first day I came to see you. I thought I'd get over it by visiting you as a friend. There are many things in your character that could cure me of you; I've tried to restrain my emo-*

tions; but I've paid too high a price for the months I've spent
with you. I do well, I think, to tell you what I feel, because
I'll recover with far less suffering if you bar me from your
house . . . But if I'm not just anybody to you, tell me. . . .[22]

Musset must have guessed that the combination of candor and irreverence, provocation and sweetness, would weaken Sand's defenses. As indeed it did. Two days later they trysted at midnight and awakened in each other's arms. "I have fallen in love, and this time seriously," declared Sand.[23]

From the beginning, the two "children of the century," as Musset would later call them, cast their relationship as a crime. They cast it, self-consciously and specifically, as an act of incest. Had Musset not wept the night of their midnight meeting, "we would have remained brother and sister," Sand wrote early on.[24] Some months later, the sister-brother relationship had been reglossed as a mother-son relationship: "Poor unhappy man, I loved you as a son," Sand would exclaim in another letter, "It's a mother's love, and I'm still bleeding from it."[25] Sister-brother, mother-son: the two relations strikingly different. The only common denominator is their incestuous nature.

This incestuous nature both Musset and Sand were committed to preserving. Where Horace Walpole shuddered at the notion that he might be breaking convention, Musset and Sand thrilled to it: "George, you believed yourself my mistress when you were only my mother," Musset would lament.[26] And with that they would quicken with emotion and jump into bed together. Where Walpole was embarrassed by the difference in years between himself and Deffand, Musset relished Sand's superior age and reminded himself of it compulsively. They relished the criminal nature of their love—and if it had not existed (as by most measures, it didn't), they would have had to invent it.

In fact, they did invent it: They invented the criminality of their affection as they invented, also, its fairy tale beauty and mythological resonance. They secured its fairy tale allure by heading off to Venice a few months after the consummation of their love and moving into a palazzo. They rode gondolas into the sunset and dressed as extraordinary creatures—Sand often as a boy, with bouffant pantaloons and a jeweled dagger at her hips; Musset as a cherubic dandy. All this color went into the letters they composed. Indeed, if Sand and Musset wrote novels about their relationship after its conclusion—*Les Confessions d'un enfant du siècle* for Musset, *Elle et lui* for Sand—their correspondence proves their most original artwork.[27] It is their correspondence that absorbed the aestheticism of their souls most completely, their correspondence in which they most perfectly mythologized their love.

"Heaven had created us for each other," Musset wrote to Sand during a short-lived break-up, "our minds, in their lofty realm, recognized each other like two mountain birds, and flew together. But the embrace was too tight—it was incest we were committing."[28]

"Yes," replied Sand, "our embrace was an act of incest—but we did not know it." (As if they had not explicitly labeled it thus from the start.) "We came together innocently, sincerely . . . do we have a single memory of our embrace that is not chaste and holy?"[29]

The lovers in these letters are saints; they are wild birds; they move in a "lofty realm." They commit "incest" like the gods of Greek mythology; at the same time, they are "holy" like the parents of Christianity. Every action between them seems fated, every sentiment looms larger than life. The touch of the novelist is everywhere apparent—which is not to say that the participants did not feel matters precisely as they wrote them and feel them the more acutely *because* they wrote them. Art both copies life and creates it. Sand and Musset felt grandly; they wrote grandly about that feeling, which, in turn, caused them to feel still *more* grandly.

Through all this, their greatest idol was truth. At no point did they feel as if they were fictionalizing their bond; quite the reverse: "You do not lie, and that is why I love you," says Sand to Musset.[30] And she *didn't* lie—at least not much. Nor did he. When he flirted with courtesans in Venice, he told her with the conscientiousness of an altar boy at confession. When he got sick and—after many weeks of delirium and mad aggression—she became infatuated with his dashing Italian doctor, she announced as much—if not instantly, then soon. "I cannot feign a love I no longer feel," she told Musset.[31]

To be honest about one's feelings can, ironically, make for "fictive"-seeming drama. Musset and Sand parted and reconciled often; their affections swerved and abated, reignited and expired on the embers—and they told each other so. Their candor allowed them to give chase and take flight over and over again, like the birds of prey they felt they were. "I still love you George," Musset wrote Sand when they parted after their Venetian sojourn.

I know that you are with another man, and yet I feel calm. . . .
Do you know what charmed me about your letter? It was your
manner of telling me about [the doctor] Pagello—of his caring for
you and your affection for him—and the frankness with which

you let me read your heart. Always treat me so; it makes me proud. My dear, the woman who speaks thus of her new lover to the one she has just left, and who still loves her, accords him the greatest proof of esteem that a man may receive from a woman.[32]

Before long, they reunited with ardor renewed. And even if, over time, they parted again and parted definitively, they retained a religious awe for the tie that had bound them. "I'm going to make a novel out of it," Musset declared. "I really want to write our story . . . I want to build you an altar, if only with my bones."[33] What he did not realize is that he had already done so.

By return post Musset received these words from Sand:

Love is a temple built by the lover to the object (more or less worthy) of his worship; what is grand in the thing is not so much the god as the altar. . . . The idol may stand for a long time or soon fall, but still, you will have built a fine house of worship.[34]

It is one of the most arresting passages ever written about the dignity of love, its errors, and its refusal of apology. Even the memory of a true passion—the effort it demands, the artistry it inspires—is, Sand says, its own reward.

Nowhere in her novels did she write anything more potent. Her novels have fallen, for the most part, into obscurity—together with Musset's poems. It is Sand's and Musset's wondrous, remorseless, bold, searching, and crafted letters that spawned the three films that have been made about them, that ensouled countless stories and legends. How can one wonder that artists have wished to dramatize their tale in their individual mediums: Sand

and Musset had already done so much of the artistic footwork themselves! Before any stage director ever touched the ballet of their lives they had already choreographed it personally. Sand might almost have skipped *Elle et lui*; Musset could have omitted *Les Confessions d'un enfant du siècle*; the gift for the children of the next century had already been bestowed. It was, and it remains, their correspondence.

* * *

THIS LEADS us to another question. If it is possible to expand our definition of art to accommodate love letters, is it not possible to expand that definition also to accommodate love *lives*? Is it not plausible that biography—like language—can be shaped into an artistic whole, an imaginative performance? Cannot experience, whether public or private, happy or sad, be the tablet upon which we inscribe our aesthetic inspiration?

* * *

IT IS 1953 and Mexico City's Galería de Arte Contemporaneo has just opened its portals. The upper crust of Mexican society is groping for cocktails. Just then a siren sounds. An ambulance pulls up and out pops a stretcher. Not here, think the passersby. They are not going to unload a patient right in front of an art opening. But they are. The patient is Frida Kahlo. It is her paintings that the crowds have assembled to view.

Kahlo was forty-six years old that day. At forty-seven, she would be dead. She had a wooden right leg, a broken spinal column, and (for long stretches of her life) a broken heart. And yet as she was wheeled over the gallery threshold, she gleamed. Her ankle-length Tehuana skirt was a kaleidoscope of color. Each of her ten fingers sported a shining ring—or two. They were not expensive rings, but they were unusual—one from a five-and-dime store in Detroit, another from the Galeries Lafayette in Paris, most from the byways of her beloved Mexico.

Hospital staff transferred Kahlo to a four-poster bed in the museum. It was not like any four-poster bed anyone has seen before. It had papier-mâché skeletons and Judas figures dangling off the horizontal bar. It boasted portraits of Stalin and of Kahlo's husband, the celebrated mural painter of Mexico, Diego Rivera. Most importantly, it had a large mirror affixed to the ceiling in which Kahlo's audience could scrutinize her face. They could study the dark eyebrows that cut an unbroken diagonal across her forehead. They could examine the magenta lipstick that had been sighted so often on the white shirts of Diego Rivera. They could watch the lipstick pucker as Kahlo mouthed vulgarities. She was not a sweet talker. Every other word from her lips had four letters—or it did when she spoke English. But her conversation was vibrant, witty, articulate, loving. She used gutter talk to speak of heaven.

"Move on," growled the guards as the crowds began to burgeon around Kahlo's bed: "Keep walking." You have to "concentrate on the exhibition itself." The museum curator was anxious. "There was a moment," he recalls, "when we had to take Frida's bed out to the narrow terrace because she could hardly breathe anymore. . . ."[35]

Not for the first time and not for the last, Frida Kahlo the woman had stolen the show from Frida Kahlo the painter. In 1972, it would be the same story. There would be the biggest retrospective to date of Kahlo's work in Mexico City, and her personality would marginalize her painting. This time Frida Kahlo would be sixteen years deceased. Her ashes would lie in an urn in Coyoacan, Mexico. And yet her character would command the occasion. The exhibit rooms "were dominated by huge blown up photographs of incidents of Frida's life," reports her biographer, "which made the jewel-like paintings look almost like punctuation points."[36]

Critics were quick to condemn this offensive imbalance. Kahlo's art was being eclipsed by her life! It is a charge that's raised with regularity for female artists. Indeed, it has become a sort of ritual lament among aesthetic puritans: *the poor artist! If only all those voyeurs paid as much attention to her art as they do to her biography!*

But is it a justified lament? Would Kahlo, for example, have echoed it? Or would she rather have welcomed the public's fascination with her life, courted it, fed it, fought for it, died for it?

There is ample evidence she would have done all of these things—that she *did*, in some sense, do them. "I suffered two grave accidents in my life," she once declared. "One in which a streetcar knocked me down. . . . The other accident is Diego."[37] Both may have been accidents, but both she exploited, studied, stylized, and raised to occasions of astonishing beauty.

She was an eighteen-year-old college prep girl when an electric train hit the bus she was riding in with her boyfriend in Mexico City and nearly split her in two pieces. She was impaled, literally, on a handrail, raped by an iron pole. Her pelvis was broken in three places, as was her spine. A foot was crushed, a leg had eleven fractures, two ribs were busted, as was her collarbone. Trapped in a full-body cast for many long months afterward and consigned to bed, she began to paint: first on her own body—on her plaster cast—and then on paper. Her father was a photographer who had dabbled in painting; so the idea was not altogether new to her. On the other hand, she lacked material. What visitors she had during her long convalescence stayed briefly and departed. So, her parents affixed a mirror over her sickbed and thus was born her first, her main, her lifelong romantic model.

Frida painted her own anguished face; she painted it when her boyfriend, Alejandro, left her; she painted it when he thrilled her, she painted it when she began to adorn it with cosmetics and earrings. She drew herself when she was aglow and she drew herself when she was abashed. In order to draw something interesting, she had to *be* something interesting. Before she could produce art on canvas she produced art in life. The effort only became more pronounced as she gained in experience and as love came to occupy stage center in her existence.

"Diego," she hollered at the most famous painter in Mexico, when she had recovered enough to walk again. He was on a scaffold, painting a mural. She had first met him years before when he had painted on the walls of her school. An incorrigible womanizer, he would flirt with the women who posed for him. To the chagrin of his second wife, Lupe Marin, he would often bed them also. So when things started to warm up for Diego, young Frida would pounce from behind a chair in the auditorium and scream, *"Watch out Diego! Here comes Lupe!"*

Perhaps Rivera recognized his imperious young antagonist

when he saw her with a portfolio under her arm; perhaps he did not. In any event, he descended to meet her when she called. "Look," she said curtly, "I have not come to flirt even though you are a woman chaser. I have come to show you my painting. If you are interested in it, tell me so, if not likewise, so that I will go to work at something else to help my parents."[38] Diego liked what he saw.

He made an appointment to view further paintings at Frida's family house in Coyoacan the following week. When he arrived, the budding artist was up a tree. She was whistling the Communist anthem, "The Internationale." Normally so feminine, she was wearing overalls. She was putting on a drama for him, as she would so often.

The first time he kissed her, the street lamps went dark for miles around. Legend has it she asked if he had planned as much. "Indeed I did," came the reply.[39] It would hardly have been surprising. The element of theater in Frida's and Diego's relationship was insistent; it was ubiquitous. They revised Descartes's credo, "I act therefore I am."

When they married, they were likened to an elephant and a dove: Diego was huge, Frida tiny; Diego was forty-two, Frida twenty-two; Diego a pasty-faced giant, Frida a chiseled and tawny little princess. Rather than diminish their differences, they emphasized them. Frida wore ever more feminine and magnificent Mexican dresses in the course of their union. As Rivera donned work boots and plain white shirts, she accumulated an ever larger collection of dangling earrings and rings and lace petticoats and brilliantly colored skirts. "Where is the circus?" cried children when the pair moved to New York for some years and appeared around town together. And, indeed, they might have been a bear and an animal trainer—a great lumbering beast and a small sparkling circus impresario; a hulking black bull and a limber little torero.

But if the Kahlo marriage was visually artistic, it was artistic in far deeper ways also. Rivera and Kahlo lived their lives with consummate gallantry, imagination, and chutzpah. Equally imbued with a love of conflict, they sparred constantly, but with extraordinary style and invention. It was a "union of lions," said observers.[40] When Diego would flirt with another woman at dinner parties, Frida would take a great swig of tequila and begin—first in a low voice, then in a booming contralto—to sing sexually explicit songs. She would sing of prostitutes and she would sing of the parts of her husband's anatomy. Before long no one could concentrate on her rival. Everyone's attention—including Diego's—was riveted on Frida.

Rifles sounded during their nightly revels. Once Diego broke a man's finger. Another time he was attacked by gun-wielding political opponents; Frida threw her small body before Diego's great paunch to protect him. He lunged to save her; the assailants fled. Not infrequently, Frida locked Diego out of her painting studio in Mexico City—connected to his own by a hanging bridge—and waited there while he wept and pleaded for entrance through the night.

Other times it was Frida who wept. If Diego was a womanizer coming into their marriage, he stayed a womanizer until the end. Sleeping around meant nothing to him. "I have put more affection into a handshake,"[41] he told Frida after bedding another model one day. It was a tough situation to accept for Frida who—despite her own penchant for promiscuity (it was the reason for the break with boyfriend Alejandro)—had counted on being rather a traditional spouse to Diego. During the early years of their marriage, she imitated his previous wife. She learned Lupe's recipes and mimicked her helpless jealousy. She brought Diego lunch baskets overflowing with flowers as he worked on his murals; she sat at the foot of the scaffold and watched him labor; she placed her own painting ambitions firmly on the sidelines. Diego's infidelities, ironically, changed all that. They prompted her to assert—or reassert—her own artistic, social, and sexual independence.

While Diego pursued his lighthearted affairs, Frida began to entertain deep-hearted ones. Her unions with the Communist dissident, Leon Trotsky; with the accomplished photographer, Nicolas Murray; the refugee art dealer, Heinz Berggruen—not to mention flirtations with painter Georgia O'Keeffe and liaisons with several actresses—were remarkable for their seriousness and for the fidelity with which all parties continued to honor and aid Frida even after her passion had run its course. It was not unusual for a discarded lover like Nicolas Murray to send Frida money when he suspected she might be short. Nor was it unusual for her to write him that "I really shouldn't complain of anything in life as long as you love me and I love you" or make him promise he would sleep with another woman "only if you find a real F.W. [fucking wonder]." [42] Frida's relationships were intense. While Diego swaggered that having sex was "like urinating," Frida forged life bonds. [43]

What is even more remarkable than the fact that Frida forged life bonds with her intermittent lovers (secondary as they always knew they were to her husband) is that she *also* built life bonds with Diego's intermittent lovers. Perhaps her best girlfriend at the time of her death was the Mexican movie star Maria Félix. Frida knew Maria because Diego had had an affair with her—probably the most serious affair during his marriage to Frida. He had proposed to Maria Félix. Maria had declined. Diego had quickly realized this was for the best, and strenuously wooed Frida anew.

Maria and Frida went on to become bosom buddies. Far from nursing a grudge against the woman who nearly stole her husband, Frida made the effort to know and understand her. In the last years of Frida's illness, Maria danced around her bed, impersonating all the offbeat public characters she knew, kissing the patient, and lying down in bed with her when she tired. Frida loved Maria Félix so much that she placed her name on the top of the list of favorite friends she'd painted in pink on her room wall. A photograph of another lover of Diego's—Pita Amor—graced the headboard of her sickbed.[44]

Frida's other and even more continual companion was her sister Cristina. Frida had three sisters and several other close relatives, but it is Cristina who attended her day in and day out, Cristina who gave Frida her hand to clasp each time she was rolled into yet another operating room. It was also Cristina who had had an extended love affair with Diego. Not a one-night stand as is sometimes suggested, but a stubborn and hurtful two-year obsession.[45]

The relationship between Cristina and Diego was the cause of Frida's worst marital suffering. It was also the occasion for what is probably her most garish and gruesome painting, a canvas she entitled "A Few Small Nips." The phrase is lifted from a Mexican news article in the early 1930s: A man had murdered his wife by slashing her naked body with a knife. Questioned by the police, he protested that no harm had been intended, the slashes were just "a few small nips." Frida was unable to confine the pain of the picture to the picture. Not only is the woman and the floor splattered with blood in her painting, but so is the wooden frame; it is covered in bright red polka dots.

Frida responded to her relationship with Diego by seizing her color palette. But where the conventional understanding is that she used her love life to feed the artwork that was her *painting*, the more accurate view may be that she used her painting to feed the artwork that was her *love life*. Frida's pictures were a way she communicated with Diego—perhaps the most vital way. He treasured her paintings, read them, and hearkened to their message. "Never before has a woman put such agonizing poetry on canvas as Frida did," he told journalists. As a painter, he felt Frida's agony more clearly when he saw images of it than when he heard her speak of it.

In all her reported conversations, Kahlo was extraordinarily feisty: Almost never did she dwell on her pain. Almost invariably she was funny and understated—a tough-talking little gangster in a bar. "They are going to cut off my paw," she declared shortly before her leg amputation: "So what?"[46] It was really only in her painting that she revealed her suffering—and there she *did*, in fact, dwell on it. Her most famous images are depictions of pain: They are images of herself in a medical corset with nails through her flesh, a Jesus figure. They are pictures of Frida with an oversized tear in her eye, pictures of Frida with her black hair spread over the floor around her—she has cut it all off. They are pictures of a young deer with a dozen arrows piercing its body. The deer has the face of Frida Kahlo.

She used these paintings to dramatize her moods to Diego. She used them as tools in the most important art project of her life: her affair with the man she loved above everything. Rather than life serving painting, this was painting serving life.

Frida's portraiture is an artistic representation of an artistic representation. It can be likened, perhaps, to architectural photography—to artful depiction of an object that is *already* an artwork. She prized her portraiture, to be sure—but she prized her love life still more. She honored its low points as well as its high points. Above everything, she honored its conflicts. Frida and Diego actually divorced at a certain moment in their lives; they divorced after ten years of marriage—and married a second time precisely one year afterward. They could not stay apart. They could not settle down tranquilly. They remained in a state of perpetual tension, drama, and passion. They were—as someone called them, "sacred monsters," "Olympian deities." [47]

It may not be everybody's love potion, this cocktail of conflict and reconciliation, theater and revolution—but it was a potent brew. Diego revered his wife above everything: "We are all clods next to Frida," he declared unambivalently.[48] She is the "center of my life," he said at other times. "If I had died without knowing her I would have died without knowing what a real woman was."[49] He asked that his ashes, when he passed away, be commingled with hers. And even as Frida filled her days with meaningful lovers, exotic pets, sublime paintings, and international honors, she found in Diego everything that mattered to her. If he was not a conventional husband, he was something far greater. He was, as she wrote in her journal, her

Beginning
Constructor

My baby
My boyfriend
Painter
My lover
"my husband" [the quotes are significant]
my friend
my mother
me
universe[50]

Diego was all in one to her: parent and child, artist and muse, means and end—as Frida was to him.

When she died in 1954, everybody was watching. Her fame as a painter had, by this time, outstripped his. But the world's focus was still first on her relationship with Diego and only second on her pictures (and third on his murals). Diego could talk as long as he wished of the way in which Frida Kahlo's work "shines like a diamond in the midst of many inferior jewels"; he could talk as long as he wished of his admiration for her brushstroke.[51] People listened. But it was his love for *her* that nailed them to their seats.

As Diego talked during Frida's opening at the Galería de Arte Contemporaneo, Frida's nephews and nieces were still drawing hearts with "Frida" and "Diego" inscribed inside. For all the rivals in their circumference, Frida and Diego were always the heroic couple, the central attraction. The central attraction brought in side attractions. Frida died flanked by her husband's ex-lovers and surrounded by gifts from her own paramours. All these persons were drawn to Frida and Diego as side shows are drawn to main shows, as candy sellers are drawn to circuses and court jesters are drawn to

Shakespearean kings. The sun itself pulls its planets close, not that they may eclipse it, but that they may revolve around it in beauty.

Frida will be remembered as an artist of love as often as she will be remembered as an artist of oil paint. And for all the protests of the academic gatekeepers, this is exactly what she would have wanted.

*   *   *

IF THE idea of love as art raises eyebrows among scholars, it raises hackles among feminist scholars. Not only is romantic love, in these circles, understood as isolated from art, it is understood as antagonistic to art. Love, the story goes, distracts women creators from their true vocation; it subjects them (often rightfully) to the world's mockery.

This was the argument of the feminist scholar Carolyn Heilbrun who recommends, in so many words, that responsible biographers ignore or minimize the "erotic plots" in the lives of their female subjects and focus exclusively on what she dubs their "quest plots"—the tales of their professional careers.[52] The irony, of course, is that an "erotic plot" in no way detracts from a writing plot, a painting plot, a philosophizing plot. "I think most deeply when I strongly feel," declared Mary Wollstonecraft. "My heart is enfolded in your thought as a branch in flame," said Margaret Fuller to her lover, George Nathan. So far from tossing a damper on intellectual activity, love ignites such activity.

The fact that love *gives rise to* art is a commonplace to all but the most conventional feminists. From here it is only a modest step to the notion that concerns us now, the more radical notion that love can *be* art; that love can be art as emphatically as a musical improvisation, an acrobatic stunt, or a dramatic soliloquy.

This does not, of course, imply that the lover exercises control over all—or even many—aspects of a love affair. But then again, neither does a painter exercise complete control over the outcome of a painting—particularly when she or he employs new colors, methods, motifs, or venues. For Diego Rivera, the *weather* determined his art. As a muralist, he was at the mercy of everything from heavy rainfalls and scorching sunbeams to the temper tantrums of wealthy patrons. When John D. Rockefeller decided he disliked the face of Lenin as it appeared on one of Rivera's murals, Rivera had either to remove the face and create a different sort of image, or assent to the destruction of his work.

What made him a great artist was not that he knew exactly what was going to happen as he worked; it was not that he controlled every aspect of his creation; it was that he possessed unflappably artistic impulses. Whether Rockefeller or a rainstorm arrested his *oeuvre*, he began again—and he began again with characteristic aplomb. So it was for Frida Kahlo. From one day to another she did not know what would happen to her work materials; having suffered the accident she had as a young girl, she did not know what would happen to the very muscles she used to hold her brush and body erect.

Neither in loving nor painting, in writing nor seducing, neither in directing a film nor in navigating a marriage, can we tell the future. "Freedom," as Sartre says, can only *ever* be "what you do with what's been done to you."[53] All art involves responding to the unknown, integrating the undesirable, and expecting the unexpected.

It does not, for that reason, need to involve all the upheaval of a Kahlo-Rivera liaison. Art and love can be traditional as well as experimental, sober as well as savage, personal as well as public. If Kahlo created an experimental artwork in her life with Rivera, her contemporary, Hannah Arendt, created a classical artwork no less brilliant in her life with her man, Heinrich Blücher.

★ ★ ★

HANNAH ARENDT is considered the most important woman philosopher of the twentieth century—though she would have objected to both terms in this equation. She hated being noted for her gender and nearly declined a historic appointment at Princeton because the university dared call her their "first tenured woman professor." She bristled, almost equally, at being named a philosopher, preferring to be understood as a political theorist.

Philosopher or political theorist, she proved one of the most intriguing, ambitious, and inflammatory thinkers the postwar period produced. Born in Germany in 1906, Arendt studied philosophy with the most controversial philosopher of the century, Martin Heidegger. Her doctoral thesis examined the concept of love. It examined love in St. Augustine—and remains a captivating first book.[54]

Perhaps it is not surprising that the love-minded Arendt had an affair with Martin Heidegger. It was an affair of grandiose proportions—an affair that marked its participants for the rest of their lives. For Martin Heidegger it was, as he admitted to his wife a quarter century later, the most passionate relationship of his whole existence. For Arendt it was the beginning of a *life* of passion.

The climax of Arendt's life of passion came neither with Heidegger nor even with her first husband. The climax came with her second husband. Heinrich Blücher met Hannah Arendt in Paris in 1936. Both had recently fled to France to escape the Nazis: Arendt because she was a Jew and could not assume university employment in Germany; Blücher because he was a Communist. In every obvious way, the two emigrés were opposites. Where Arendt was passionately Semitic, Blücher was proudly German; he was related, in fact, to the legendary Prussian general who had fought Napoleon. Where Arendt had studied not merely with Heidegger but with Karl Jaspers, Edmund Husserl, and several other luminaries of 1920s Europe, Blücher hated book learning and had dropped summarily out of high school. Where Arendt was unusually well bred and well mannered, Blücher was crude, wild, surly, and pugnacious. He was the son of a single mother who had worked in a laundromat. He did not know how to hold a fork or, for years after meeting Arendt, a job. Where Arendt loved to write, Blücher loathed it. Where she was shy in public, he commanded an auditorium of students or militants, Frenchmen or Germans, as easily as a dinner date.

What drew them together was conversation. Over a decade and a half into their marriage—for they married in 1940—the critic Alfred Kazin still marveled at the soirées he attended in their company. It was not the guests or the cocktails, it was them.

They were vehemently involved in working out a common philosophy. . . . Between clenched lips holding a pipe, Heinrich growled his thought out as if he were still on the battlefield— against wrong-headed philosophers. Hannah, despite her genteel

training, also talked philosophy as if she were standing alone . . .
against powerful forces of error. She . . . joined him in the most
passionate seminar I would ever witness between a man and a
woman living together. . . .[55]

Blücher—though not a writer—collaborated with Arendt on
the writing of her most important books. Perhaps the most celebrated of them all—*The Origins of Totalitarianism* (written soon
after the pair married and emigrated to New York)—was a *folie-
à-deux*. Blücher would head for the New York Public Library, read
everything he could find that related to the topic, and report back
to Arendt; he would also interview emigré acquaintances on their
personal experience of totalitarianism. Arendt, in the meantime, sat
at the typewriter. It often takes two to generate the best ideas—an
interlocutor and an answerer. Blücher was Arendt's interlocutor.

They rejoiced in each other's successes: "I am filled with
pride for my Stups the Clever and the Wise who could persuade
the American faculty," wrote Arendt to Blücher when he was
appointed—without any formal education worth mentioning
and without good English—to teach philosophy to the students
of Bard College in New York.[56] He shared with Arendt all his insights on the thinkers he taught there—Jesus, Buddha, Homer,
Heraclitus, Zarathustra. She responded to these insights ardently
in her written work. Blücher, however, shone in the classroom.
He chose to be buried at Bard College. So did his wife.

Deep into a marriage that would last thirty years, or until
Blücher's death in 1970, they wrote each other love poems. It was
the only kind of writing Blücher consented to do. In his entire
lifetime, Blücher—husband to an intellectual who published over

three million words—brought to press a single brief article. It was
poems in which he expended his energy—unpublished poems
that he addressed to Hannah Arendt: "I must be you," he wrote,

> . . . *You more Me than me,*
> *I more You than you,*
> *So I more Me than me*
> *And you more you than you . . .*[57]

She wrote him verse in return. It may not have been the strongest writing she ever did, but it was the strongest loving. As the
poet and scholar, Randall Jarrell, commented, they comprised a
"Dual Monarchy" when they were together.[58] Different but equal.
Ever connected—but with a space between them.

As she grew increasingly famous, Arendt traveled through the
United States and through Europe. Blücher often stayed behind.
In 1949 she revisited her once-loved Heidegger—who, thanks to
his confused flirtation with the Nazi regime during World War II,
had become a disappointment to her. She reconnected with him
in an electric way. She wrote Blücher about it in great detail—
confident, as she said, that he would "judge the whole business
correctly."[59] She was grateful "not to have forgotten" the worth of
Heidegger. Profoundly moved by her encounter, she felt like she
was talking to him for the first time.

Heidegger's wife was bitterly jealous of Arendt. Blücher was not
in the least bit jealous of Heidegger. "Let them be jealous," those
hamstrung souls, he wrote Arendt happily: "There waits here at
home for you your not at all jealous [husband], who, instead of
being jealous, really loves you. . . ." "Yes," Arendt responded, "our

steps go in unison. . . . These fools who think themselves loyal if they give up their active lives and bind themselves together into an exclusive One; they then have not only no common life, but generally no life at all. If it weren't so risky," she proffered, *"one should tell the world what a marriage really is."*[60]

They *should* have told the world. Instead, they told each other. Their story, however, speaks for itself. It was not based on strict fidelity. If Blücher kept Arendt on a long leash, she returned the favor. Both were alluring personalities, attractive to the opposite sex. Both experimented with their attractiveness. But their own union was set in stone—fire and brimstone. They vowed honesty to each other—and they practiced it. Blücher understood his wife's lifelong intimacy with Heidegger; she understood his ardor, during one of her absences, for a young Russian Jewess. The love between the two thinkers was not exclusive, but inclusive. It asked. It comprehended. It cherished. And it survived.

When Blücher died of a heart attack after a dinner with friends one night in 1970, Arendt was profoundly in love with him. He was profoundly in love with her. She died in exactly the same way in 1975—on a sofa after a night with friends. Today, they are buried in the same grave. "Grand passions," Arendt wrote in one of her most compelling essays, "are as rare as masterpieces."[61] It is a quote from Balzac, but it could be a quote from Arendt. It could be a quote from Blücher.

Not only are grand passions as rare as masterpieces; they *are* masterpieces.

* * *

WHEN I was in high school my English teacher told our class that the most important thing about life was to live it as if it were a good novel—as if, she said, it were a good film script. "Would audiences *walk out* during the movie of your life?" she asked confrontationally. Most of us answered silently in the affirmative. Our sheltered and unimaginative lives could not detain a viewer.

It will come as no surprise that my English teacher got in trouble with the school authorities. She was supposed to be instructing us about the thrill of literature, not the thrill of autobiography. She was intended to be helping us *recognize* the heroes in the novels we read—not compete with them.

It turns out that the distinction may have been irrelevant to several of the artists and writers who would become my favorites. For every Samuel Johnson or Immanuel Kant who had *no* life I could identify outside of words, there were six artists I loved—often women—who led heart-stoppingly vivid lives. This does not mean they led painless lives. But just as fictional stories need not be blithe to be artful, life stories need not be easy to be artful. Some of my idols paid for the drama of their loves in blood as well as ink—but it was no lesser achievement for being so costly.

The author of *Paradise Lost*, John Milton, once said that a poet's life should be his most perfectly formed poem.[62] Perhaps one reason we have so many plays and verses, novels and films about certain lovers is that they have already done so much of the stylization, dramatization, and mythification on our behalf. Far from being a rebuke to art, their life—*our* life, the life of anyone who lives deliberately, gracefully, inventively, and fearlessly—can be a *piece* of art.

Waging Love:
Toward a New Definition of Eros

ROMANTIC LOVE, at the start of this century, is cause for embarrassment. What it once partook of the heroic and the transcendent has been lost. Undermined by cynicism, marginalized by recreational sex, rendered suspect by our culture's obsession with safety, and displaced, in part, by the worship of family values, it has also suffered—and suffered gravely—from the side effects of feminism. To this day, a woman in love is a woman who must relinquish her feminist credentials. Witness the case, quite recently, of the political columnist, social critic, and poet, Katha Pollitt.

After a decades-long career writing tough-minded political polemics, she published a *New Yorker* essay—and then an essay collection—foregrounding her faithless lover.[1] Reader interest flared, but the response among feminist intellectuals was withering. Few of them failed to mention and mock Pollitt's own, now defunct, feminist credentials: "It must be my problem," wrote the *Los Angeles Times* staff critic, but "[w]atching a feminist I've admired my entire life dissolve into a whingeing puddle in her late 50s is painful."[2] The *New York Times* reviewer shared her pain, or her scorn, anyway: "Have you heard the latest? 'Men are rats.' This directly from the desk of Katha Pollitt, a longtime feminist columnist. . . ."[3] Never mind that Pollitt never comes close to stating men are rats. What she stated was rather: Men *matter.* Men matter to women intellectuals. We get excited about them, obsessed with them, sometimes injured by them. It is for this suggestion that she was pilloried—not for the *New York Times* critic's easy putdown: *that* would have gone over just fine.

Men are allowed, indeed, supposed, to be louts. What they are not supposed to be is objects of importance to women. The more intelligent you claim to be, the more ironical and distant must be your relation to love. If this has been true in female circles for some time, it has trickled into male circles as well. It has trickled, also, into the arts. Where once upon a time love poetry was the most abundant poetry written, it is now among the rarest—particularly in high-brow publications. Adolescents are still allowed to write love poems. Famous poets are not—or only if they demonstrate Latin American provenance or prodigious restraint. In literary verses—as in literary essays—issues of class, race, family, anatomy, and geography have largely supplanted concerns about romantic love.

It is really only in Hollywood—or in Hollywood-like genres— that love retains real clout. And even there it is on the defensive: Readers of celebrity news now know a great deal more about Angelina Jolie's and Brad Pitt's kids than they do about their love. Pregnancy, childbirth, and adoption make bigger headlines than romance.

It is to the credit of contemporary feminism that it has not only claimed new rights for women but also reclaimed old ones it had lost along the way. Among the rights feminism has *re*claimed for women is the right to relish motherhood. The media's focus on pregnancy is part and parcel of this phenomenon—but so are the "mommy wars" raging in cerebral newspapers and magazines. Not only are women pop stars modeling maternity for the masses, but women thinkers are debating it for the intelligentsia—at ever-increasing length. To stay at home or go to work, to breast feed or bottle feed, to strap your infant to your bosom or hire a nanny; all this is discussed with a gravity once reserved for international diplomacy. And that is a good thing.

Feminism has brought many other good things. It's brought half the human population the right to be ambitious, the right to be political, the right to be sexually playful. One of the few things feminism has not yet brought womankind—and indeed has helped torpedo—is the right to be romantic. All other doors stand open. We can run for president or stay in the nursery; cruise for sex or plan a family. Just about the only thing we cannot do is *love*. And yet this is what gives the other enterprises vitality and meaning. Love is the music that makes the other steps we take in life flow, the song that allows our otherwise tentative motions to cohere. It is the bridge between sex and maternity—but, more importantly, it is the sky above these activities. It is at once the glue and the god.

We must do for amorous passion what has been done for contented motherhood. If there are books, today, called *Maternal Desire*, books that make parenting sexy, there ought to be books—a whole lot of books—that make romantic love honorable—not only for film buffs but for philosophers; not only for young people but for old, not only for men but for women.[4]

The Nobel Prize–winning author, J. M. Coetzee, laments, in his last novel, the decline of *longing*. "Is it too much," he asks in *Diary of a Bad Year* (2007), "to say that the music we call Romantic has an erotic inspiration—that it unceasingly pushes further, tries to enable the listening subject to leave the body behind, to be rapt away . . . to become a living soul? If this is true then the erotics of Romantic music could not be more different from the erotics of the present day. In young lovers today one detects not the faintest flicker of that old metaphysical hunger, whose code word for itself was yearning (*Sehnsucht*)."[5]

Let us prove him wrong. Despite lavish evidence of his correctness—evidence I see, suffer from, and assail—I increasingly believe that he *is* wrong. The "yearning" is there, among the women and men I know and esteem most. If, in the foregoing pages, I enlist examples from literature and literary biography, it is not because I think the best is in the past. It is not because I believe the greatest models are behind us. I use these cultural touchstones because I believe, with C.S. Lewis, that "what is new usually wins its way by disguising itself as the old."[6] But even more strongly I believe that we must create our own models in this new century, models that encompass, consume, and transcend the models of old.

This book is not a backwards summons to a time of long-stemmed roses and cabbage-patch courtship. It is an invitation to risk, an incitement to unruliness, a cry to battle.

As I write these words, I bear the bodily scars of a loss or two in love. I have been derailed by love, hospitalized by love, flung around five continents, shaken, overjoyed, inspired, and unsettled by love. But as I think upon it now—a couple of weeks away from giving birth to a little girl—I wish her something of the same. I feel new. Ready for the next round. And full of heady hope for my sisters, my suitors, my brothers, and lovers, my—yes—daughter.

We stand poised, I think, at the opening of a new era. An era not of sobriety and self-protectiveness, of feminist resentment and masculine "backlash," but an era of revived romantic hope, of greater trust between genders and fresh daring among lovers. We have been pragmatic and pedestrian about our erotic lives for too long; there is impatience in the air. There is impatience among lifelong feminists like Katha Pollitt, resistance among crusty white males like J. M. Coetzee. There is rebellion among young women around me, and among the men who keep them company.

Love, we know somewhere within ourselves, transcends ordinary expectations and experience. Love gives more and it takes more. It is a metaphysical minefield—or a mine. It glitters, illuminates, endangers. The stakes are real. You win some. You lose some. You are never undamaged. But you are, with any luck, undaunted.

Acknowledgments

I WOULD LIKE TO THANK, first of all, the astonishing individuals I have loved. I would like to thank my first boyfriend, Michel Goussu—choir director at Paris's Saint Sulpice church (made notorious by *The Da Vinci Code*)—for setting the bar so high on quotidian romance. I would like to thank Chris McCully, the fiercest poet the British Isles ever bore, and once my fiancé. I would like to thank the father of my newborn child, Vasilis Tsakonas, for taking me into his proud Cretan heart despite our resplendent differences. If our love was impossible, it was also fiery and stubborn— as he is. I would like to thank the teacher who reintroduced me to writing after I'd abandoned it. Michael Bonin inspires all whom he touches, and anyone who witnesses him in a classroom today is as lucky as I was yesterday. I would like to thank every person who has arrested my heart. Each has taught me more than I can express, more than I am able to admit.

I would like to thank the women who have changed me. They are women in books, women who have written books, and women who deserve books to be written about them. They are lovers and rebels, fighters and feminists, tragic and comic heroines, women who loved too much, women who were fools for lesser things than love, women who blundered, explored, took risks; women (like Mary Wollstonecraft) who didn't want kids but had them by accident, and women (like Frida Kahlo) who wanted kids more than anything, and got eternity instead.

I want to thank my spectacular literary agent, Sarah Burnes. Sarah is not an agent but an event: half celebration, half high-powered colloquy. She is heartfelt and canny, tender and tenacious, erudite and shrewd, a romantic and a supermom, a friend and a consummate professional, a strategist and a stream of sunlight. She sustained me in times of terror; buoyed me in moments of languor. Without her belief in this project, I would have faltered along the way.

I want to thank Terry Karten, my editor at HarperCollins, for her strong faith in this book—and for lending it a finer and braver form than ever it would have had without her. I want to thank her also for tolerating my idiosyncracies, for suffering me to make the mistakes I had to make, and making them in the particularly recalcitrant way I had to make them. This, also, is the mark of a great editor.

Let me thank the first editor I ever had, Steve Wasserman, then at the *Los Angeles Times Book Review*. It is he who brought me into the public sphere; he who entrusted me with my first published review essay. Next came Lewis Lapham, whose midnight phone call informing me "you can write anything you want for *Harper's*," began my scribbling career for real. Let me thank Benjamin Schwarz for picking up from there and offering me the best magazine home I can imagine at the *Atlantic Monthly*.

Let me thank, finally, my wise and wide-minded university mentors: Stephen Yenser, in particular, and Jonathan Post, with whom I did literary graduate work at UCLA. I would like to thank also the late Diane Middlebrook—author of splendid biographies of splendid women—as well as treasured confidante during the first year of my English Ph.D. program at Stanford.

The manuscipt for this book has had few readers but formidable ones. My mother, Christa Nehring, is a shockingly good critic in spite of the fact that she refuses to criticize me in English. My father, Wolfgang Nehring, is never to be fooled with. Roy Robins—a brilliant editor and writer in London whom I have yet to meet face to face—has helped me immeasurably, subjecting *A Vindication of Love* to page by page analyses as thrilling and invigorating as they are discriminating and toughminded. Karin Badt, whose chutzpah and can-do creativity never cease to startle me, blew wind beneath my often tired wings.

There are so many other muses and friends, allies and advisors whose attention shaped this work that I cannot enumerate them with the dignity they demand. I will mention only one, therefore: the incendiary, rousing, riveting, understated, overanxious, bitter and sweet companion of my last decade, Russell Jacoby. What I have done these last years I have done, always, with him in heart. He has critiqued me, taught me, challenged me, moved me, ensouled me, and aided me in ways at once editorial and emotional, mundane and magnificent. I thank him so much. I love him so much.

Finally: there is my daughter. Eurydice. She hasn't been around long. She was born in Paris four months ago, at this writing. And yet: my horizons are softer and wider for her. If her cry has shortened my work day, her smile has given me an eternity of joy.

Select Bibliography

Abelard, Peter and Heloise. *The Letters of Abelard and Heloise.* Translated by Betty Radice. New York: Penguin, 2003.

Abrams, M.H., ed. *The Norton Anthology of English Literature, 5th Ed., Vol. 1.* New York: W.W. Norton & Co., 1986.

Alighieri, Dante. *The Divine Comedy.* Translated by John Ciardi. New York: Penguin Group, 2003.

_____. *La Vita Nuova.* Translated by Barbara Reynolds. New York: Penguin Group, 2004.

_____. *New Life.* Translated by J.G. Nichols. London: Hesperus Press, 2003.

Appignanesi, Lisa. *Simone de Beauvoir.* New York: Penguin Books, 1988.

Arendt, Hannah and eds. Joanna Vecchiarelli Scott, Judith Chelius Stark. *Love and Saint Augustine.* Chicago: University of Chicago Press, 1996.

Arnim, Bettina von and Johann Wolfgang von Goethe. Translated by Bettina von Arnim. *Correspondence with a Child.* Lowell, MA: Daniel Bixby, 1841.

Ascher, Carol. *Simone de Beauvoir: A Life of Freedom*. Boston: Beacon Press, 1981.

Austen, Jane. *Pride and Prejudice*. Edited by and introduced by Vivien Jones. New York: Penguin, 2003.

Bair, Deirdre. *Simone de Beauvoir: A Biography*. New York, Simon & Schuster, 1990.

Balzac, Honoré de. *La Comédie Humaine*. Translated by Anatole Cerfberr. Philadelphia: G. Barrie & Son, 1987.

Barish, David P. and Judith Eve Lipton. *The Myth of Monogamy: Fidelity and Infidelity in Animals and People*. New York: W.H. Freeman and Company, 2001.

Beauvoir, Simone de. *Adieux: A Farewell to Sartre*. Translated by Patrick O'Brian. New York: Pantheon Books, 1984.

_____. *All Said and Done*. Translated by Patrick O'Brian. New York: Putnam, 1974.

_____. *Force of Circumstance*. Translated by Richard Howard. *Vol. 2: Hard Times*. New York: Paragon House, 1992.

_____. *Letters to Sartre*. Translated by Quintin Hoare. New York: Arcade, 1993.

_____. *The Second Sex*. Translated by H. M. Parshley. New York: Vintage Books, 1989.

_____. *A Very Easy Death*. Translated by Patrick O'Brian. New York: Pantheon, 1985.

Behrendt, Greg and Liz Tuccillo. *He's Just Not That Into You: the No-Excuses Guide to Understanding Guys*. New York: Simon & Schuster, 2004.

Bentley, Toni. "Life, and My Evil Ex-Boyfriend," in *New York Times Book Review*, September 23, 2007.

Bernières, Louis de. Foreword to Dante Alighieri, *New Life*. Translated by J.G. Nichols. London: Hesperus Press, 2003.

Béroul, *The Romance of Tristan*. Edited by Alan S. Fedrick. New York: Penguin Classics, 1970.

Bishop, Elizabeth. *The Complete Poems, 1927–1979*. New York: Farrar, Straus and Giroux, 1984.

Bizet, Georges. *Carmen*. Translated and introduced by Ellen H. Bleiler. New York: Dover Publications, 1983.

Bloom, Allan. *Love and Friendship*. New York: Simon and Schuster, 1993.

Borges, Jorge Luis. *Other Inquisitions, 1937–1952*. Translated by Ruth L. C. Simms. Austin: University of Texas Press, 1964.

Bowen, Marjorie and George Preedy. *This Shining Woman: Mary Wollstonecraft, 1759–1797*. New York, London: D. Appleton-Century Company, Incorporated, 1937.

Brontë, Charlotte. *Jane Eyre*. New York: Harper & Bros., 1899.

Brontë, Emily. *Wuthering Heights*. Edited by David Daiches. New York: Penguin, 1988.

Burge, James. *Heloise & Abelard: A New Biography*. New York: HarperCollins, 2006.

Capper, Charles. *Margaret Fuller: An American Romantic Life: The Private Years, Vol. I*. New York: Oxford University Press, 1994.

_____. *Margaret Fuller: An American Romantic Life: The Public Years, Vol. II*. New York: Oxford University Press, 2007.

Carter, Angela. "Colette," *London Review of Books Anthology One*. Edited by Michael Mason. London: Junction Books, 1981.

Casanova, Giacomo. *The Story of My Life*. New York: Penguin Classics, 2001.

Chaucer, Geoffrey. *The Canterbury Tales*. Edited by V.A. Kolve and Glending Olson. New York: W.W. Norton & Co., 2005.

Chevigny, Bell Gale. *The Woman and the Myth: Margaret Fuller's Life and Writings*. Boston: Northeastern University Press, 1994.

Choderlos de Laclos, Pierre. *Liaisons Dangereuses*. New York: Oxford University Press, 1995.

Coetzee, J.M. *Diary of a Bad Year*. New York: Penguin, 2007.

Coontz, Stephanie. *Marriage, a History: From Obedience to Intimacy, or How Love Conquered Marriage*. New York: Viking Penguin, 2005.

Costa-Prades, Bernadette. *Simone de Beauvoir*. Paris: Maren Sell, 2006.

Cowan, Dr. Connell and Dr. Melvyn Kinder. *Smart Women/Foolish Choices: Finding the Right Man Avoiding the Wrong Ones*. New York: Signet, 1986.

Coppola, Sofia, dir. *Lost in Translation*. Perfs. Bill Murray, Scarlett Johansson. Focus Features, 2003.

Cravieri, Benedetta. *Madame du Deffand and Her World*. Translated by Teresa Waugh. Boston: David R. Godine, 1994.

Crosland, Margaret. *Simone de Beauvoir: The Woman and Her Work*. London: Heinemann, 1992.

Dickinson, Emily. *The Complete Poems of Emily Dickinson*. Edited by Thomas H. Johnson. Boston: Little, Brown and Co., 1960.

_____. *The Master Letters of Emily Dickinson*. Edited by R.W. Franklin. Amherst, MA: Amherst College Press, 1986.

Dowd, Maureen. *Are Men Necessary?: When Sexes Collide*. New York: G.P. Putnam's Sons, 2005.

Dworkin, Andrea. *Intercourse*. New York: The Free Press, 1987.

_____. *Pornography: Men Possessing Women*. New York: G.P. Putnam, 1981.

Dziech, Billie Wright, Robert W. Dziech II, and Donald B. Hordes. "'Consensual' or Submissive Relationships: The Second-Best Kept Secret." *Duke Journal of Gender Law and Policy* 6 (1999): 83–112.

Dziech, Billie Wright and Linda Weiner. *The Lecherous Professor: Sexual Harassment on Campus*. Boston: Beacon Press, 1984.

Eco, Umberto. "God Isn't Big Enough for Some People." *The Telegraph* (February 27, 2005).

Ehrenreich, Barbara, Elizabeth Hess, and Gloria Jacobs. *Re-Making Love: The Feminization of Sex*. Garden City, NY: Doubleday, 1986.

Eliot, T.S. *The Complete Poems and Plays, 1909–1950*. New York and Orlando: Harcourt Brace and Co., 1967.

Emerson, Ralph Waldo. *The Collected Letters of Ralph Waldo Emerson, Volume II, Essays: First Series*. Edited by Alfred R. Fergusan and Jean Ferguson Carr. Cambridge, MA: President and Fellows of Harvard College, 1979.

_____. *The Collected Works of Ralph Waldo Emerson*. Edited by Ralph L. Rusk. Cambridge, MA: Harvard University Press, 1994.

_____. *Essays and Lectures*. New York, Penguin Putnam, 1983.

_____. *The Letters of Ralph Waldo Emerson*. Edited by Ralph L. Rusk. New York: Columbia University Press, 1991.

_____. *Selected Writings of Ralph Waldo Emerson*. Edited by William H. Gilman and Introduction by Dr. Charles Johnson. New York: Penguin, 2003.

Emerson, Ralph Waldo, W.H. Channing, and J.F. Clarke. *Memoirs of Margaret Fuller Ossoli, Vol. I*. Boston: Roberts Brothers, 1884.

Ensler, Eve. *The Vagina Monologues*. New York: Villard Books, 2001.

Epstein, Daniel Mark. *What Lips My Lips Have Kissed: The Loves and Love Poems of Edna St. Vincent Millay*. New York: Henry Holt, 2001.

Evans, Mary. *Love: An Unromantic Discussion*. Cambridge, UK: Blackwell Publishers, 2003.

Faderman, Lillian. *Odd Girls and Twilight Lovers: A History of Lesbian Life in Twentieth-Century America*. New York: Columbia University Press, 1991.

Fallaize, Elizabeth. *Introduction to Simone de Beauvoir: A Critical Reader*. London: Routledge, 1998.

Fein, Ellen and Sherrie Schneider. *The Rules: Time-Tested Secrets for Capturing the Heart of Mr. Right.* New York: Grand Central Publishing, 2007.

Firestone, Shulamith. *The Dialectic of Sex: The Case for Feminist Revolution.* New York: Bantam Books, 1970.

Flanagan, Caitlin. "Wifely Duty: Marriage Used to Provide Access to Sex. Now It Provides Access to Celibacy," *The Atlantic Monthly* 291, no. 1 (Jan-Feb 2003): 172.

Flaubert, Gustave. *Madame Bovary.* Translated by Geoffrey Wall and Michelle Roberts. 1992, New York: Penguin Classics, 2003.

Francis, Claude and Fernande Gontier. *Simone de Beauvoir: A Life, A Love Story.* New York: St. Martin's Press, 1987.

Franklin, R.W., ed. *The Master Letters of Emily Dickinson.* Amherst, MA: Amherst College Press, 1986.

Freedman, Diane P., ed. *Millay at 100: A Critical Reappraisal.* Carbondale, IL: Southern Illinois University Press, 1995.

Fuller, Margaret. "Bettine Brentano und Guenderode," *The Dial: A Magazine for Literature, Philosophy, and Religion, Vol. II.* Boston: E.P. Peabody, 1842.

_____. *The Letters of Margaret Fuller, Vol. 2.* Edited by Robert N. Hudspeth. Ithaca, NY: Cornell University Press, 1983.

_____. *My Heart Is a Large Kingdom: Selected Letters of Margaret Fuller.* Edited by Robert N. Hudspeth. Ithaca, NY: Cornell University Press, 2001.

_____. *Summer on the Lakes.* Urbana and Chicago: University of Illinois Press, 1991.

_____. *Woman in the Nineteenth Century.* Edited by Larry J. Reynolds. New York: W.W. Norton & Co., 1997.

García Márquez, Gabriel. *Love in the Time of Cholera.* Translated by Edith Grossman. New York: Penguin Books, 1985, 1988.

Gass, William H. *Reading Rilke: Reflections on the Problem of Translation.* New York: Alfred A. Knopf, 1999.

Gilson, Etienne. *Heloise and Abelard.* Ann Arbor: University of Michigan Press, 1960.

Giorcelli, Cristina and Charles Capper, eds. *Margaret Fuller: Transatlantic Crossings in a Revolutionary Age.* Madison: University of Wisconsin Press, 2008.

Goethe, Johann Wolfgang von. "Brief an Graefin Auguste zu Stolberg," in *Werke, Vol. 1: Gedichte und Epen.* Edited by Erich Trunz. Hamburg: Christian Wegner Verlag, 1964.

_____. *Faust, Parts 1 and 2*. Edited by Cyrus Hamlin and translated by Walter Arndt. New York: W.W. Norton & Co, 2000.

_____. *Sorrows of Young Werther and Selected Writings*. Translated by Catherine Hutter and introduction by Hermann J. Weigand. New York: Signet, 1962.

Gioia, Dana. *The Gods of Winter*. Saint Paul, MN: Graywolf, 1991.

Godwin, William. *Memoirs of the Author of A Vindication of the Rights of Woman*. Edited by Pamela Clemit and Gina Luria Walker. Ontario: Broadview, 2001.

Goldman, Emma. *Anarchism and Other Essays*. Port Washington, NY: Kennikat Press, 1969.

Gordon, Lyndall. *Vindication: A Life of Mary Wollstonecraft*. New York: HarperCollins, 2005.

Griffin, Susan. "Rape: The All-American Crime." *Ramparts Magazine* (Sept. 1971): 26–35.

Grimm Brothers. *The Complete Fairy Tales of the Brothers Grimm*. Translated by Jack Zipes. New York: Bantam Books, 1987.

Grymes, Peg. *The Romance Trap*. Dublin, Ireland: Brandon, 1996.

Hamilton, Edith. *Mythology*. New York: Little Brown & Co., 1999.

Hawthorne, Nathaniel. *The Scarlet Letter*. Edited by Brian Harding. New York: Oxford University Press, 1998.

Hays, Mary. "Memoirs of Mary Wollstonecraft" in Mary Wollstonecraft, *Vindication of the Rights of Woman: A Norton Critical Edition*. Edited by Carol Poston. New York: W.W. Norton, 1988.

Heilbrun, Carolyn. *Writing a Woman's Life*. New York: W.W. Norton, 1988.

Herrera, Hayden. *Frida: A Biography of Frida Kahlo*. New York: HarperCollins, 1983.

Higginson, Thomas Wentworth. *Margaret Fuller Ossoli* (American Men of Letters series). Boston: Houghton, Mifflin, and Co., 1884.

Hofstadter, Daniel. *The Love Affair as a Work of Art*. New York: Farrar, Straus and Giroux, 1996.

Homer. *The Iliad*. Translated by Richmond Lattimore. Chicago: University of Chicago Press, 1961.

_____.*The Odyssey*. Translated by.Richmond Lattimore. New York: HarperCollins, 1999.

Hunt, Morton. *The Natural History of Love*. New York: Anchor, rev. and updated, 1994.

Hustvedt, Siri. *A Plea for Eros: Essays*. New York: Picador, 2006.

James, Heather. *Shakespeare's Troy: Drama, Politics, and the Translation of Empire*. Cambridge, UK: Cambridge University Press, 1997.

James, Laurie. *Men, Women, and Margaret Fuller: The Truth That Existed Between Margaret Fuller and Ralph Waldo Emerson and Their Circle of Transcendental Friends*. New York: Golden Heritage Press, 1990.

Jonson, Ben. *Ben Jonson and the Cavalier Poets*. Edited by Hugh Maclean. New York: W.W. Norton & Co., 1975.

Kazin, Alfred. *New York Jew.* New York: Random House, 1978.

Kipnis, Laura. *Against Love: A Polemic*. New York: Pantheon Books, 2003.

Kleist, Heinrich von. *Penthesilea*. Translated by Joel Agee. New York: HarperCollins, 2000.

Kornfield, Eva. *Margaret Fuller: A Brief Biography with Documents*. New York: Bedford/St. Martin's, 1996.

Krauss, Nicole. *The History of Love: A Novel*. New York: W.W. Norton & Co., 2005.

Kruks, Sonia. "Beauvoir's Time/Our Time: The Renaissance in Simone de Beauvoir Studies." *Feminist Studies* 31.2 (2005):286–309.

Lamartine, Alphonse de. *Poetic Meditations*, in *Six French Poets of the Nineteenth Century*. Edited and translated by E.H. and A.M. Blackmore. Oxford, UK: Oxford University Press, 2000.

Lacy, Norris J., ed. *The Lancelot-Grail Reader: Selections from the Medieval French Arthurian Cycle*. New York: Garland Publishing Co., 2000.

Larkin, Philip. *Collected Poems*. Edited and introduction by Anthony Thwaite. London: Faber and Faber, 2003.

Leach, William. *True Love and Perfect Union: The Feminist Reform of Sex and Society*. Middletown, CT: Wesleyan University Press, 1989.

Leon, Celine. "Beauvoir's Women: Eunuch or Male?" in *Critical Essays on Simone de Beauvoir*. Edited by Elaine Marks. Boston: G.K. Hall, 1987.

Levy, Ariel. *Female Chauvinist Pigs: Women and the Rise of Raunch Culture*. New York: The Free Press, 2005.

Lewis, C.S. *The Allegory of Love: A Study in Medieval Translation*. Oxford; New York: Oxford University Press, 1953.

Liechtenstein, Ulrich von. *The Service of Ladies*. Translated by J.W. Thomas and introduction by Kelly DeVries. Woodbridge, Suffolk, UK: Boydell Press, 2004.

Marlowe, Christopher and Sylvan Barnet, eds. *Doctor Faustus*. New York: Signet Classic, 2001.

Marneffe, Daphne de. *Maternal Desire: On Children, Love, and the Inner Life*. New York: Little, Brown & Co., 2004.

Mason, Michael, ed. *London Review of Books Anthology One*. London: Junction Books, 1981.

Mehren, Joan von. *Minerva and the Muse: A Life of Margaret Fuller Ossoli*. Amherst: University of Massachusetts Press, 1995.

Mews, Constant J. *Abelard and Heloise*. Oxford, UK: Oxford University Press, 2004.

_____. *The Lost Love Letters of Heloise and Abelard: Perceptions of Dialogue in Twelfth-Century France*. Translated by Neville Chiavaroli and Constant J. Mews. New York: Palgrave, 2001.

Milford, Nancy. *Savage Beauty: The Life of Edna St. Vincent Millay*. New York: Random House, 2001.

Millay, Edna St. Vincent. *Collected Poems*. Edited by Norma Millay. New York: Harper & Row, 1956.

Millett, Kate. *Sexual Politics*. New York: HarperCollins, 1970.

Miller, Perry. *Margaret Fuller: American Romantic*. Ithaca, NY: Cornell University Press, 1963.

Moi, Toril. *Simone de Beauvoir: The Making of an Intellectual Woman*. New York: Oxford University Press, 1994, 2008.

Montaigne, Michel de. *The Complete Essays of Montaigne*. Translated by Donald Frame. Stanford, California, Stanford University Press, 1958.

Milton, John. *Selected Prose Writings of John Milton*. Introduction by Ernest Myers. New York: D. Appleton and Co., 1884.

Musset, Alfred de. *The Confession of a Child of the Century*. Translated by Kendall Warren. Chicago: C. H. Sergel, 1892.

Nehring, Cristina. "Last the Night: The Abiding Genius of Edna St. Vincent Millay," *Harper's* (July 2002), p. 74–81.

Ortega y Gasset, José. *On Love*. Translated by Tony Talbot. New York: Meridian, 1957.

Ovid. *The Art of Love*. Translated by Rolfe Humphries. Bloomington: Indiana University Press, 1957.

_____. *Metamorphoses*. Translated by David Raeburn. New York: Penguin, 2004.

Patai, Daphne. *Heterophobia: Sexual Harassment and the Future of Feminism*. Lanham, MD: Rowman & Littlefield Publishers, 1988.

Pater, Walter. *The Renaissance: Studies in Art and Poetry*. New York: The Macmillan Co, 1899.

Pankhurst, Christabel. *The Great Scourge and How To End It*. London: E. Pankhurst, 1913.

Perel, Esther. *Mating in Captivity*. New York: HarperCollins, 2006.

Petrarch. *Petrarch's Lyric Poems: The Rima Sparse and Other Lyrics*. Edited by Robert M. Durling. Cambridge, MA: Harvard University Press, 1976.

Plato. *Selected Dialogues of Plato: The Benjamin Jowett Translation*. Translated by Benjamin Jowett. New York: Modern Library/Random House, 2001.

Pollitt, Katha. *Learning to Drive, and Other Life Stories*. New York: Random House, 2007.

Polwhele, Richard. "Unsex'd Females," in Mary Wollstonecraft, *Vindication of the Rights of Woman: A Norton Critical Edition*. Edited by Carol Poston. New York: W.W. Norton, 1988.

Réage, Pauline. *Story of O*. Translated by John P. Hand. New York: Blue Moon Books, 1998.

Reynolds, Susan Salter. "And Another Thing: Learning to Drive and Other Life Stories," in *Los Angeles Times Book Review*, September 9, 2007.

Richardson, Samuel. *Clarissa: Or the History of a Young Lady*. Edited by Angus Ross. New York: Penguin, 1986.

_____. *Pamela: Or Virtue Rewarded*. Edited by Thomas Keymer and Alice Wakely. Oxford; New York: Oxford University Press, 2001.

Rilke, Rainer Maria and William H. Gass. *Reading Rilke: Reflections on the Problem of Translation*. New York: Alfred A. Knopf, 1999.

_____. *Rilke on Love and Other Difficulties: Translations and Considerations of Rainer Maria Rilke*. New York: W.W. Norton & Co, 2004.

Rivera, Diego and Gladys March, *My Art, My Life: An Autobiography*. New York: Citadel Press, 1960.

Rochefoucauld, *Maxims*. Translated by Stuart D. Warner and Stéphane Douard. South Bend, IN: St. Augustine's Press, 2001.

Rose, Phyllis. *Parallel Lives: Five Victorian Marriages*. New York: Alfred A. Knopf, 1983.

Rowley, Hazel. *Tête-à-Tête: Simone de Beauvoir and Jean-Paul Sartre*. New York: HarperCollins, 2005.

Rougemont, Denis de. *Love in the Western World*. Princeton, NJ: Princeton University Press, 1983.

Saint-Exupéry, Antoine de. *Night Flight*. Translated by Stuart Gilbert. New York: Harcourt, Brace & Co, 1932.

_____. *The Wisdom of the Sands*. Translated by Stuart Gilbert. New York: Harcourt, Brace & Co, 1950.

Sand, George. *Correspondance de George Sand*. Edited by Georges Lubin. Paris: Garnier Frères, 1966.

_____. *Correspondance de George Sand et d'Alfred de Musset*. Bruxelles: E. Deman, 1904.

_____. *Correspondance de George Sand et d'Alfred de Musset*. Edited by Louis Evrard. Monaco: Editions de Rocher, 1956.

_____. *Elle et lui*. Paris: Michel Lévy Frères, 1869.

Sade, Marquis de. *The Complete Marquis de Sade*. Edited by John S. Yankowski and translated by Paul J. Gillette. Los Angeles: Holloway House, 2005.

Sartre, Jean-Paul. *Being and Nothingness*. Translated by Hazel E. Barnes. New York: Washington Square Press, 1992.

_____. *Witness to My Life: The Letters of Jean-Paul Sartre to Simone de Beauvoir*. Translated by Lee Fahnestock and Norman MacAfee. New York: Charles Scribner's Sons, 1992.

_____. *Words*. Translated by Bernard Frechtman. New York: Fawcett World Library, 1966.

Sewall, Richard B. *The Life of Emily Dickinson, Vol. 2*. New York: Farrar, Straus and Giroux, 1974.

Shakespeare, William. *Antony and Cleopatra*. New York: Washington Square Press New Folger Edition, 1999.

_____. *The Riverside Shakespeare*. Edited by G. Blakemore Evans. Boston: Houghton Mifflin Co., 1974.

_____. *Measure for Measure*. Edited by Brian Gibbons. Cambridge, UK: Cambridge University Press, 2006.

_____. *A Midsummer Night's Dream*. New York: Washington Square Press New Folger Edition, 1993.

_____. *Romeo and Juliet*. New York: Washington Square Press New Folger Edition, 1992.

Shalit, Wendy. *A Return to Modesty: Discovering the Lost Virtue*. New York: Simon & Schuster, 2000.

_____. *Girls Gone Mild: Young Women Reclaim Self-Respect and Find It's Not Bad To Be Good*. New York: Random House, 2007.

Sheehy, Gail. *Sex and the Seasoned Woman*. New York: Random House, 2006.

Shelley, Percy B., Donald H. Reiman, and Doucet Devin Fischer. *Shelley and His Circle, 1773–1822*. Cambridge, MA: Harvard University Press, 1961.

Stendhal. *Love*. Translated by Gilbert and Suzanne Sale. New York: Penguin Books, 1975.

_____. *The Charterhouse of Parma*. Translated by Margaret Mauldon. Oxford; New York: Oxford University Press, 1999.

_____. *The Red and the Black*. Translated by Roger Gard. New York: Penguin, 2002.

Taylor, G.R. Stirling. *Mary Wollstonecraft: A Study in Economics and Romance*. London: Martin Secker, 1911.

Taylor, Thomas. "Vindication of the Rights of Brutes" in Mary Wollstonecraft, *Vindication of the Rights of Woman: A Norton Critical Edition*. Edited by Carol Poston. New York: W.W. Norton, 1988.

Thesing, William B., ed. *Critical Essays on Edna St. Vincent Millay*. New York: G. K. Hall & Co., 1993.

Todd, Janet, ed. *A Wollstonecraft Anthology*. Bloomington: Indiana University Press, 1977.

_____. *Mary Wollstonecraft: A Revolutionary Life*. New York: Columbia University Press, 2000.

Tolstoy, Leo. *Anna Karenina*. Edited by John Bayley and translated by Richard Pevear and Larissa Volokhonsky. New York: Penguin Classics, 2003.

Tomalin, Claire. *The Life and Death of Mary Wollstonecraft*. New York: Harcourt, Brace, Jovanovich, 1975.

Troyes, Chrétien de. *Lancelot, or The Knight of the Cart*. Translated by Ruth Harwood Cline. Athens, GA: University of Georgia Press, 1990.

Walpole, Horace. *Correspondence with Hannah More*. Edited by W.S. Lewis, Robert A. Smith, and Charles H. Bennett. New Haven, CT: Yale University Press, 1961.

_____. *The Letters of Horace Walpole, Earl of Orford*. Edited by Peter Cunningham. London: Richard Bentley, 1858.

Wang, Orrin N.C. "The Other Reasons: Female Alterity and Enlightenment Discourse in Mary Wollstonecraft's *A Vindication of the Rights of Woman*." *Yale Journal of Criticism* 5, no. 1 (1991): 129–49.

Wardle, Ralph Martin. *Mary Wollstonecraft: A Critical Biography*. Lawrence: University of Kansas Press, 1951.

Warhol, Robyn R. and Diane Price Herndl, eds. *Feminism: An Anthology of Literary Theory and Criticism*. New Brunswick, NJ: Rutgers University Press, 1997.

Wharton, Edith. *The Age of Innocence*. New York: W.W. Norton & Co., 2003.

Wilson, Edmund. "The All-Star Literary Vaudeville," *New Republic* 47 (30 June 1926): 158–63.

Wollstonecraft, Mary. *Collected Letters of Mary Wollstonecraft*. Edited by R. Wardle. Ithaca, NY: Cornell University Press, 1979.

_____. *Mary Wollstonecraft: Letters to Imlay*. Edited by Charles Kegan Paul. Published by Charles Kegan Paul, 1879.

_____. *Vindication of the Rights of Woman: A Norton Critical Edition*. Edited by Carol Poston. New York: W.W. Norton, 1988.

_____. *Vindication of the Rights of Men* in *A Wollstonecraft Anthology*. Edited by Janet Todd. Bloomington: Indiana University Press, 1977.

Wollstonecraft, Mary. *Letters Written During a Short Residence in Sweden, Norway, and Denmark*. London: J. Johnson, 1796.

Yeats, William Butler. *Yeats's Poems*. Edited by A. Norman Jeffares. London: Macmillan, 1989.

Young-Bruehl, Elisabeth. *Hannah Arendt: For Love of the World*. New Haven, CT: Yale University Press, 2004.

Notes

1. See Mary Hays, "Memoirs of Mary Wollstonecraft" (1798) in Mary Wollstonecraft, *Vindication of the Rights of Woman: A Norton Critical Edition*, ed. Carol Poston (New York: W. W. Norton, 1988), p. 229; Richard Polwhele's "Unsex'd Females" (1798) in *Vindication: A Norton Critical Edition*, pp. 235-7; Thomas Taylor, "Vindication of the Rights of Brutes" (1792) in *Vindication: A Norton Critical Edition*, pp. 229-31; Horace Walpole, *Correspondence with Hannah More*, eds. W.S. Lewis, et al. (New Haven, CT: Yale University Press, 1961), p. 397.

    Embarrassment among Wollstonecraft's twentieth- and twenty-first-century commentators takes many forms. The well-intended apologias of biographer Janet Todd are only one instance. In an overview of recent scholarship, Orrin N.C. Wang writes in the *Yale Journal of Criticism* (1991) that contemporary feminists still essentially view Wollstonecraft as "an unstable woman whose life proves her error" ("The Other Reasons: Female Alterity and Enlightenment Discourse in Mary Wollstonecraft's *A Vindication of the Rights of Woman*," *Yale Journal of Criticism* 5, no. 1 (1991): 129-49). One of the very few scholars to part company with this crowd of shamefaced attackers is Lyndall

Gordon, whose 2005 biography, *Vindication: A Life of Mary Wollstone-craft* (New York: HarperCollins, 2005), diagnoses and attempts to cure the same illness I do: "Mary Wollstonecraft's unguardedness," she writes, "has made her an easy target. Godwin's Memoirs . . . exposed her to attacks in the late 1790s, sustained through much of the following century and renewed in our time" (p. 4). And despite Gordon's eloquent campaign to stem the tide, the attacks continue.

2. For an account of the positive early reception of Wollstonecraft's work and the negative early reception of her life, see R. M. Janes, "On the Reception of Mary Wollstonecraft's *A Vindication of the Rights of Woman*," in *A Vindication of the Rights of Woman: A Norton Critical Edition*, pp. 285-97.

3. Simone de Beauvoir, *The Second Sex* (New York: Vintage Books, 1989), p. 667.

4. Marjorie Bowen and George Preedy, *This Shining Woman: Mary Wollstonecraft*, 1759–1797 (New York, London: D. Appleton-Century Company, Incorporated, 1937), p. 14.

5. Edmund Wilson, "The All-Star Literary Vaudeville," *New Republic* 47 (30 June 1926): 162.

6. See editor's introduction in William B. Thesing, ed., *Critical Essays on Edna St. Vincent Millay* (New York: G. K. Hall & Co., 1993). "One hundred years after Edna St. Vincent Millay's birth," writes Thesing, ". . . the talk at conferences and the tone of essay revaluations focus on what went 'wrong'[with Millay], on the possible reasons for the decline and fall of a literary reputation. . . ." (p. 1). See also: Diane P. Freedman, ed., *Millay at 100: A Critical Reappraisal* (Carbondale: Southern Illinois University Press, 1995).

7. For more information on the sinking of Edna St. Vincent Millay's reputation among the American poetry elite, see my essay, "Last the Night: The Abiding Genius of Edna St. Vincent Millay," *Harper's*, July 2002, pp. 74-81.

8. William Butler Yeats, "The Choice" in *Yeats's Poems*, edited and annotated by A. Norman Jeffares (London: Macmillan, 1989), p. 362.

9. William Shakespeare, "Sonnet 127" to "Sonnet 152," *The Riverside Shakespeare* (Boston: Houghton Mifflin Co., 1974), pp. 1772-7.

10. Soon after Beauvoir's death in 1986, "a volatile mix of adulation and hostility" emerged among the very scholars who one might think owed her most (Elizabeth Fallaize, *Introduction to Simone de Beauvoir: A Critical Reader* [London: Routledge, 1998], p. 7). Once the heroine of women's liberation, Beauvoir suddenly became the "antagonist." Fem-

inist essays on her started to "display a quite extraordinary antipathy to their subject" (Fallaize, p. 7). Before long, they either disappeared altogether or turned "peculiarly nasty, condescending, sarcastic, sardonic, or dismissive" (Sonia Kruks, "Beauvoir's Time/Our Time: The Renaissance in Simone de Beauvoir Studies," *Feminist Studies* 31.2 [2005]: 289); Elizabeth Fallaize, 1998, p. 7; Toril Moi, *Simone de Beauvoir: The Making of an Intellectual Woman* (Oxford: Oxford University Press, 1994, 2008), p. 94.

By the time Deirdre Bair published the first full-length biography in 1990, Beauvoir's personal life with Sartre had come in for such harsh criticism that Bair was accosted at readings and upbraided during interviews by people who seemed to hold her personally responsible for Beauvoir's slavish behavior with her lover (Deirdre Bair, *Simone de Beauvoir: A Biography* [New York: Simon & Schuster, 1990]). "Why should we even continue to read Simone de Beauvoir's writing when the life that produced the theory was such a lie?" they demanded in so many words. "She told us she lived a perfect feminist life . . . she inspired us, and now we don't have that inspiration anymore. We believed her and she let us down." Feeling "like a slowly deflating balloon," Deirdre Bair published a painful *New York Times Magazine* piece entitled "Do as she Said, not as she Did" (*New York Times* [November 18, 1990]). In many ways, the recent history of feminist Beauvoir criticism is the history of "Electras trying to murder their sexist mother" (Celine Leon, "Beauvoir's Women: Eunuch or Male?" in *Critical Essays on Simone de Beauvoir*, Elaine Marks, ed. [Boston: G.K. Hall, 1987], p. 153).

11. Christabel Pankhurst, *The Great Scourge and How To End It* (London: E. Pankhurst, 1913), pp. 78-9.

12. For a history of this malaise, see William Leach, *True Love and Perfect Union: The Feminist Reform of Sex and Society* (Middletown, CT: Wesleyan University Press, 1989); Peg Grymes, *The Romance Trap* (Dublin, Ireland: Brandon, 1996).

13. Shulamith Firestone, *The Dialectic of Sex: The Case for Feminist Revolution* (New York: Bantam Books, 1970), p. 126.

14. Andrea Dworkin, *Pornography: Men Possessing Women* (New York: G.P. Putnam, 1981), p. 105.

15. Susan Griffin, "Rape: The All-American Crime," *Ramparts Magazine* (Sept. 1971): 30.

16. Kate Millett, *Sexual Politics* (New York: Ballantine, 1978); Andrea Dworkin, *Intercourse* (New York: The Free Press, 1987), p. 194.

17. Lillian Faderman, *Odd Girls and Twilight Lovers: A History of Lesbian Life in Twentieth-Century America* (New York: Columbia University Press,

1991), p. 207. See the wider study of this phenomenon in academia by Daphne Patai, *Heterophobia: Sexual Harassment and the Future of Feminism* (Lanham, MD: Rowman & Littlefield Publishers, 1988).

18. Mary Evans, *Love: An Unromantic Discussion* (Cambridge, UK: Blackwell Publishers, 2003) p. 143; Laura Kipnis, *Against Love: A Polemic* (New York: Pantheon Books, 2003), p. 47.

19. Gail Sheehy, *Sex and the Seasoned Woman* (New York: Random House, 2006).

20. Ariel Levy, *Female Chauvinist Pigs: Women and the Rise of Raunch Culture* (New York: The Free Press, 2005).

21. Barbara Ehrenreich, et al., *Re-making Love: The Feminization of Sex* (New York: Anchor Press, 1986), p. 195.

22. Michel de Montaigne, *Essays by Montaigne*, edited by the author of "The gentle life" (London: Sampson Low, Son & Marston, 1869), pp. 116-8.

23. Ralph Waldo Emerson, "Friendship" in *The Essays of Ralph Waldo Emerson*, ed. Alfred R. Ferguson and Jean Ferguson Carr (Cambridge, MA: Belknap Press, 1987), p. 127. My emphasis.

24. Carolyn Heilbrun, *Writing a Woman's Life* (New York: W.W. Norton, 1988), pp. 48-52.

25. Phyllis Rose, *Parallel Lives: Five Victorian Marriages* (New York: Alfred A. Knopf, 1983), p. 7.

26. Emma Goldman, *Anarchism and Other Essays* (Port Washington, NY: Kennikat Press, 1969), p. 223.

27. Dante Alighieri, *The Divine Comedy*, trans. John Ciardi (New York: Penguin Group, 2003); Shakespeare, *Antony and Cleopatra*, in *The Riverside Shakespeare*, ed. G. Blakemore Evans, et al. (Boston: Houghton Mifflin Co., 1974).

28. Peter Abelard and Heloise, *The Letters of Abelard and Heloise*, trans. Betty Radice (New York: Penguin, 2003); Petrarch, *Petrarch's Lyric Poems: The Rima Sparse and Other Lyrics*, ed. Robert M. Durling (Cambridge, MA: Harvard University Press, 1976).

29. Umberto Eco, "God Isn't Big Enough for Some People," *The Telegraph* (February 27, 2005).

ONE Cupid Doffs His Blindfold: *Love as Wisdom*

1. Ben Jonson, "Song: To Celia," *Ben Jonson and the Cavalier Poets*, ed. Hugh Maclean (New York: W.W. Norton & Co., 1975), p. 28.

2. Ovid, *The Art of Love*, trans. Rolfe Humphries (Bloomington: Indiana University Press, 1957), p. 190.

3. 1 Corinthians 13:12.

4. William Shakespeare, "Sonnet 130," *The Riverside Shakespeare*, ed. G. Blakemore Evans, et al. (Boston: Houghton Mifflin Co., 1974), p. 1773 (l.1).

5. William Shakespeare, *A Midsummer Night's Dream*, in *The Riverside Shakespeare*, ed. G. Blakemore Evans, et al. (Boston: Houghton Mifflin Co., 1974), p. 225 (1.1.235-9).

6. William Shakespeare, "Sonnet 137," *The Riverside Shakespeare*, p. 1774 (l. 1-2).

7. "Sonnet 148," ibid., p. 1776 (l. 1-4).

8. "Sonnet 148," ibid. (l. 12-14).

9. "Sonnet 147," ibid. (l. 13-14).

10. Stendhal, *The Charterhouse of Parma*, trans. Margaret Mauldon (Oxford: Oxford University Press, 1999); Stendahl, *The Red and the Black*, trans. Roger Gard (New York: Penguin, 2002).

11. Stendhal, *On Love*, trans. Gilbert and Suzanne Sale (New York: Penguin Books, 1975), p. 45.

12. Ibid.

13. Ibid.

14. Ibid., p. 47.

15. Ibid., p. 51.

16. Ibid., p. 55.

17. Ralph Waldo Emerson, *The Collected Letters of Ralph Waldo Emerson*, Volume II, Essays: First Series, ed. Alfred R. Ferguson and Jean Ferguson Carr (Cambridge, MA: President and Fellows of Harvard College, 1979), p. 127.

18. Joan von Mehren, *Minerva and the Muse: A Life of Margaret Fuller Ossoli* (Amherst: University of Massachusetts Press, 1995), p. 338.

19. Stendhal, *Love*, trans. Gilbert and Suzanne Sale (New York: Penguin Books, 1975), p. 60.

20. C.S. Lewis, *The Allegory of Love: A Study in Medieval Translation* (London: Oxford University Press, 1936, rpt. 1953), p. 2.

21. Ibid., p. 3.

22. Ibid.

23. Stephanie Coontz, *Marriage, A History: From Obedience to Intimacy, or How Love Conquered Marriage* (New York: Viking Penguin, 2005).

24. Morton Hunt, *The Natural History of Love* (New York: Alfred A. Knopf, 1959; rpt., New York: Anchor, rev. and updated, 1994), p. 144.

25. Plato, "Phaedrus," in *Selected Dialogues of Plato: The Benjamin Jowett Translation* (New York: Modern Library/Random House, 2001), pp. 150-1 (251a-b).

26. Ibid., p. 120 (231a).

27. Ibid., p. 122 (233b).

28. Dr. Connell Cowan and Dr. Melvyn Kinder, *Smart Women/Foolish Choices: Finding the Right Men Avoiding the Wrong Ones* (New York: Signet, 1986).

29. Plato, *Selected Dialogues of Plato*, p. 124 (234c-d).

30. Ibid., p. 127 (236b).

31. Ibid., p. 131 (238c).

32. Ibid., p. 135 (241b).

33. Ibid., (241b-c).

34. Ibid., pp. 138-9 (242d).

35. Ibid., p. 138 (243a).

36. Christopher Marlowe, *Doctor Faustus*, ed. Sylvan Barnet (New York: Signet Classic, 1969, 2001), p. 74 (5.1.95-6).

37. Plato, *Selected Dialogues of Plato*, p. 139 (243b).

38. Ibid.

39. Ibid., p. 149 (249d).

40. My italics. Ibid., p. 140 (244b).

41. Ibid., p. 142 (245a).

42. Ibid. (245a).

43. Ibid. (245b).

44. Allan Bloom, *Love and Friendship* (New York: Simon & Schuster, 1993), p. 431.

45. Plato, *Selected Dialogues of Plato*, p. 205 (173c).

46. Ibid., p. 209-10 (176a-e).

47. Ibid., p. 260 (211c).

48. Ibid., p. 259-60 (211c).

49. Ibid., pp. 258-9 (210d-e).

50. C.S. Lewis, *The Allegory of Love*, pp. 4-5.

51. Jean-Paul Sartre, *Being and Nothingness* (New York: Washington Square Press, 1992); Simone de Beauvoir, *The Second Sex* (New York: Vintage Books, 1989).

52. Angela Carter, "Colette," *London Review of Books Anthology One*, ed. Michael Mason (London: Junction Books, 1981), p. 135.

53. Simone de Beauvoir, *Letters to Sartre* (New York: Arcade, 1992), pp. 184 and 148.

54. Hazel Rowley, *Tête-à-Tête: Simone de Beauvoir and Jean-Paul Sartre* (New York: HarperCollins, 2005), xiii.

55. Ibid., p. 84.

56. Simone de Beauvoir, *Force of Circumstance, Vol. 2: Hard Times* (New York: Paragon House, 1992), p. 380. My emphasis.

57. Brothers Grimm, *The Complete Fairy Tales of the Brothers Grimm*, p. 45.

58. Ibid.

59. Homer, *The Odyssey*, trans. Richmond Lattimore (New York: Harper Perennial, 1991), Book X.

60. Author's translation. Alphonse de Lamartine, "Isolation" from *Poetic Meditations*, in *Six French Poets of the Nineteenth Century*, ed. and trans. E.H. and A.M. Blackmore (Oxford; New York: Oxford University Press, 2000), pp. 4-5.

61. William Shakespeare, "Sonnet 105," *The Riverside Shakespeare*, p. 1768 (l.1).

62. Edna St. Vincent Millay, *Collected Poems*, ed. Norma Millay (New York: Harper & Row, 1956), p. 75.

63. T.S. Eliot, "Four Quartets: Burnt Norton" in *The Complete Poems and Plays, 1909–1950* (New York and Orlando: Harcourt Brace and Co., 1967), p. 118.

two The Power of Power Differentials:
Love as Inequality

1. Jorge Luis Borges, *Other Inquisitions, 1937–1952*, trans. Ruth L.C. Simms (Austin: University of Texas Press, 1964) p. 99.

2. Billie Wright Dziech, et al., eds., "'Consensual' or Submissive Relationships: The Second-Best Kept Secret," *Duke Journal of Gender Law and Policy* 6 (1999): 92.

3. David P. Barish and Judith Eve Lipton, *The Myth of Monogamy: Fidelity and Infidelity in Animals and People* (New York: W.H. Freeman and Company, 2001), p. 76.

4. Chrétien de Troyes, *Lancelot, or The Knight of the Cart*, trans. Ruth Harwood Cline (Athens: University of Georgia Press, 1990), p. 34.

5. Charlotte Brontë, *Jane Eyre* (New York: Harper & Bros., 1899), p. 97.

6. Plato, *Symposium*, in *Selected Dialogues of Plato: The Benjamin Jowett Translation* (New York: Modern Library/Random House, 2001), p. 217 (251a-b).

7. Ibid., p. 309 (181d).

8. Ibid., p. 307 (178c).

9. Ibid., p. 261 (212e).

10. Ibid., p. 267 (216d).

11. Ibid. (217a).

12. Ibid., p. 268 (217a-b).

13. Ibid. (217c).

14. Ibid.

15. Ibid., p. 269 (217d-e; 218b-c).

16. Ibid. (218c).

17. Ibid., p. 270 (219b).

18. My emphasis. Ibid., p. 271 (219d.)

19. Ibid., p. 271 (219e).

20. Ibid., p. 267 (217a).

21. La Rochefoucauld, *Maxims*, trans. Stuart D. Warner and Stéphane Douard (South Bend, IN: St. Augustine's Press, 2001), p. 17.

22. The following account will draw upon Ulrich von Liechtenstein, *The Service of Ladies*, trans. J.W. Thomas, intro. Kelly DeVries (Woodbridge, Suffolk, UK: Boydell Press, 2004).

23. The following account will refer to Chrétien de Troyes, *Lancelot, or The Knight of the Cart*, trans. Ruth Harwood Cline (Athens: University of Georgia Press, 1990).

24. Brothers Grimm, "Snow White," in *The Complete Fairy Tales of the Brothers Grimm*, trans. Jack Zipes (New York: Bantam Books, 1987), pp.181-8.

25. Brothers Grimm, *The Complete Fairy Tales*, pp. 193-6.

26. Ibid., pp. 669-670.

27. Ibid., p. 477.

28. Ibid.

29. Ibid.

30. Ibid., p. 480.

31. Georges Bizet adapted *Carmen*, the French opera, in 1875 from Prosper Mérimée's 1845 work of the same title. This paragraph will refer to Bizet's *Carmen*. *Bizet's Carmen*, trans. and intro. Ellen H. Bleiler (New York: Dover Publications, 1983).

32. Ibid., p. 64.

33. Siri Hustvedt, *A Plea for Eros: Essays* (New York: Picador, 2006).

34. Jane Austen, *Pride and Prejudice,* ed. and intro. Vivien Jones (New

York: Penguin, 2003); Emily Brontë, *Wuthering Heights*, ed. David Daiches (New York: Penguin, 1988).

35. Jane Austen, *Pride and Prejudice*, p. 186.

36. Emily Brontë, *Wuthering Heights*, p. 98.

37. Emily Dickinson, "No. 273," *The Complete Poems of Emily Dickinson*, ed. Thomas H. Johnson (Boston: Little, Brown, 1960), p. 124.

38. Richard B. Sewall, *The Life of Emily Dickinson* (New York: Farrar, Straus and Giroux, 1974), p. 518.

39. Emily Dickinson, *The Master Letters of Emily Dickinson*, ed. R.W. Franklin (Amherst, MA: Amherst College Press, 1986), p. 12.

40. Ibid.

41. Ibid., p. 15.

42. Ibid.

43. Ibid., p. 16.

44. Ibid., p. 19.

45. Ibid., p. 32. The order of Dickinson's Master Letters has been for some time in dispute. I am here following the order proposed by Dickinson's most important biographer, Richard Sewall. I find this order most convincing and organic even though I wish to quote the letter in this chapter not from Sewall's biography but rather from the collected master letters whose editor in fact, prefers a different order from Sewall's.

46. Ibid., p. 36.

47. Ibid., p. 39.

48. Ibid., p. 43.

49. Ibid., pp. 43-44.

50. Ibid., p. 36. My emphasis.

51. Ibid., p. 32.

52. Ibid., p. 39.

53. Ibid., pp. 43-44.

54. Ibid., p. 44.

55. Ibid., p. 29. My emphasis.

56. Ibid.

57. Ibid., p. 44.

58. Edna St. Vincent Millay, *Collected Poems*, ed. Norma Millay (New York: Harper & Row, 1956), p. 602. For biographical information on Edna St. Vincent Millay, see Nancy Milford, *Savage Beauty: The Life of Edna St. Vincent Millay* (New York: Random House, 2001).

59. Millay, *Collected Poems*, p. 127.

60. Eugen Boissevain, quoted in Daniel Mark Epstein, *What Lips My Lips Have Kissed: The Loves and Love Poems of Edna St. Vincent Millay* (New York: Henry Holt, 2001), p. 182.

61. Millay, *Collected Poems*, p. 571.

62. Maureen Dowd, *Are Men Necessary?: When Sexes Collide* (New York: G.P. Putnam's Sons, 2005).

THREE The Blade Between Us: *Love as Transgression*

1. Silesian proverb, qtd. by Christa F. Nehring, private conversation.

2. Beroul, *The Romance of Tristan*, cont. and ed. Alan S. Fedrick (New York: Penguin Classics, 1970); William Shakespeare, *A Midsummer Night's Dream* in *The Riverside Shakespeare*, ed. G. Blakemore Evans, et al. (Boston: Houghton Mifflin Co., 1974).

3. William Shakespeare, *A Midsummer Night's Dream* in *The Riverside Shakespeare*, ed. G. Blakemore Evans, et al. (Boston: Houghton Mifflin Co., 1974).

4. *Bizet's Carmen*, trans. and intro. Ellen H. Bleiler (New York: Dover Publications, 1983).

5. Nathaniel Hawthorne, *The Scarlet Letter*, ed. Brian Harding (Oxford, UK: Oxford University Press, 1998).

6. "Pyramus and Thisbe" in Edith Hamilton, *Mythology* (New York: Little, Brown and Co., 1999), pp. 105-7; William Shakespeare, *Romeo and Juliet*, in *The Riverside Shakespeare*; Brothers Grimm, "Rapunzel," in *The Complete Fairy Tales of the Brothers Grimm*, trans. Jack Zipes (New York: Bantam Books, 1987), 42-5.

7. Caitlin Flanagan, "Wifely Duty: Marriage Used to Provide Access to Sex. Now It Provides Access to Celibacy," *Atlantic Monthly* 291, no. 1 (Jan-Feb 2003): 172.

8. *Lost in Translation*. Dir. Sofia Coppola. Perfs. Bill Murray, Scarlett Johansson. Focus Features, 2003.

9. Wendy Shalit, *A Return to Modesty: Discovering the Lost Virtue* (New York: Simon & Schuster, 2000); Wendy Shalit, *Girls Gone Mild: Young Women Reclaim Self-Respect and Find It's Not Bad To Be Good* (New York: Random House, 2007); Edith Wharton, *The Age of Innocence* (New York: W.W. Norton & Co., Inc., 2003).

10. Peter Abelard and Heloise, *The Letters of Abelard and Heloise*, trans. Betty Radice (New York: Penguin, 2003); Chrétien de Troyes, *Lancelot, or The Knight of the Cart*, trans. Ruth Harwood Cline (Athens: University of Georgia Press, 1990); William Shakespeare, *Romeo and Juliet*, in *The Riverside Shakespeare*; William Shakespeare, *Antony and Cleopatra*,

in *The Riverside Shakespeare*; William Shakespeare, *Measure for Measure*, in *The Riverside Shakespeare*; Choderlos de Laclos, *Liaisons dangereuses* (Oxford, UK: Oxford University Press, 1998); Marquis de Sade, *The Complete Marquis de Sade*, ed. John S. Yankowski, trans. Paul J. Gillette (Los Angeles: Holloway House, 2005); Gustave Flaubert, *Madame Bovary* (1992, New York: Penguin Classics, 2003); Leo Tolstoy, *Anna Karenina* ed. John Bayley, trans. Richard Pevear and Larissa Volokhonsky (New York: Penguin Classics, 2003); Giacomo Casanova, *The Story of My Life* (2000, New York: Penguin Classics, 2001); Pauline Réage, *Story of O*, trans. John P. Hand (New York: Blue Moon Books, 1998).

11. Peter Abelard and Heloise, *The Letters of Abelard and Heloise*, trans. Betty Radice (New York: Penguin, 2003), p. 80.

12. William Shakespeare, *Romeo and Juliet*, in *The Riverside Shakespeare*, ed. G. Blakemore Evans, et al. (Boston: Houghton Mifflin Co., 1974), p. 1068 (2.2.33).

13. My emphasis. Ibid., p. 1068 (2.2.38-42).

14. Ibid., p. 1068 (2.2.71-2).

15. William Shakespeare, *Measure for Measure*, in *The Riverside Shakespeare*, p. 562 (2.2.179-85).

16. Denis de Rougemont, *Love in the Western World* (Princeton, NJ: Princeton University Press, 1983).

17. Ovid, *The Art of Love*, trans. Rolfe Humphries (Bloomington: Indiana University Press, 1957), p. 65.

18. Ibid., p. 66.

19. Ibid., p. 171.

20. Ibid., p. 170.

21. C.S. Lewis, *The Allegory of Love: A Study in Medieval Translation* (London: Oxford University Press, 1936, 1953), p. 2.

22. Ibid., pp. 2-3.

23. Béroul, *The Romance of Tristan*, ed. Alan S. Fedrick (New York: Penguin Classics, 1970).

24. Johann Wolfgang von Goethe, *Sorrows of Young Werther and Selected Writings*, trans. Catherine Hutter and intro. Hermann J. Weigand (New York: Signet, 1962).

25. Béroul, *The Romance of Tristan*, p. 64; Denis de Rougemont, *Love in the Western World*.

26. Ibid., p. 99.

27. Ibid., p. 113.

28. Ibid., p. 142.

29. Ibid., pp. 163-4

30. I shall leave the issue of separation in *Tristan* for the next chapter ("Love as Absence"), and limit my comments here to the subject of transgression.

31. Béroul, *The Romance of Tristan*, p. 163.

32. "To burn always with this hard, gemlike flame, to maintain this ecstasy, is success in life," in Walter Pater, *The Renaissance: Studies in Art and Poetry* (New York: The Macmillan Co, 1899), p. 250.

33. Béroul, *The Romance of Tristan*, p. 98.

34. Ibid., p. 142.

35. Denis de Rougemont, *Love in the Western World* (1939; Princeton, NJ: Princeton University Press, 1983), p. 41.

36. Ibid., pp. 232-3.

37. Esther Perel, author of the 2006 bestseller, *Mating in Captivity*, proposes that we go wild in bed, make animalistic noises, act savage, etc. At the same time the majority of her clients appear to live lives of exemplary success and prudence. Esther Perel, *Mating in Captivity* (New York: HarperCollins, 2006).

38. Denis de Rougemont, *Love in the Western World*, p. 287.

39. Simone de Beauvoir, *The Prime of Life*, trans. Peter Green (Cleveland and New York: The World Publishing Co., 1962), p. 24.

40. Simone de Beauvoir, *Letters to Sartre* (New York: Arcade, 1993), p. 255.

41. Sartre, *Witness to My Life: The Letters of Jean-Paul Sartre to Simone de Beauvoir*, trans. Lee Fahnestock and Norman MacAfee (New York: Charles Scribner's Sons, 1992), p. 200.

42. Hazel Rowley, *Tête-à-Tête: Simone de Beauvoir and Jean-Paul Sartre* (New York: HarperCollins, 2005), pp. 58-61, 175-7, 214-223.

43. Nancy Milford, *Savage Beauty: The Life of Edna St. Vincent Millay* (New York: Random House, 2001).

44. Ibid., 358-9.

45. Ibid., 349.

46. Edna St. Vincent Millay, *Collected Poems*, ed. Norma Millay (New York: Harper & Row, 1956) p. 631.

47. Nancy Milford, *Savage Beauty*, p. 273.

FOUR **There Must Be Two Before There Can Be One:**
Love as Absence

1. Ralph Waldo Emerson, "Friendship," in *Essays and Lectures* (New York:

Penguin Putnam, 1983). My adaptation. The original reads: "There must be very two before there can be very one. . . ."

2. John Fowles, *The Magus* (Boston: Little, Brown, 1966), p. 103.

3. Antoine de Saint-Exupéry, *The Wisdom of the Sands* (New York: Harcourt, Brace & Co, 1950), p. 145.

4. Denis de Rougemont, *Love in the Western World*, trans. Stuart Gilbert (1939; Princeton, NJ: Princeton University Press, 1983), p. 37.

5. Michael Palmer writes this in the front flap of Dante Alighieri, *The New Life* (New York: New York Review Books, 2002).

6. Dante Alighieri, *The Divine Comedy*, trans. John Ciardi (New York: Penguin Group, 2003).

7. Dante Alighieri, *New Life*, trans. J.G. Nichols (London: Hesperus Press, 2003), p. 3.

8. Ibid.

9. Louis de Bernières, Foreword to Dante Alighieri, *New Life* (London: Hesperus Press, 2003), xiii.

10. Dante Alighieri, *New Life*, p. 5.

11. Ibid., pp. 64 and 66.

12. Denis de Rougemont, *Love in the Western World*, p. 37.

13. Dante Alighieri, *New Life*, p. 7.

14. Ibid., p. 9.

15. Ibid.

16. Ibid., p. 10.

17. Ibid., p. 12.

18. Ibid.

19. Ibid., p. 14.

20. Ibid., p. 15.

21. Ibid., p. 27.

22. Ibid., p. 39.

23. Ibid., p. 38.

24. Ibid., pp. 51-2.

25. Ibid., p. 52.

26. Ibid.

27. Ibid., p. 53.

28. Ibid.

29. Ibid., p. 65.

30. Dante Alighieri, *La Vita Nuova*, trans. Barbara Reynolds (New York: Penguin Group, 2004), pp. 11-12.

31. Ibid., p. 73. My emphasis.

32. Ibid.

33. Ellen Fein and Sherrie Schneider, *The Rules: Time-Tested Secrets for Capturing the Heart of Mr. Right* (1995; New York: Grand Central Publishing, 2007).

34. Ralph Waldo Emerson, "Love," in *Essays and Lectures* (New York, Penguin Putnam, 1983).

35. Ralph Waldo Emerson, "Friendship," in *Essays and Lectures* (New York, Penguin Putnam, 1983), p. 351.

36. Ibid.

37. Ibid., p. 353.

38. Eve Ensler, *The Vagina Monologues* (New York: Villard Books, 2001).

39. Ralph Waldo Emerson, "Friendship," p. 351.

40. Lyndall Gordon, *Vindication: A Life of Mary Wollstonecraft* (New York: HarperCollins, 2005), pp. 332-3.

41. Ibid., p. 320.

42. Ralph Waldo Emerson, "Friendship," p. 350.

43. Diego Rivera and Gladys March, *My Art, My Life: An Autobiography* (New York: Citadel Press, 1960), p. 242.

44. Emily Dickinson, "No. 872," *The Complete Poems of Emily Dickinson*, ed. Thomas H. Johnson (Boston: Little, Brown and Co., 1960), p. 415.

45. Ibid., "No. 640," p. 317.

46. Ibid.

47. Richard B. Sewall, *The Life of Emily Dickinson, Vol. 2* (New York: Farrar, Straus and Giroux, 1974), pp. 563-4.

48. Thomas Wentworth Higginson, quoted in Richard B. Sewall, *The Life of Emily Dickinson, Vol. 2* (New York: Farrar, Straus and Giroux, 1974), p. 539.

49. Emily Dickinson, "No. 97," *The Complete Poems of Emily Dickinson*, p. 35.

50. Thomas Wentworth Higginson, in Richard B. Sewall, *Life of Emily Dickinson*, p. 655.

51. Ibid., p. 450.

52. Emily Dickinson, "No. 239," *The Complete Poems of Emily Dickinson*, p. 109.

53. Rainer Maria Rilke, *Rilke on Love and Other Difficulties: Translations*

and Considerations of Rainer Maria Rilke (1975, New York: W.W. Norton & Co, 2004), p. 28.

54. Luke 15:11-32.

55. Ralph Waldo Emerson, "Friendship," p. 350-1.

56. Daude de Pradas, in Morton M. Hunt, *The Natural History of Love*, p. 142.

FIVE **"On My Blood I'll Carry You Away":** *Love as Heroism*

1. Translation by William H. Gass. Ibid., p. 53-4.

2. Greg Behrendt and Liz Tuccillo, *He's Just Not That Into You: The No-Excuses Guide to Understanding Guys* (New York, Simon & Schuster, 2004), p. 16.

3. Dr. Connell Cowan and Dr. Melvyn Kinder, *Smart Women/Foolish Choices: Finding the Right Men Avoiding the Wrong Ones* (New York: Signet, 1986), p. 90.

4. Greg Behrendt and Liz Tuccillo, *He's Just Not That Into You*, p. 17.

5. Dr. Connell Cowan and Dr. Melvyn Kinder, *Smart Women/Foolish Choices*, pp. 104-6.

6. Ovid, *The Art of Love*, trans. Rolfe Humphries (Bloomington: Indiana University Press, 1957).

7. Ibid., p.137.

8. Rolfe Humphries, "Introduction," in Ovid, *The Art of Love*, pp. 5-7.

9. Ovid, *Metamorphoses*, trans. David Raeburn (New York: Penguin, 2004).

10. The original statement, from Samuel Johnson's "Preface" in his 1765 edition of Shakespeare, is: "A quibble was to him the fatal apple for which he was content to lose heaven, or stoop from his elevation." Heather James, *Shakespeare's Troy: Drama, Politics, and the Translation of Empire* (Cambridge, UK: Cambridge University Press, 1997), p. 3.

11. Ovid, *The Art of Love*, p. 80.

12. Ibid., p. 74. My emphasis.

13. Ibid., p. 15.

14. Ibid., p. 29.

15. Ibid., p. 30.

16. Ibid., p. 130.

17. M.H. Abrams, ed., *The Norton Anthology of English Literature*, 5th Ed., *Vol. 1* (1962; New York: W.W. Norton & Co., 1986), p. 93.

18. Quotations have been modernized by the author. When I have employed a different word to express the Wife of Bath's meaning than

she uses it appears in brackets, except when it is the word suggested in the margin by the editor, in which case I have simply substituted it into the text. Geoffrey Chaucer, *The Canterbury Tales*, ed. V.A. Kolve and Glending Olson (New York: W.W. Norton & Co., 2005), p. 102 (l. 6-8).

19. Ibid., p. 102 (l. 9-13).

20. Ibid., p. 102 (l. 26, 28-9).

21. Ibid., p. 105 (l.152, 158-9). My emphasis.

22. Ibid., p. 104 (l. 105, 110-11).

23. Ibid., p. 107 (l. 223).

24. Ibid., p. 113 (l. 489).

25. Ibid., p. 107 (l. 207-8).

26. Ibid., p. 114 (l. 549).

27. Ibid., p. 115 (l. 578-9).

28. Ibid., p. 115 (l. 580-1).

29. Ibid., p. 116 (l. 632-3).

30. Ibid., p. 113 (l. 506-7).

31. *New Life,* J. G. Nichols, translator, p. 116 (l. 637).

32. Ibid., p. 117 (l. 680).

33. Op. Cit., p. 120 (l. 788-93).

34. Op. Cit., p. 120 (l. 795-8).

35. Op. Cit., (l. 800).

36. Op. Cit., (l. 802).

37. Op. Cit., (l. 805).

38. Op. Cit., (l. 818).

39. Op. Cit., (l. 814-5).

40. William Shakespeare, *Antony and Cleopatra*, in *The Riverside Shakespeare*, ed. G. Blakemore Evans, et al. (Boston: Houghton Mifflin Co., 1974), p. 1351 (1.3.9-10).

41. Ibid., p. 1370 (3.11.57-61).

42. Ibid. (3.12.59 and 66-7). My emphasis.

43. Ibid., p. 1380 (4.15.16).

44. Ibid., p. 1381 (4.15.65-8).

45. Ibid. (4.15.76-8).

46. Ibid., p. 1380 (4.15.22 and 30).

47. Ibid. (4.15.32).

48. Ibid., p. 1381 (4.15.68).

49. Homer, *The Iliad*, trans. Richmond Lattimore (Chicago: University of Chicago Press, 1961); *The Odyssey*, trans. Richmond Lattimore (New York: HarperCollins, 1999).

50. The reference book that Kleist consulted is Benjamin Hederich's *Mythological Lexicon*, published in 1724.

51. First published in Germany in 1808. Heinrich von Kleist, *Penthesilea*, trans. Joel Agee (New York: HarperCollins, 2000).

52. This fact and the account that follows can be found in the introduction of Kleist, *Penthesilea*, trans. Joel Agee.

53. Ibid., p. 3.

54. Ibid., p.38.

55. Ibid., p.38.

56. Ibid., p. 38.

57. Ibid., p. 56.

58. Ibid.

59. Ibid., p. 60.

60. Ibid., pp. 141-2

61. Ibid., p. 161.

62. Ibid., p. 162.

63. Ibid.

64. Ibid., p. 164.

65. Percy B. Shelley, Kenneth Neill Cameron, editor, *Shelley and His Circle 1773-1822* (Cambridge, MA: Harvard University Press, 1961), p. 955.

66. Mary Wollstonecraft, *A Vindication of the Rights of Men*, in *A Wollstonecraft Anthology*, Janet Todd, ed. (Bloomington: Indiana University Press, 1977), pp. 73, 82-3.

67. Mary Wollstonecraft, *A Vindication of the Rights of Woman* (1972; New York: Penguin Classics, 1992), p. 50.

68. Ibid., p. 39.

69. Ibid.

70. Ibid., p. 57.

71. Ibid., p. 58.

72. Mary Wollstonecraft, Letter XLIV to Gilbert Imlay, *Collected Letters of Mary Wollstonecraft*, ed. R. Wardle (Ithaca, NY: Cornell University Press, 1979), p. 291.

73. Lyndall Gordon, *Vindication: A Life of Mary Wollstonecraft* (New York: HarperCollins, 2005), p. 144.

74. William Godwin in Lyndall Gordon, *Vindication: A Life of Mary Woll-stonecraft*, p. 290.

75. Ibid., p. 312.

76. Ibid., p. 313.

77. Ibid., p. 314.

78. William Godwin, *Memoirs of Mary Wollstonecraft Godwin*, quoted in Todd, *A Wollstonecraft Anthology*, p. 16.

79. Janet Todd, *Mary Wollstonecraft: A Revolutionary Life* (New York: Columbia University Press, 2000), p. 356.

80. Lyndall Gordon, *Vindication: A Life of Mary Wollstonecraft*, p. 315.

81. "The Vision of Liberty," *Anti-Jacobin Review and Magazine* IX (1801), in Todd, *A Wollstonecraft Anthology*, p. 17.

82. G.R. Stirling Taylor, *Mary Wollstonecraft: A Study in Economics and Romance* (London: Martin Secker, 1911), p. 63.

83. My emphasis. Todd, *A Wollstonecraft Anthology*. A notable exception to the trend in tepid 20th-21st-century Wollstonecraft biographies is Lyndall Gordon's excellent *Vindication: A Life of Mary Wollstonecraft* (New York: HarperCollins, 2005).

84. Mary Wollstonecraft and Gilbert Imlay, *Letters Written During a Short Residence in Sweden, Norway, and Denmark* (London: J. Johnson, 1796), p. 214.

85. Janet Todd, *Mary Wollstonecraft: A Revolutionary Life* (New York: Columbia University Press, 2000), p. 160.

SIX "Anonymous Except for Injury": *Love as Failure*

1. Dana Gioia, "Counting the Children," in *The Gods of Winter* (Saint Paul, MN: Graywolf, 1991).

2. Jorge Luis Borges, quoted in Yasmina Reza, *L'Aube le soir ou la nuit* (Paris: Flammarion, 2007), p. 17. My translation.

3. Dante, *New Life*, p. 46.

4. Quoted in Morton M. Hunt, *The Natural History of Love* (New York: Alfred A. Knopf, 1959), p. 143.

5. Peter Abelard and Heloise, *The Letters of Abelard and Heloise*, trans. Betty Radice (New York: Penguin, 2003), p. 51.

6. Ibid.

7. Ibid., p. 14.

8. Ibid., p. 51.

9. Ibid., p. 11.

10. Ibid.

11. Ibid., p. 16.

12. Ibid., p. 80.

13. Ibid., p. 17.

14. Ibid.

15. Ibid., p. 18.

16. Ibid., p. 54.

17. Ibid., p. 3.

18. Ibid., pp. 40-1.

19. Ibid., p. 47.

20. Ibid., p. 50.

21. My emphasis. Ibid., p. 54.

22. My emphasis. Ibid.

23. Ibid., p. 56.

24. Ibid.

25. Ibid., p. 62.

26. Ibid.

27. Ibid., p. 65.

28. Ibid., p. 68.

29. Ibid., p. 69.

30. Ibid.

31. Ibid.

32. Stevie Smith, "Not Waving But Drowning," *The Collected Poems of Stevie Smith* (London: Allen Lane, 1975), p.111.

33. My emphasis, *Abelard and Heloise*, p. 70.

34. Ibid., p. 79.

35. Ibid., p. 81.

36. Ibid., p. 79.

37. Ibid., p. 84.

38. Ibid.

39. "The Arundel Tomb," in Philip Larkin, *Collected Poems*, ed. and intro. Anthony Thwaite (London: Faber and Faber, 2003), p. 111.

40. Peter Abelard and Heloise, *Abelard and Heloise*, p. 93.

41. Ibid., p. 94.

42. Ibid., p. 147.

43. Constant J. Mews, interview with Rachel Kohn, ABC Radio (Australia), 13 Feb. 2000. Also see Constant J. Mews, *The Lost Love Letters of Heloise and Abelard: Perceptions of Dialogue in Twelfth-century France*,

trans. Neville Chiavaroli and Constant J. Mews (New York: Palgrave, 2001).

44. Peter Abelard and Heloise, *Abelard and Heloise*, p. 51.

45. Johann Wolfgang von Goethe, *Faust, Parts 1 and 2*, ed. Cyrus Hamlin, trans. Walter Arndt (New York: W.W. Norton & Co, 2000).

46. Johann Wolfgang von Goethe, *Sorrows of Young Werther and Selected Writings*, trans. Catherine Hutter and intro. Hermann J. Weigand (New York: Signet, 1962), p. 8.

47. Ibid., p. 26.

48. Ibid., p. 60.

49. Ibid., p. 82.

50. Ibid., p. 35.

51. Ibid., p. 54.

52. Ibid., p. 57.

53. Ibid., p. 55.

54. Ibid., pp. 43, 108.

55. Ibid., p. 50.

56. Ibid., p. 30-1.

57. Ibid., p. 122.

58. Ibid., p. 127.

59. Ibid.

60. Ibid., p. 124.

61. Ibid.

62. Ibid., p. 131.

63. Etienne Gilson, *Heloise and Abelard* (Ann Arbor: University of Michigan Press, 1960), xiii.

64. Petrarch, "Poem 133," *Petrarch's Lyric Poems: The Rima Sparse and Other Lyrics*, ed. Robert M. Durling (Cambridge, MA: Harvard University Press, 1976), p. 270.

65. Goethe, *Sorrows of Young Werther*, p. 85.

66. Ibid., p. 78.

67. My translation. "Alles geben die Goetter ihren Lieblingen ganz; alle Freuden die Unendlichen, alle Schmerzen die Unendlichen—ganz." Johann Wolfgang von Goethe, "Brief an Graefin Auguste zu Stolberg," in Werke, *Vol. 1: Gedichte und Epen*, ed. Erich Trunz (Hamburg: Christian Wegner Verlag, 1964), p. 142.

68. Lyndall Gordon, *Vindication: A Life of Mary Wollstonecraft* (New York: HarperCollins, 2005), pp. 364, 369-70.

69. Bell Gale Chevigny, *The Woman and the Myth: Margaret Fuller's Life and Writings* (Boston: Northeastern University Press, 1994), p. 142.

70. Bronson Alcott, in Perry Miller, *Margaret Fuller: American Romantic* (Ithaca, NY: Cornell University Press, 1963), xxi.

71. Ibid., ix.

72. Ibid., x.

73. Thomas Wentworth Higginson, *Margaret Fuller Ossoli* (American Men of Letters series), (Boston: Houghton Mifflin, and Co., 1884), pp. 290-1.

74. Margaret Fuller, "Bettine Brentano und Guenderode," *The Dial: A Magazine for Literature, Philosophy, and Religion*, Vol. II (Boston: E.P. Peabody, 1842), p. 19.

75. Margaret Fuller, *Woman in the Nineteenth Century*, ed. Larry J. Reynolds (New York: W.W. Norton & Co., 1997).

76. William Henry Channing, in *Margaret Fuller, American Romantic*, ed. Perry Miller (Ithaca, NY: Cornell University Press, 1963), p. xix.

77. Margaret Fuller's diary quoted in Laurie James, *Men, Women, and Margaret Fuller* (New York: Golden Heritage Press, 1990), p. 51.

78. Ibid., p. 189.

79. Ibid., p. 184.

80. Margaret Fuller, *The Letters of Margaret Fuller, Vol. 2*, ed. Robert N. Hudspeth (Ithaca, NY: Cornell University Press, 1983), p. 81.

81. Ibid., p. 90.

82. Ibid.

83. Elizabeth Bishop, *The Complete Poems, 1927–1979* (New York: Farrar, Straus and Giroux, 1984).

84. Margaret Fuller, *The Letters of Margaret Fuller, Vol. 3*, p. 209.

85. Margaret Fuller, *The Letters of Margaret Fuller, Vol. 2*, p. 32.

86. Ibid.

87. Ralph Waldo Emerson, *Selected Writings of Ralph Waldo Emerson*, ed. William H. Gilman and intro. Dr. Charles Johnson (New York: Penguin, 2003), p. 52.

88. Charles Capper, *Margaret Fuller: An American Romantic Life: The Private Years, Vol. I* (New York: Oxford University Press, 1994), xii.

89. Margaret Fuller, *The Letters of Margaret Fuller, Vol. 3*, p. 211.

90. Bettina von Arnim, Johann Wolfgang von Goethe, *Correspondence with a Child* (Lowell, MA: Daniel Bixby, 1841).

91. Ibid., p. 316-7.

92. Ralph Waldo Emerson, *The Letters of Ralph Waldo Emerson*, ed. Ralph L. Rusk (New York: Columbia University Press, 1991).

93. Ralph Waldo Emerson, *The Collected Works of Ralph Waldo Emerson, Vol. 5: English Traits* (Cambridge, MA: Harvard University Press, 1994), p. xl.

94. Ralph Waldo Emerson, *The Letters of Ralph Waldo Emerson*, p. 236.

95. Ibid.

96. Ibid.

97. Ibid., p. 235.

98. Ibid.

99. Ralph Waldo Emerson, *Journals*, quoted in Laurie James, *Men, Women, and Margaret Fuller*, p. 325.

100. Margaret Fuller, *The Letters of Margaret Fuller, Vol. 4*, p. 50.

101. Ibid., p. 73.

102. Ibid., p. 95.

103. Ibid., p. 96.

104. Ibid., p. 93.

105. Ibid., p. 162.

106. Margaret Fuller, *Summer on the Lakes* (Urbana and Chicago: University of Illinois Press, 1991), p. 61.

107. Laurie James, *Men, Women, and Margaret Fuller*, p. 184.

108. Ralph Waldo Emerson, W.H. Channing, and J.F. Clarke, *Memoirs of Margaret Fuller Ossoli, Vol. I* (Boston: Roberts Brothers, 1884), p. 296.

109. September 25, 1840. Ralph Waldo Emerson, *The Letters of Ralph Waldo Emerson*, p. 227.

110. Bell Gale Chevigny, *The Woman and the Myth: Margaret Fuller's Life and Writings* (Boston: Northeastern University Press, 1994), p. 106.

111. October 21, 1849. Margaret Fuller, *My Heart Is a Large Kingdom: Selected Letters of Margaret Fuller*, ed. Robert N. Hudspeth (Ithaca, NY: Cornell University Press, 2001), p. 305.

112. "There is evidence that while the Elizabeth was breaking upon the rocks of Fire Island on July 19, 1850, she herself might have been rescued had she wanted to make the effort. If this is so then in full view of America, she elected to perish with her husband and baby." The form of this evidence is under dispute, but it is alluded to in Fuller scholarship time and again, perhaps most resonantly in Perry Miller, *Margaret Fuller: American Romantic* (Ithaca, NY: Cornell University Press, 1963), xxviii.

113. "Rezsoe Seres Commits Suicide; Composer of 'Gloomy Sunday'," *New York Times* (January 14, 1968, Sunday), p. 84.

114. Jean-Paul Sartre, *Words*, trans. Bernard Frechtman (New York: Fawcett World Library, 1966), p. 40.

115. Claude Lanzmann, quoted in Hazel Rowley, *Tête-à-Tête: Simone de Beauvoir and Jean-Paul Sartre* (New York: HarperCollins, 2005), p. 220.

116. Margaret Fuller, "Bettine Brentano und Guenderode," in *The Dial: A Magazine for Literature, Philosophy, and Religion, Vol. II* (Boston: E.P. Peabody, 1842), p. 322.

SEVEN Carving In the Flesh: *Love as Art*

1. Rainer Maria Rilke, *On Love and Other Difficulties: Translations and Considerations of Rainer Maria Rilke* (New York: W.W. Norton & Co., 2004), p. 62.

2. José Ortega y Gasset, *On Love*, trans. Tony Talbot (New York: Meridian, 1957), p. 25.

3. Simone de Beauvoir, *The Second Sex* (New York: Vintage Books, 1989), p. 657.

4. Stendhal, *Love*, trans. Gilbert and Suzanne Sale (New York: Penguin Books, 1975), p. 57.

5. The quote in Horace Walpole's letters reads, "This world is a comedy to those who think, and a tragedy to those who feel!" Horace Walpole, *The Letters of Horace Walpole, Earl of Oxford*, ed. Peter Cunningham (London: Richard Bentley, 1858), p. 501.

6. Samuel Richardson, *Clarissa: Or the History of a Young Lady*, ed. Angus Ross (New York: Penguin, 1986); *Pamela: Or Virtue Rewarded*, ed. Thomas Keymer and Alice Wakely (Oxford, UK: Oxford University Press, 2001); Gabriel García Márquez, *Love in the Time of Cholera* (New York: Penguin Books, 1988).

7. Nicole Krauss, *The History of Love: A Novel* (New York: W.W. Norton & Co., 2005).

8. Lytton Strachey, in *Madame du Deffand and her World*, by Benedetta Cravieri, trans. Teresa Waugh (Boston: David R. Godine, 1994), p. 259. First published in Milan, Italy in 1982.

9. Horace Walpole to H.S. Conway, January 12, 1766, in *Horace Walpole's Correspondence*, Vol. 39, ed. W.S. Lewis (New Haven, CT: Yale University Press, 1974), p. 42.

10. Cravieri, *Madame du Deffand and her World*, p. 268.

11. Ibid., pp. 264-5.

12. Madame du Deffand to Horace Walpole, April 19, 1766 in *Horace Wal-*

pole's Correspondence with Madame du Deffand and Wiart, ed. W.S. Lewis and W.H. Smith (New Haven, CT: Yale University Press, 1939), pp. 3-6.

13. Madame du Deffand to Horace Walpole, April 21, 1766, in ibid., p. 7.

14. Translation slightly modified by author. Ibid., p. 281.

15. Madame du Deffand to Horace Walpole, May 14, 1766, in ibid., p. 37.

16. Horace Walpole to Madame du Deffand, May 20, 1766, in ibid., p. 44.

17. Madame du Deffand to Horace Walpole, May 25, 1766, in ibid., p. 52.

18. Portrait of Horace Walpole by Madame du Deffand dated November 1766, in ibid., p. 72.

19. Ibid., p. 73.

20. Madame du Deffand to Horace Walpole, April 4, 1767, in ibid., p. 279.

21. Ibid.

22. Alfred de Musset to George Sand, July 1833, in *Correspondance de George Sand et d'Alfred de Musset*, ed. Louis Evrard (Monaco: Editions de Rocher, 1956), p. 27-8. Dan Hofstadter discusses the Sand-Musset relationship in *The Love Affair as a Work of Art* (New York: Farrar, Straus and Giroux, 1996), p. 136. I have found Hofstadter's discussion of love letters-as-art in general and George Sand's correspondence in particular very useful in this chapter. I do, however, disagree with him in several areas of both discussions. I disagree with him first of all about the fundamental artistic distinction between paper letters and present-day e-mails, believing as I do that a brilliant e-mailer is a brilliant letter-writer and a sloppy or clichéd e-mailer is a sloppy or clichéd letter-writer. If George Sand were alive today she would, I am confident, put the same number and quality of thoughts into a cyber-communication as she did between the too-much-romanticized leaves of an eighteenth-century letter.

I also disagree with Hofstadter on George Sand's fundamental dishonesty. Hofstadter makes a very great deal out of what seems to me a fairly small footnote: that George Sand lightly revised a small handful of the letters in her prodigious (25-volume!) correspondence before releasing them for publication. Given the sharp limelight and self-consciousness in which she lived, together with the superabundance of her publishing, this is hardly unexpected or sinister. That she revised these letters to cast herself in a subtly more moral light than she otherwise might have enjoyed also stands to reason. The alterations she made seem fairly modest: the fact of which Hofstadter makes most—that she implies she began cheating on Alfred de Musset a few weeks after she in fact started cheating on him—seems to me less shocking than it does to him. What is extraordinary about the Sand-

Musset correspondence is surely not how much it leaves out but how (extremely) much it includes. As it stands today, it is one of the most compromising, pornographically explicit, morally tolerant, and soul-searching correspondences ever published.

23. Sand to Sainte-Beuve, August 25, 1833, in *Correspondence de George Sand*, Vol. II ed. Georges Lubin (Paris: Garnier Frères, 1966), p. 407.

24. George Sand, quoted in Belinda Jack, *George Sand: A Woman's Life Writ Large* (London: Chatto and Windus, 1999), p. 230.

25. Sand, quoted in Hofstadter, *The Love Affair as a Work of Art*, p. 151.

26. George Sand, *Correspondance de George Sand et d'Alfred de Musset* (Bruxelles: E. Deman, 1904), p. 25.

27. Alfred de Musset, *The Confession of a Child of the Century*, trans. Kendall Warren (Chicago: C. H. Sergel, 1892); George Sand, *Elle et lui* (Paris: Michel Lévy Frères, 1869).

28. George Sand, *Correspondance de George Sand et d'Alfred de Musset*, p. 25.

29. Sand to Musset, April 15, 1834, in *Correspondance de George Sand, Vol II*, p. 563.

30. Sand, quoted in Hofstadter, *The Love Affair as a Work of Art*, p. 151.

31. Sand, quoted in ibid., p. 141.

32. Musset to Sand, April 30, 1834, in *Correspondance de George Sand et d'Alfred de Musset*, p. 56.

33. Ibid.

34. Sand, quoted in Hofstadter, *The Love Affair as a Work of Art*, p. 148.

35. Hayden Herrera, *Frida: A Biography of Frida Kahlo* (New York: HarperCollins, 1983), p. 408.

36. Ibid., xii.

37. Ibid., p. 107.

38. Ibid., p. 87.

39. Ibid., p. 94.

40. Ibid., p. 107.

41. Hayden Herrera, *Frida*, p. 98.

42. Ibid., p. 237-8.

43. Ella Wolfe quoting Diego Rivera, ibid., p. 366.

44. Ibid., p. 371.

45. The Academy Award-winning film *Frida*, based largely but not completely on Hayden Herrera's biography (1983), suggests Diego and Cristina slept together once, were caught, and desisted. This is not the case.

46. Hayden Herrera, *Frida*, p. 416.

47. Ibid., p. 360.

48. Ibid., p. 362.

49. Ibid., p. 378.

50. Ibid., p. 379.

51. Ibid., p. 362.

52. Carolyn Heilbrun, *Writing a Woman's Life* (New York: W.W. Norton, 1988), p. 48.

53. While this sentence is widely attributed to Jean-Paul Sartre, I have been unable to find a source for it in his writings.

54. Hannah Arendt and eds. Joanna Vecchiarelli Scott, Judith Chelius Stark, *Love and Saint Augustine* (Chicago: University of Chicago Press, 1996).

55. My emphasis. Alfred Kazin, *New York Jew* (New York: Random House, 1978), pp. 303-4.

56. Elisabeth Young-Bruehl, *Hannah Arendt: For Love of the World* (New Haven, CT: Yale University Press, 2004), p. 271.

57. Ibid., p. 265.

58. Ibid., p. 267.

59. Ibid., p. 247.

60. Ibid., p. 265.

61. Ibid.; Honoré de Balzac, *La Comédie Humaine*, trans. Anatole Cerfberr (Philadelphia: G. Barrie & Son, 1987), p. 33.

62. John Milton, "Apology to Smectynius" in *Selected Prose Writings of John Milton*, intro. Ernest Myers (New York: D. Appleton and Co., 1884), pp. 59-67.

Waging Love: *Toward a New Definition of Eros*

1. Katha Pollitt, *Learning to Drive and Other Life Stories* (New York: Random House, 2007).

2. Susan Salter Reynolds, "And Another Thing; Learning to Drive and Other Life Stories," *Los Angeles Times Book Review*, September 9, 2007, p. 7.

3. Toni Bentley, "Life, and My Evil Ex-Boyfriend," *New York Times Book Review*, September 23, 2007, p. 17.

4. Daphne de Marneffe, *Maternal Desire: On Children, Love, and the Inner Life* (New York: Little, Brown and Company, 2004).

5. J.M. Coetzee, *Diary of a Bad Year* (New York: Penguin, 2007), p. 138.

6. C.S. Lewis, *The Allegory of Love: A Study in Medieval Translation* (London: Oxford University Press, 1953), p. 11.

Index

About the author

About the book

Read on

Insights,
Interviews
& More ...

Meet Cristina Nehring

Russell Jacoby

CRISTINA NEHRING grew up in Los Angeles, Switzerland, and Germany, and now lives in Paris, France. She is an award-winning essayist, literary critic, and travel writer, known for her fiery polemics and frequently contrarian positions. Trained as a Shakespearean and specialist of sixteenth- and seventeenth-century love poetry, her own loves have taken her from the limestone cliffs of northern England to the red shores of southern France and the black-clad mountains of western Crete. In 2008, she gave birth to an adored daughter, Eurydice Rafaella, whose battle with childhood leukemia is the inspiration for her current work: a book of provisional wisdom. ∾

On Writing
A Vindication of Love

I WROTE *A VINDICATION OF LOVE*
largely on an island in Greece.
I remember long afternoons huddled
over notes in a seaside café where
people ate barefoot and kids deposited
their inflatable plastic swans. As
darkness fell, I would duck into hotel
lobbies, fondling the walls behind
couches in search of electric outlets
into which to plug my tiny Mac.
I typed away among the hotel guests,
deleting, reformulating, ordering a
glass of wine to justify my presence
and tame my inner editor. Come 2 a.m.,
I flashed what I hoped was a winning
smile at the janitorial staff and darted
into the night to meet my boyfriend.

He was a waiter at a local taverna—
a beauty of a boy, proud and original
and difficult. Since coming to western
Crete to be at his side, I'd lived a double
life. Nobody here knew I was a writer.
I knew no *other* writer. I knew no
other reader, as a matter of fact. My
boyfriend's home did not contain a
single book when I moved in—nor
did it have a desk. It did, however,
accommodate two or three chickens
that wandered in and out from the
neighboring coop. My LaserJet printer
rested on top of his washing machine
and rattled when he cleaned his white
shirts for work.

A mentor in the U.S. informed me ▶

I was committing "career suicide." As a first-time author, I could not afford to disappear so entirely from the public sphere before I had ever, well, entered it.

I was as shocked as anyone when the book on which I had labored on the periphery of the literate world landed on the cover of the *New York Times Book Review*. This does not mean that I had not tried to write it in a way that would reach people; that could challenge, fundamentally, the way we think about our love lives in contemporary society. As my *Times* reviewer noted with wry indulgence: "This is not a book without ambition." Isn't. Wrongly or rightly, I felt I had something urgent to say to my fellow women and men. If I had to speak to them from hiding, I would not be the first. If I had to speak while practicing what I preached (while risking all for love, as per my book), I hoped I wouldn't be the last.

The fact, however, that I was actually heard has given me a faith in the "process" I might never otherwise have had. It has seemed to me a miracle that so many readers—public and private—have attended to and embraced and adapted and improvised upon my arguments in *Vindication*. I have received letters from men and women that bear witness to the fact that romantic idealism is alive and active in the hearts of both sexes. I have pored over reviews that have inspired and taught me. I have learned from my readers of poems which have become closely-held favorites—like the Jack Gilbert poem quoted in *Slate* by Meghan O'Rourke: "Nobody remembers that Icarus also flew." Indeed, we don't remember—but we should. For to burn one's wings on the sun, one has to see a hell of a lot of light. It may be worth it.

If *Vindication* was read and understood, it was also misread and misunderstood, sometimes grievously. This is not too surprising, inasmuch as I intended to provoke, to unsettle, to puncture contemporary pieties. While maintaining an overarching argument about the need to reclaim, reheroize, and reinvent romantic love for our (post-hedonist, post-feminist) age, I tried to introduce, in every chapter, a discrete sub-argument. Each one of these arguments was selected as much to offset a present-day excess, to topple some sacred cow in our common conceptual barnyard, as it was to erect an alternative model of love. Thus, for instance, one chapter (*Love as Wisdom*) attacks the cliché of romantic passion as irrationality. Another (*Love as Heroism*) takes aim at the contemporary cult of safe sex, and safe love. A third (*Love as Inequality*) questions our knee-jerk ▶

criminalization of power differences in a relationship; a fourth (*Love as Failure*) attempts to widen the narrow notion we have of amorous "success." A final chapter (*Love as Art*) posits that love is not the *distraction* from feminist, political, and artistic achievement we are often told, but possibly the highest form of such achievement.

A number of critics seem to have noticed only one or another of these several arguments—and to have distorted that one beyond recognition. Thus the philosopher, Martha Nussbaum, believes I want everybody to fail—i.e. to kill themselves and die for love. Writing a 4,000-word piece on *Vindication* for the *New Republic*, she insists the book is an ode to suffering. A Texas college instructor writing for the *Philadelphia Enquirer* claims I want to return to a system of gender discrimination in which men "lord" it over women—inexplicably ignoring the fact that the vast majority of examples evoked in my discussion of power show women "lording it over" men. Thanks to misapprehensions like these, some people have wondered if *Vindication* is anti-feminist.

In fact, *Vindication* takes its title from the woman generally considered the mother of modern feminism, Mary Wollstonecraft, whose *A Vindication of the Rights of Woman* inaugurated the women's movement in the eighteenth century. If I sometimes criticize Wollstonecraft's followers *for joining hands with patriarchal bigots* and mocking their own sisters for falling in love, it is not in order to renounce feminism, but in order to reclaim feminism for full-hearted contemporary women and men. It is not to turn the movement backward, but to take it forward, to nudge it past the anti-romantic bias in which it has occasionally been entangled—almost always in direct contradiction to the personal example of its pioneers, who, like Wollstonecraft, Margaret Fuller, Frida Kahlo, Simone de Beauvoir, and even the medieval Heloise, were surprisingly often lovers as ardently as they were writers, revolutionaries, explorers, and artists.

But perhaps the worst misunderstandings of *Vindication* come from individuals who have never laid eyes on it. This may be the curse of our blog-around-the-clock age: people no longer take the time to read (or even locate) a book before they pronounce upon it on their personal opinion page. I have had many an entrepreneurial and eloquent blogger admit to me in confidence that he had not, in fact, seen the book at the time he publically dubbed it a "defense of rash flings" or a celebration of short-term dalliances with "mustachioed strangers." These same bloggers also have told me ▸

many things I didn't know about my biography—that I'm recently divorced, having an affair behind my husband's back, regretting my decisions as I travel through my forties, and so on. I'm in my thirties, as a matter of fact, and have never been either married or divorced. The typical length of a relationship profiled in the pages of *Vindication* is . . . a lifetime. One need think only of Werther and Lotte. Heloise and Abelard. Tristan and Iseult. Beauvoir and Sartre. Edna St. Vincent Millay and Eugen Boissevain. Hannah Arendt and Heinrich Blücher. Frida Kahlo and Diego Rivera.

Admittedly, I also examine a few relationships—like Wollstonecraft's with Gilbert Imlay—which lasted only several years (and produced thousands of letters and a deeply loved daughter). Not all the relationships I praise are married relationships (though at least a third of them are). This does not mean *Vindication* is anti-marriage. The most that might be said is that *Vindication* is anti-cynical marriage, anti-routinized marriage, anti-pragmatic marriage. *Vindication* is anti-risk aversion. To quote Jack Gilbert's poem again: "Anything worth doing is worth doing badly." Anything worth doing is worth doing temporarily. It is worth doing as gracefully and courageously and magnanimously as one's partner permits, one's situation permits, one's temperament and—yes—occasionally one's health permits.

Speaking of health. There is a final question that has been raised about *Vindication* which is whether its calls to passion, risk, romantic idealism—are only livable when one is unencumbered by responsibility for a child. I write today as the mother of a child I love without measure. I write as the mother of a child with whom I was pregnant while finishing *Vindication* and to whom I dedicated the book. Mary Wollstonecraft herself had two children—two daughters. In the midst of her most extravagant and emotionally perilous romance with Imlay she sailed around the then-known world alone with Fanny and an adolescent nursemaid. Her letters reverberate with passionate tenderness for Fanny. Wollstonecraft would have given her life for her first daughter. She did give her life for her second. She died giving birth to Mary Shelley.

I would die for my daughter, Eurydice, in a moment. I would prefer to live for her. She has leukemia, so it is a question I think about every day. Eurydice will need chemotherapy by year's end—and perhaps a bone marrow transplant. Since her birth in 2008, my writing life has been under siege. My romantic forays have been rendered more difficult, to be sure. ▶

But love, whether romantic or parental—can very well become stronger through difficulty. "The wind extinguishes a small flame but fans a big one into a fire so great it can warm a village." Or a marriage. Or a state. The human heart is large; it contains multitudes.

I do not, in fact, believe that commitment to a child or children detracts from what one can offer one's partner, one's lover, one's partner in crime. Schedules can show signs of strain. But the human heart is great; it contains multitudes.

Vindication is not a self-help book, though I am aware it is sometimes placed in self-help sections. I am not proselytizing. I am only telling tales and confiding, in a literary way, what has fired me as an individual. Probably the most quoted and misinterpreted part of the book is a line from the epilogue in which I confessed: "I have been derailed by love, hospitalized by love, flung around five continents, shaken, overjoyed, inspired, and unsettled by love."

At the risk of seeming absurd: I meant that as a positive. And yet, I am not offering myself as a model to follow, dear Reader. Wherever you are. Whoever you are. And I do feel odd and real affection for you, if you've read this far, pondered about love with me this long. I have taken real hits. But if my observers are remorseful, I'm not. The whole purpose of the most-quoted sentence in *Vindication* was to lead to this one, never quoted: "As I think upon it now—a couple of weeks away from giving birth to a little girl—I wish her something of the same."

What we have here is an expression of gratitude, not a sigh of contrition. In spite—and perhaps *because*—of the globetrotting, the wounds, the wins, the bright lights, and stark shadows, I feel lucky to be alive. I wish the richness I've known, the reboundability, the resonance, the *quality of life* on the child I adore.

It did not occur to me when I wrote this that the crux with Eurydice might be less *quality* of life than *length* of life. We will need to learn to multitask, Eurydice and I: to fight for endurance as well as speed, longevity as well as levity, light as well as heat. If we can do this, then surely we can also prove what legions of women and men greater than ourselves have in the past: that the ardor of a child and parent can enflame and ensoul—not ensnare and enfeeble—the intimacy of two lovers. It's "not a breach," as John Donne once said, "but an expansion . . . *like gold to airy thinness beat.*" ∾

A Dozen Only Slightly Quirky Benchmarks in the History of Love

1. Ovid, *The Art of Love*
   A rowdy and irreverent advice column for lovers from the fourth century BC. Dismiss your awe of the ancients and enjoy this aphoristic, silly, wise frolic through the land of broken and hopeful hearts.

2. Plato, *Symposium*
   A necessary classic. Half a dozen drunken philosophers (including Socrates) sit down to dinner and discuss love. Read and replicate.

3. The Tristan Myth, as related and discussed in Denis de Rougemont, *Love in the Western World*
   One of my favorite works of scholarship of all time, this book relates the primal Western myth of Tristan and Iseult better than any single manuscript that has come down to us from the Middle Ages. Superb, original, readable analysis of this tale and of others.

4. *The Letters of Abelard and Heloise* (those of Heloise in particular)
   After Abelard's castration and retirement to a monastery, the two outrageous medieval lovers were reduced to letter writing. But what letters they are. Heloise is the first truly great female prose stylist of

the Western tradition—and one of its most fiery, blunt, and blasphemous lovers.

5. William Shakespeare,
Antony and Cleopatra
   Packed with deathless verse, this Shakespeare play is a study of games people play in love—not cynically but often (despite appearances) idealistically. The play bristles with big themes: death, duty, daring, suicide, sex—and big lines, like those of Antony to Cleopatra after he has followed her ship out of battle: "My heart was to thy rudder tied by th'strings/ . . . O'er my spirit they full supremacy thou knew'st and that/Thy beck might from the bidding of the Gods command me."

6. John Donne, *Songs and Sonnets*, especially "The Sun Rising," and "Batter My Heart"
   From the brilliant seventeenth-century poet whose career was ruined by rash elopement comes to us this compendium of poems both sublime and ridiculous, religious and raunchy. Some of the most powerful verses about God can be read equally (one might argue) as poems about women: see, in particular, Holy Sonnet 4.

7. Jane Austen, *Pride and Prejudice*
   Perhaps the most romantic novel ever written. The tale of the plucky Elizabeth Bennett and the severe, snobby, yet passionate Mr. Darcy is ▶

testimony to the transformative effect of love.

8. Emily Dickinson,
The Complete Poems
Steer clear of the over-anthologized "fly buzz" poems and plunge, instead, into blood-stained verses of barely constrained desire like "As the starved maelstrom laps the navies." Savor the sexily self-imposed distances of "I cannot live with you," the affecting consolation of "Success is counted sweetest," and the quiet heroism of "I took my power in my hand." Be not deceived by Dickinson's childlike tone: the woman is a powerhouse.

9. Edna St. Vincent Millay,
Collected Poems, especially the sonnets in *Fatal Interview*
Millay wrote the sonnets in *Fatal Interview* at the height of her poetic powers and in the throes of an affair with a far younger man. It details, in searing imagery and unfashionably musical lines, the rise and fall of a great love. See also her proudly insouciant verses: "What lips my lips have kissed," and "Safe upon the solid shore the ugly houses stand." " 'Wolf,' cried my cunning heart/At every sheep it spied" is one of the most poignant nursery rhymes ever written—it also

heartbreakingly predicts Millay's own manner of death.

10. Graham Greene,
The End of the Affair
This story of a liaison in Blitz-torn London touches every note on the register of romantic passion from sexual obsession and guilt to painful renunciation and redemption. Compellingly narrated, the novel has plot twists as ingenious as any thriller, but Greene surprises most of all by creating a love triangle that unexpectedly rescues its members from doom to a sort of salvation.

11. Simone de Beauvoir,
A Transatlantic Love Affair: Letters to Nelson Algren
If ever you thought intellectually prickly feminists don't make emotionally abandoned lovers, think again. This book may have you wishing the French philosopher had left her famous Parisian compatriot, Sartre, for the gritty Chicago novelist she addresses in these pages.

12. Jack Gilbert,
Refusing Heaven: Poems
One of the reasons this crystalline book—and author—has fallen into neglect is undoubtedly the subject ▶

A Dozen Only Slightly Quirky Benchmarks in the History of Love *(continued)*

matter: women and love. Women in love. Sons and lovers. Old-fashioned? No. This volume is timeless, as are its luminous reflections on failure and tenderness, transience and gratitude. ᔍ